D0736020

# THE COEN BROTHERS

## INTERVIEWS

CONVERSATIONS WITH FILMMAKERS SERIES
PETER BRUNETTE, GENERAL EDITOR

Photo credit: Associated Press

# THE COEN BROTHERS

## BROTHERS

## INTERVIEWS

EDITED BY WILLIAM RODNEY ALLEN

UNIVERSITY PRESS OF MISSISSIPPI/JACKSON

www.upress.state.ms.us

The University Press of Mississippi is a member of the Association of American University Presses.

Copyright © 2006 by University Press of Mississippi

All rights reserved

Manufactured in the United States of America

First Edition 2006

∞

Library of Congress Cataloging-in-Publication Data

The Coen brothers : interviews / edited by William Rodney Allen.
    p. cm. — (Conversations with filmmakers series)
  Filmography:
  Includes index.
  ISBN-13: 978-1-57806-888-3 (cloth : alk. paper)
  ISBN-10: 1-57806-888-6 (cloth : alk. paper)
  ISBN-13: 978-1-57806-889-0 (pbk. : alk. paper)
  ISBN-10: 1-57806-889-4 (pbk. : alk. paper)
    1. Coen, Joel—Interviews. 2. Coen, Ethan—Interviews. 3. Motion picture producers and directors—United States—Interviews. I. Coen, Joel. II. Coen, Ethan. III. Allen, William Rodney. IV. Series.

  PN1998.3.C6635C64   2006
  791.4302'33092273—dc22                                    2005034188

British Library Cataloging-in-Publication Data available

# CONTENTS

# INTRODUCTION

LATE AT NIGHT, a supposedly dead man enters a deserted bar. He's hoping to find some cash his former boss (who had contracted his murder) owes him. He doesn't find the cash, but he does discover the boss—apparently dead in his office chair, a bullet through his chest. A baby strapped in a car seat sits contentedly in the middle of a desert road, having gotten there by first being kidnapped by an infertile hick husband and wife, then by a couple of dim-witted escaped cons who'd taken him, plastic seat and all, into their latest bank robbery before leaving him on the roof of their getaway car. A black hat, as free from context as a *chapeau* in a Magritte painting, tumbles over and over in the wind through a forlorn forest. Waking up beside a woman he has slept with for the first time, a screenwriter finds her dead, their bed a sea of blood. High in an art deco skyscraper, a fat executive climbs up onto a long boardroom table, calmly checks his watch, sets his feet, then sprints past his still-seated peers and dives through the window to his death. A pregnant midwestern policewoman, her gun drawn, follows the sound of an engine through snow-filled woods until she comes upon a kidnapper/murderer grinding up the remains of his partner in a wood chipper. And all of this mayhem is somehow . . . well . . . *funny.*

After all, none of it's real. We've just bought our movie tickets and entered the singular cinematic world of Joel and Ethan Coen—or at least the first half of it so far, up to their watershed 1996 film *Fargo*. Striking scenes from their more recent movies would be as easy to catalogue; if nothing else, the Coens' movies are memorable. And as different from each other as their eleven major films to this point have been, uniting them all is something critics have come to call "that Coen brothers feeling." This book, a collection of the most extensive, most probing of their interviews conducted over the span of twenty years and covering all their films to date, aims to illuminate the contours of that distinctive Coen brothers landscape: the tricky moving camera work; the omnipresent black humor; the addiction to the voiceover; the distancing ploy of setting movies in the past; the complicated use of cinematic genres to pay homage and simultaneously to introduce an element of mockery; the love of highly ornate verbiage and out-of-date and even invented slang; the fascination with sudden, off-kilter violence; the rare but moving moments when characters at least temporarily find some sort of transcendence in the midst of their tawdry, compromised lives.

To put it more broadly and concretely, even to build a Frankenstein monster of a Coen brothers movie: a fat man wearing a toupee (without exception referred to as a "rug") yammers on in a smoke-filled room about how all his fellow criminals lack ethics, or about how dry cleaning is the wave of the future, while outside, by the pool, the camera skims over the water toward a cynical, fast-talking lawyer or Bible salesman or movie mogul who uses his gift of gab to scam some hayseed or writer into negotiating with the kidnappers or becoming the temporary patsy of some corporate suits or writing a wrestling picture—just before the shouting man with the shotgun sets fire to the hotel, the UFO lands, and the levee breaks and floods the whole shebang. Then an out-of-context wise blind black man or cowpoke observes, chorus-like, that all the hubbub is simply another case of the whole dern human comedy perpetuatin' itself. It's quite a rumpus. Much ado.

Yet despite all the incongruity, tomfoolery, and cartoonish, slapstick violence, there's usually something intellectually serious going on in the Coen brothers' films. That seriousness may be strained through the filters of time period and genre and irony and technique, but it's there all right—as surely as that Zippo lighter is there under the dead fish on the boss's desk in *Blood Simple*. Granting the brothers' insistence on their indebtedness to the hard-boiled detective fiction of James M. Cain, Raymond Chandler, and Dashiell Hammett, and to the films based on some of their novels, the bedrock of the Coens' intellectual world is really good old-fashioned existentialism. Princeton philosophy major Ethan, in addition to writing his senior paper on Wittgenstein, certainly seems to have absorbed his Sartre and Camus. Both of those philosophers argued that man finds himself in an absurd world, where he must act despite having only incomplete knowledge, with no moral absolutes to guide him. Trapped inside the prison of his own mind, he finds that his freedom is more a curse than a blessing, and that anguish is his natural state of mind as he objectifies and misunderstands others while being misunderstood in return. This bleak metaphysic underlies the film noir world of *Blood Simple* (1984), the gangster milieu of *Miller's Crossing* (1990), the theater-of-the-absurd cosmos of *Barton Fink* (1991), the mechanical though superficially comic urban landscape of *The Hudsucker Proxy* (1994), the morose, endless midwestern snowscapes of *Fargo* (1996), and, most purely, in the black-and-white existential gloom of *The Man Who Wasn't There* (2001). The Coens' "sunnier" films simply depict the comic side of existential absurdity and non sequitur: their rousing *Raising Arizona* (1987), their comic masterpiece *The Big Lebowski* (1998), their exuberant "hayseed comedy" *O Brother, Where Art Thou?* (2000), and their uncharacteristically breezy latest entertainments, *Intolerable Cruelty* (2003) and *The Ladykillers* (2004).

In their more than twenty years of making movies, the Coens have granted scores of interviews, far more than it would be possible to include in one volume. This necessarily selective collection is aimed at providing comprehensiveness of coverage of their cinematic careers, as well as freshness of insight into their techniques, influences, and methods of working together. All the major interviews are here: the early, extensive one on *Blood Simple* conducted by the late Hal Hinson, five interviews from the influential French film journal *Positif*, the indispensable *Playboy* and *Vogue* interviews, conversations with internet magazines like *indieWire* and *The Onion*, and more recent interviews from British sources (*The Ladykillers* being a remake of a British film). Arranged in chronological order, these interviews appear here as they were originally published, except that I have silently corrected obvious typos and errors of fact.

Over the years, the Coens have gained something of a reputation for being difficult interview subjects. Some of their interrogators have described them as bored, mildly annoyed, elliptical, or flippant. But in the Coens' defense, many of the same obvious or personal questions come up over and over in the interviews—"Do you two ever fight?" probably being the winner in this category. The Coens' wit in handling these predictable queries always makes for interesting reading, with their comical answers often being as revealing as their "straight" ones respecting the nature of their working relationship. As one interviewer punned, the Coen brothers are "joined at the quip."

The early interviews stress the importance of the Coens' contribution to the much vaunted "independent film" explosion of the 1980s. Given such precursors as John Cassavetes and John Sayles in the 1970s, it's hardly fair to credit the Coens with inventing the independent movie. Still, the fact that two suburban kids from Minneapolis who started out with home video cams managed to raise almost a million dollars to shoot *Blood Simple*—and then got a distributor for it, and then made money on it—well, that certainly got everyone's attention. Moreover, the genre of the movie—film noir—now probably seems more novel than it did at the time. While the Coens talk a great deal in these interviews about the influence of older noir movies of the 1930s and 1940s, when they were growing up as aspiring filmmakers in the late 1970s and early 1980s they were aware of three contemporary, successful revivals of the noir film. Roman Polanski's *Chinatown* (1974), starring Jack Nicholson; another film noir starring Nicholson, Bob Rafelson's remake *The Postman Always Rings Twice* (1981); and Lawrence Kasdan's *Body Heat* (1981) all provided a commercially viable, "revivalist" context for *Blood Simple*. As the brothers freely admit, their first effort was a "phony" movie—meaning one taken not from life but based on other films.

The habit of looking at reality through the lens of earlier genre films would become one of the defining traits of "that Coen brothers feeling." Similarly, in *Blood Simple* (immediately following the pessimistic first image of their cinematic career—a blown-out tire tread on an empty stretch of Texas road), a voiceover by actor M. Emmet Walsh would set the pattern that has become perhaps the signature feature of the Coen brothers' work. And that first voiceover would end with the grim, existential observation that "down here [in Texas], you're on your own."

The brothers stress in the interviews that with their second film they wanted to try something entirely different. Thus evolved their experiment in what I like to call "yokel color." Traveling due west from Texas in terms of locale, the Coens set *Raising Arizona* in the desert/ suburban world of the Southwest—with which, as had been the case with Texas (excepting Joel's single term in film school in Austin), they were personally unfamiliar. As Ethan says, theirs was an "Arizona of the mind" rather than of the map. And the spooky grimness of *Blood Simple* was replaced with the over-the-top cartoon kookiness of *Raising Arizona*. Perhaps the emblematic image for the brothers' first "hayseed" movie would be the Roadrunner tattoo on protagonist H. I. ("Hi") McDunnough's arm. Like the Looney Toons desert bird perpetually pursued by Wile E. Coyote, Hi is habitually on the run; and, similarly, despite the absurd dangers he encounters out on the desert roads, he's a survivor who manages to keep moving on to the next outlandish episode.

The interviews on *Raising Arizona* point out another crucial element in the Coens' success: pitch-perfect casting. In addition to the virtuoso performance by the twenty-four-year-old Nicolas Cage, the movie bene-fited enormously from the acting of Holly Hunter (as Ed, Hi's wife) and John Goodman (as escaped con Gayle Snopes). These two actors would become part of the revolving door of go-to players who would appear again and again in the Coen brothers' movies, giving their cinematic world a feeling of wholeness and even family-like cohesion. Just as William Faulkner's mythical Yoknapatawpha County and recurrent characters would give unity to his fiction, the reappearance of Frances McDormand, John Goodman, John Turturro, Steve Buscemi, and sev-eral other actors is the glue holding together the Coens' imaginary universe. And Faulkner's impact on the Coens is pervasive: from identifying their two escaped cons in *Raising Arizona* as members of Faulkner's legendary white-trash Snopes clan, to the elevated diction incongruously employed by all their hayseeds, to their obvious depic-tion of Faulkner as a character in *Barton Fink*, the Coens show unmis-takable signs of Faulkner's influence. One could easily imagine the Coens adapting *As I Lay Dying* to the screen, with John Turturro playing the shiftless Anse Bundren.

The interviewers all seem to have one big question concerning the Coens' gangster film, *Miller's Crossing*: what's with the hat? Mysteriously, the movie begins with what the Coens say was the first image that came to them as they started writing the screenplay, a black hat being blown by the wind through some woods. The viewer keeps expecting a human being to show up in the shot, but that never happens. And the scene isn't a "flash forward" that's explained later. In fact, in one of the movie's few references to hats, the major character, a gangster called Tom, confesses to his (and his boss Leo's) girlfriend Verna that he has had a disturbing dream of his hat blowing in the wind. When Verna asks if the hat had turned into something else, Tom says, no, it stayed a hat. Thus begins a series of "symbolic" images throughout the Coens' films that some critics have found hard or even impossible to interpret. But the *Miller's Crossing* hat as symbol seems pretty obvious: Tom says to Verna that nothing is so foolish as a man chasing his hat. That's an understandable sentiment, given that a hat is the essence of the gangster's uniform, as vital as his cigarette or even his gun. His hat protects him from the elements and from too much scrutiny. A man who has lost his hat has lost his head, maybe even his life—just as a man in *Miller's Crossing* will lose his life out in the same woods, presumably, through which the symbolic hat blows at the beginning of the film.

Other concerns about the Coens' third film running through the interviews include the charges by some reviewers that the intricately plotted and cleverly written film lacked heart; that there was little chemistry between the romantic leads, Gabriel Byrne and Marcia Gay Harden; that it depicted the Coens' first Jewish character, the crooked bookie Bernie Bernbaum, in a stereotyped and offensive way (especially considering Bernbaum was created by two Jewish screenwriters). Moreover, the movie came out at the same time as did two other gangster films, *The Godfather III* and *GoodFellas*, and found itself swamped by their success. Though not the box-office disaster *The Hudsucker Proxy* would prove to be, *Miller's Crossing* was a disappointment financially, and the interviews reveal how the brothers tried to deal with the pressure to keep at least one set of eyes on the bottom line—the only line that often matters in the movie business.

In their next film, the genre-busting, nearly surrealistic *Barton Fink*, the Coens for the first time really hit their stride. The movie would go on to win the prestigious Palme d'Or at the Cannes Film Festival. The story of an intellectual Jewish playwright who leaves New York in 1941 to come to Hollywood to write screenplays, *Barton Fink* would be the brothers' closest thing to an autobiographical movie. But it would be an autobiography of the life of the Coens' minds, not of literal fact, for the interviews reveal how the Coens show off a dizzying array of artistic influences in the film. Barton resembles the left-wing playwright Clifford Odets, who also wrote for Hollywood; the one play of Barton's we learn about is called *Bare Ruined Choirs*, a title taken from a Shakespeare sonnet; the character W. P. Mayhew is an obvious though skewed version of Faulkner; the stain on the ceiling in Barton's strange room in the Hotel Earle is straight out of another tale about a self-important, failed writer, Flannery O'Connor's short story "The Enduring Chill"; and the whole movie is not Capraesque but Kafkaesque, with its melting wallpaper, irrational murder, and inferno of a finale.

In terms of film influences, interviewers have detected elements of Roman Polanski's *The Tenant*, Stanley Kubrick's *The Shining*, David Lynch's *Eraserhead*, as well as of the movie that would be so important an influence on *O Brother, Where Art Thou?*, Preston Sturges's *Sullivan's Travels*. Barton's life spirals out of control as he suffers from writer's block and gradually discovers that his "friend" Charlie Meadows (John Goodman) is actually a thrill killer, and by the end of the film the melting wallpaper and dead woman in Barton's bed and burning hotel combine to form a surreal vision of hell. Barton escapes from the flames, carrying a package presumably containing the head of the woman he had found dead in his bed. He wanders out onto the beach, where he sits down and talks with a bathing beauty who assumes the exact pose of a bathing beauty in a picture that had hung on the wall in Barton's hotel room. While interviewers have puzzled over the symbolic meaning of the picture's being "reenacted" in "real" life (the Coens, as always, have been reluctant to say), that one seems pretty easy. As Shakespeare famously observed, the artist's job is to hold a mirror up to nature; put another way, art should imitate life. But Barton has it backwards. He thinks life should conform to the artistic visions he dreams up in his head. He doesn't really care about depicting the reality of his subject, the "common man" he's always claiming to write about. Common man Charlie Meadows (note his initials) nails Barton when he yells "You don't *listen.*" In the last scene, when Barton finally exits the hotel (which is symbolic of his own mind), he finds that there is a real world out there. Rather than staring at a picture of a pretty young woman, he has the chance to interact with an actual one. Maybe then he can begin to learn that life is primary, art secondary. But probably not. When Barton asks the woman "Are you in pictures?" she replies "Don't be silly."

In their next movie, the Coens didn't take the advice they had given out so copiously to Barton Fink: they made a cerebral, self-reflexive, grandiose, very expensive dark comedy that was a disaster at the box office. *The Hudsucker Proxy*, written years earlier with Sam Raimi, was superficially a "screwball" comedy, a Frank Capraesque fantasy like *It's a Wonderful Life* in which all's well that ends well, even if that requires a deus ex machina. But at its heart, *Hudsucker* is a tough-minded satire of Hollywood. Like the Hudsucker Corporation itself, Tinseltown is an "industry" turning out a standard, shiny product on the assembly line, each unit fitted with an unrealistic promise of a happy ending designed to assure the common man he's really a fine fellow—much better than the rich, cynical people who smoke the big cigars and make all the money *selling him that image of himself*. It's telling that the real major character in the film is not the corporate patsy Norville Barnes (Tim Robbins), but the big city itself, and especially the skyscraper head-quarters of Hudsucker Industries. Set late in the 1950s, the Hudsucker building is art deco 1930s, in characteristic Coen brothers scrambled chronological style. And the Hudsucker Corporation is a ruthless machine, from the bowels of its mailroom to the clock in its spire. It's a place where a rube like Norville wouldn't have a chance, unless the big corporate manipulator Sidney J. Mussberger (Paul Newman) wanted him to—for Mussberger's own purposes.

As the interviews show, while the Coens acted stoically about the commercial failure of *Hudsucker*, they realized that after making three straight movies that collectively lost millions of dollars, they were start-ing to edge out onto professional thin ice. In vulgar parlance, they needed a hit. They needed a less intellectual, "warmer" movie—some-thing more like their one big success, *Raising Arizona*. And, fortunately, with *Fargo*, they managed to create exactly that. The "warmest" movie ever set in the frozen snowscapes of the upper Midwest, *Fargo* won the moviegoers' hearts as well as their minds. While its violent plot was driven by one of the Coens' standard motifs, kidnapping, *Fargo* wasn't really a genre crime film; and rather than being all head and no heart, it was centered on a character with plenty of heart—with two, in fact, since she is pregnant. Frances McDormand's matter-of-fact, small-town policewoman Marge Gunderson would ironically turn out to be the most memorable dramatic character of the Coens' career (complimented by Jeff Bridges's masterful turn as The Dude in their next and best comic film, *The Big Lebowski*). Her performance would win the Academy Award for Best Actress, and, all told, *Fargo* would be nominated for seven Academy Awards. Every bit as strong as McDormand's acting was William H. Macy's great performance as Jerry Lundegaard, a way-in-over-his-head car salesman.

Marge turned out to be so charming almost despite the Coen brothers' intentions. In one interview Ethan admits that in terms of the script, before the movie was made, he thought of Marge as rather annoying. But McDormand's ability to present, comically but sympathetically, Marge's simple love of her community, her husband, her baby on the way, even the mounds of food she eats all through the film—that was a revelation. Thereafter, the Coens' main characters would be more believable as realistic human beings and less like abstract embodiments of ideas. The brothers' trademark violence would recede, and when present would become less gratuitous, more genuinely tragic, as in *The Man Who Wasn't There*. Part of this evolution was probably the result of both Joel's and Ethan's becoming parents shortly after they made *Fargo*. The wonder boys, it seems, were growing up and maturing.

Then came The Dude, and he fit *right in there*. Featuring enough zany invention to power three or four conventionally funny movies, *The Big Lebowski* showed the Coens at the height of their very considerable comic powers. Their anti-hero of the new Wild West (Los Angles circa 1991), the continually stoned, unemployed league bowler Jeffrey Lebowski would have been a memorable character no matter who acted the part; but with Jeff Bridges playing him, he was immortal. The Coens' famous pitch-perfect casting reached a whole new level in this film, with Bridges channeling The Dude, John Goodman ranting as his Vietnam vet bowling partner, Steve Buscemi smirking but clueless as their mascot, John Turturro strutting as their Hispanic bowling nemesis, Julianne Moore vamping as the artistic feminist daughter of the *other* Jeffrey Lebowski (the confusion over the two Lebowskis powers the movie's kidnapping plot), and the incomparable Sam Elliott drawling as a sardonic cowboy narrator simply called The Stranger.

The interviews reveal that the brothers saw the intricate twists and turns of the movie's plot as beside the point, and they were bemused by reviewers who complained that it finally didn't make sense. Alfred Hitchcock had spoken of the object the characters are after in a film as the "McGuffin." The McGuffin really isn't that important by itself, but simply provides a way to get the characters interacting with each other. In *The Big Lebowski*, the McGuffin is the supposed million dollar ransom the other Jeffrey Lebowski had incongruously asked The Dude to deliver to his young trophy wife's supposed abductors. And those kidnappers include, or seem to include, porn stars, German nihilists, and even the young trophy wife herself. The hilarity of the film comes from The Dude's unhurried, ineffectual efforts to untangle the mess while staying stoned, keeping to his bowling schedule, and not getting all "un-Dude" about the whole thing. His side-kick Walter (Goodman), who lives to vent his pent-up anger on inappropriate targets, constantly offers his self-assured, totally wrong assessments of the situation, exponentially compounding The Dude's problems. But when things get too balled up, Walter at least always has his one-size-fits-all answer: "Let's bowl."

Then there are The Dude's dreams, set to the music of the celestial Bob Dylan or the lowly Kenny Rogers, which feature The Dude flying after Julianne Moore as she rides a magic carpet, or teaching her how to bowl in a great Busby Berkeley–inspired dance number. And when Sam Elliott finally comes out of his voiceover role to sit down at the bar with The Dude and swap philosophical observations over White Russians and sarsaparilla—well, *that about wraps her up.* As these interviews repeatedly show, a measure of the movie's success is that it's hardly possible to talk about it without lapsing into Dude- or cowboy-speak. There's even a loose organization of fans that puts on a *Big Lebowski* convention every year, with the participants dressing as their favorite characters from the movie. At the very least, the Coens should get a kickback from the American Bowling Congress for adding thousands of new bowlers to league rosters across the country.

Continuing in their comic vein in 2000, the Coens would present the new twenty-first century with a film set in the 1930s, the exuberant chain-gang farce *O Brother, Where Art Thou?* Its musical score—artfully written and assembled by Carter Burwell (who had done such good work for the Coens in previous films) and T-Bone Burnett—almost becomes a character unto itself in a movie bursting with American roots music from the likes of the Cox Family, Ralph Stanley, and Allison Krauss and her band Union Station. Set in Depression Mississippi, this film features George Clooney's first appearance for the Coens—as Ulysses Everett McGill, the fast-talking convict who escapes from the chain gang with John Turturro and Tim Blake Nelson. These three are supposedly pursuing the McGuffin of buried treasure, but the real point is McGill's attempt to get back into the arms of his skeptical wife, played by Holly Hunter. The interviews reveal the Coens' confession that their credited co-screenwriter, Homer, was only the loosest of influences on the plotting of this picaresque romp through the political, musical, and criminal landscape of the fabled Mississippi Delta. Preston Sturges's *Sullivan's Travels*, which features a Hollywood screenwriter who hopes to (but never does) make a movie about the common man called *O Brother, Where Art Thou?*, was a far more substantial source than the *Odyssey*. It's typically obtuse of the Coens that they managed to "remake" a movie that never existed. But with their great comic zest, and their typically strong casting (which also included a fine turn by John Goodman as confidence man Big Dan Teague), the brothers made *O Brother* a very popular film—one of their most solid financial successes to date.

*The Man Who Wasn't There* was a return to the Coens' film noir beginnings, but it had a polished look (a credit to the Coens' director of photography since *Barton Fink*, Roger Deakins) and a subtlety of theme far beyond anything in *Blood Simple*. Billy Bob Thornton, working with the Coens for the first time, plays Ed Crane, the non-entity of a barber whose wife Doris (Frances McDormand) cheats on him with her boss Big Dave (James Gandolfini), setting the James M. Cain–like murder plot into motion. Through all the movie's twists and turns, Thornton's Crane remains passive, and mostly silent—except in his terse but nevertheless Hamlet-like voiceovers, which reveal the depth of his existential anguish and longing to be more than just a cipher who cuts hair. Set in 1948 in California, the film seethes with postwar anxiety about male heroism, or the lack thereof, in World War II (Ed Crane had been rejected by the draft board for having flat feet, while Big Dave falsely claims to have been a war hero in the Pacific); the relentless pursuit of enough money to obtain the American dream (Ed blackmails Big Dave, then is scammed by a man offering him a chance to get in on the ground floor of the dry cleaning industry); and even the fear of invasion from outer space (newspapers have articles about a UFO landing in Roswell, New Mexico, and Big Dave's spooky wife claims she and her husband were abducted on a camping trip by aliens).

But *The Man Who Wasn't There*'s emotional centerpiece is Ed's odd relationship with Birdy (beautifully portrayed by Scarlett Johansson), a teen-aged, modestly talented classical pianist. After hearing her play at a party, Ed decides that her pedestrian Beethoven is the most beautiful thing he's ever heard, and that she must make the most of her talent (as he never was able to) and study with "the best." But when "the best" says Birdy should probably consider a career as a typist, Ed's hopes for pursuing the higher life crash to the ground—especially when Birdy offers to console him with oral sex as they drive home. This clumsy, unwanted move results in a car crash, the ur-symbol at least since Fitzgerald's *The Great Gatsby* of the American dream's ending up in the ditch. The film itself ends with Ed's electrocution for a murder he didn't commit. In his last voiceover, he expresses the hope that in the afterlife he might have a chance to tell his dead wife Doris "all the things they don't have words for here." *The Man Who Wasn't There* is beautifully filmed, masterfully acted, poignantly written—in short, full of the best of that Coen brothers feeling.

Finally, *Intolerable Cruelty* and *The Ladykillers* are, in a sense, extensions of *O Brother, Where Art Thou?* All three films are farcical comedies driven by high-powered Hollywood stars, and all three are more mainstream in their sensibilities than the Coens' more idiosyncratic work (*Barton Fink, The Hudsucker Proxy, The Man Who Wasn't There*). Unlike *O Brother*, however, these two most recent movies are, respectively, a collaborative screenwriting project (with John Romano, Robert Ramsey, and Matthew Stone) and a remake (albeit an extensive one) of a 1955 British comedy written by William Rose. The interviews on these two most recent films include much discussion of whether or not the Coens have changed their stripes and "gone Hollywood." Actually, though, that charge is probably a nice change for the Coens, who for most of their careers have been criticized for being too intellectual, too "indie"-minded, or just too plain weird.

In *Intolerable Cruelty*, George Clooney seems to have an even better time with his role than he did in *O Brother*, if that's possible. As the amoral divorce lawyer Miles Massey, who falls for the equally amoral gold digger Marylin Rexroth (Catherine Zeta-Jones), Clooney gives one of the most zestful comic performances since the heyday of Cary Grant. His double takes, spit takes, and, presumably, even his outtakes as he plays the wolf to Zeta-Jones's femme fatale are a wonder to watch. Filled with great dialogue ("One husband at a time," "I assume you're a carnivore," "I'm in a meeting," "Love is good"), skipping through the Coens' usual maze of plot reversals, flagging a little only in its concluding game show gag, *Intolerable Cruelty* is mainstream all right, but with a vengeance. It's a carnivore of a comedy.

In *The Ladykillers*, the Coens' first actual remake of an earlier film, Tom Hanks makes a valiant effort to become the brothers' new George Clooney by portraying yet another shady, self-serving character with a silver tongue. The leader of a gang of less-than-mastermind criminals who rent a basement in a house next to a floating Mississippi casino and tunnel into its vault, Hanks (Professor Goldthwait Higginson Dorr, Ph.D.) dons an anachronistic getup complete with cape that makes him look like a cross between Edgar Allan Poe and Colonel Sanders. But Hanks has a long row to hoe in the Coens' version of a 1950s British comedy transposed into modern-day Mississippi, because the result is a loose pastiche of chronology, architecture, music, and literary/cinematic allusion. Reviewers were generally disappointed in the film, faulting it for its crude, slapstick hijinks and foul language, its lack of human warmth, and its perilous approach to offensiveness in terms of its racial humor. True, the Coens have always been equal opportunity offenders of ethnic political correctness. But their subjection of Irma P. Hall (playing landlady Marva Munson) to crude phallic sight gags (Dorr wondering at Marva's proud display of her late husband's long home-made fife), to proudly giving money to Bob Jones University, and even to bellowing out the ultimate racial epithet—twice—well, this may be going a politically incorrect bridge too far.

And what *about* that *Ladykillers's* bridge, a gothic wonder from which so many bodies are dumped onto the trash barges that move like clockwork under its vast span? What's a gargoyle-festooned bridge from the set of *Batman* doing in modern-day Mississippi? Admittedly, though, the best visual allusion of the movie happens there. At the end, all the members of the hapless gang have managed to kill themselves rather than Mrs. Munson, and Dorr himself is dispatched when a raven straight out of Poe lights on the head of one of the bridge's gargoyles, which snaps off at just the right moment to crack the Professor on the head and send him over the rail. His cape catches the understructure of the bridge, leaving him suspended for a moment like a hanged man. But then the cape tears, dropping him down onto yet another passing trash barge; his cape, however, rises and flutters in the wind, in an ironic allusive nod to the hopeful feather that floats above Forrest Gump and his little son at the end of Tom Hanks's signature film. Fittingly, one of the Coens' last cinematic images so far is a wry, subtle, emotionally reversed "negative" of an allusion to another movie. No doubt about it—*that's* that Coen brothers feeling.

Well, as The Stranger might say, I guess I've introduced 'em enough. Now it's time for the Coens to speak for themselves.

As customary with all books in this series, the interviews herein have not been edited from the form of their initial publication. Consequently the reader will at times encounter repetitions of both questions and answers but it is the feeling that the significance of the same questions being asked and the consistency (or inconsistency) of responses will prove of value to readers in their unexpurgated form.

I owe thanks to several people who helped make this book possible. Drew Houpt, the Coen brothers' assistant, was invaluable in facilitating the project. I'm of course indebted to those interviewers of the Coens and to the editors of the various publications in which their interviews appeared, who allowed me to republish their work. My editors at the University Press of Mississippi, Peter Brunette (the general editor of the series) and Anne Stascavage, were most helpful and supportive. And over the years, through the development of several of my books, Seetha Srinivasan, the director of the UPM, has been simply the best guide and colleague I could imagine.

Closer to home, the Louisiana School for Math, Science, and the Arts generously supported this project with a grant from the Richard G. Brown Fund. I'm indebted to Catherine Calhoun and Erin Callais, my research assistants, who worked with me on this book with enthusiasm, efficiency, and good humor. I owe many thanks to Cary Mangum for his technical know-how, as well as to Jennifer Mangum and Emily Shumate for their encouragement and insights. Randy Allen, my bowling partner as the result of our seeing *The Big Lebowski*, read portions of my manuscript and contributed a lot to this book. My friend Paul Smith was with me through every step of the project, and I owe him more than I can say. Thanks as well to Paul's sons in the movie business, Matt and Lucas, and to Paul's wife Lauren. I'm deeply grateful to my friend and writing partner Mike Henry for making possible "PECOS," "Three Bad Years," and "A House Divided," three of our unproduced screenplays that still play pretty well, at least to us, in the theater of the mind. My pal Nancy James, who knows everyone in Hollywood, got me onto the set of *The Ladykillers* and introduced me to the Coens. This book is dedicated to her.

As always, I owe it all to my wife Cindy, and to our daughters, Emily and Claire.

And I thank Joel and Ethan Coen.

WRA

# CHRONOLOGY

| | |
|---|---|
| 1954 | Joel Coen born November 29 in Minneapolis, Minnesota, to Edward and Rena Coen. |
| 1957 | Ethan Coen born September 21 in Minneapolis. |
| 1971 | Joel enters Simon's Rock of Bard College in Great Barrington, Massachusetts. |
| 1973 | Joel enters New York University as a film studies major. |
| 1974 | Ethan enters Simon's Rock of Bard College. |
| 1975 | Ethan enters Princeton University as a philosophy major. |
| 1979 | Joel enters the graduate film studies program at the University of Texas, but quits the program after one semester. His brief first marriage ends in divorce. |
| 1980 | Ethan, having graduated from Princeton, moves to New York. Joel joins Ethan in New York and works as a production assistant, then editor, on various low-budget films, while Ethan works part-time as a typist. The Coens meet independent horror filmmaker Sam Raimi. The Coens begin writing *Blood Simple*. |
| 1982 | The Coens shoot *Blood Simple*. |
| 1983 | The Coens edit *Blood Simple*. |
| 1984 | The Coens search for a distributor for *Blood Simple*, finally getting a deal with Ben Barenholtz's company, Circle Releasing. Joel marries Frances McDormand. |
| 1985 | *Blood Simple* released. *Crimewave,* the Coen brother's collaboration with Sam Raimi, released. Ethan marries for the first time, but soon divorces. |
| 1987 | *Raising Arizona* released. |

1990    *Miller's Crossing* released. Ethan marries film editor Tricia Cooke.

1991    *Barton Fink* released. At the Cannes Film Festival, *Barton Fink* wins as Best Picture (Palme d'Or), Joel wins as Best Director, and John Turturro wins as Best Actor.

1994    *The Hudsucker Proxy* released, premiering at the Sundance Film Festival in Park City, Utah.

1996    *Fargo* released.

1997    *Fargo* nominated for an Academy Award for Best Picture. Joel and Ethan win the Oscar for Best Original Screenplay, Joel wins the Oscar for Best Director, Frances McDormand wins the Oscar for Best Actress, and William H. Macy wins the Oscar for Best Supporting Actor. The Writers' Guild of America gives the Coen brothers its award for Best Screenplay for *Fargo*.

1998    *The Big Lebowski* released.

1998    Ethan's collection of stories, *Gates of Eden*, published.

2000    *O Brother, Where Art Thou?* released.

2001    *The Man Who Wasn't There* released, winning Joel the prize at Cannes for Best Director.

2003    *Intolerable Cruelty* released.

2004    *The Ladykillers* released.

# FILMOGRAPHY

1985
BLOOD SIMPLE
Director: **Joel Coen**
Writers: **Joel Coen, Ethan Coen**
Producer: **Ethan Coen**
Director of Photography: Barry Sonnenfeld
Production Designer: Jane Musky
Original Music: Carter Burwell, Jim Roberge
Editors: **Roderick Jaynes** (a pseudonym for Joel and Ethan), Don Wiegmann
Casting: Julie Hughes, Barry Moss
Cast: John Getz (Ray), Frances McDormand (Abby), Dan Hedaya (Julian Marty), M. Emmet Walsh (Loren Visser)
35 mm, color
97 minutes

1985
CRIMEWAVE
Director: Sam Raimi
Writers: **Ethan Coen, Joel Coen**, Sam Raimi
Producers: Robert Tapert, Bruce Campbell
Director of Photography: Robert Primes
Editors: Michael Kelly, Kathy Weaver
Music: Arlon Ober, Joseph Loduca (jazz)
Cast: Louise Lasser (Helen Trend), Paul L. Smith (Faron Crush), Brion James (Arthur Coddish), Sheree J. Wilson (Nancy), Edward R. Pressman

(Ernest Trend), Bruce Campbell (Renaldo "The Heel"), Reed Birney
(Vic Ajax)
35 mm, color
86 minutes


1987
RAISING ARIZONA
Director: **Joel Coen**
Writers: **Joel Coen**, **Ethan Coen**
Producers: **Ethan Coen**, Mark Silverman
Director of Photography: Barry Sonnenfield
Editor: Michael R. Miller
Production Designer: Jane Musky
Original Music: Carter Burwell
Casting: Donna Isaacson, John Lyons
Cast: Nicolas Cage (H. I. McDunnough), Holly Hunter (Edwina "Ed"
McDunnough), Trey Wilson (Nathan Arizona, Sr.), John Goodman
(Gale Snopes), William Forsythe (Evelle Snopes), Sam McMurray
(Glen), Frances McDormand (Dot), Randall "Tex" Cobb (Leonard
Smalls)
35 mm, color
94 minutes


1990
MILLER'S CROSSING
Director: **Joel Coen**
Writers: **Joel Coen**, **Ethan Coen**
Producers: **Ethan Coen**, Mark Silverman
Director of Photography: Barry Sonnenfield
Editor: Michael Miller
Production Designer: Dennis Gassner
Original Music: Carter Burwell
Casting: Donna Isaacson, John Lyons
Cast: Gabriel Byrne (Tom Reagan), Marcia Gay Harden (Verna), John
Turturro (Bernie Bernbaum), Jon Polito (Johnny Caspar), J. E. Freeman
(Eddie Dane), Albert Finney (Leo), Mike Starr (Frankie), Al Mancini

(Tic-Tac), Richard Woods (Mayor Dale Levander), Thomas Toner
(O'Doole), Steve Buscemi (Mink)
35 mm, color
115 minutes

1991
BARTON FINK
Director: **Joel Coen**
Writers: **Joel Coen**, **Ethan Coen**
Producers: **Ethan Coen**, Graham Place
Director of Photography: Roger Deakins
Editors: **Roderick Jaynes**, Michael Barenbaum
Production Designer: Dennis Gassner
Original Music: Carter Burwell
Casting: Donna Isaacson, John Lyons
Cast: John Turturro (Barton Fink), John Goodman (Charlie Meadows),
Judy Davis (Audrey Taylor), Michael Lerner (Jack Lipnick), John
Mahoney (W. P. Mayhew), Tony Shalhoub (Ben Geisler), Jon Polito (Lou
Breeze), Steve Buscemi (Chet)
35 mm, color
116 minutes

1994
THE HUDSUCKER PROXY
Director: **Joel Coen**
Writers: **Joel Coen**, **Ethan Coen**, Sam Raimi
Producers: **Ethan Coen**, Graham Place
Director of Photography: Roger Deakins
Editor: Thom Noble
Production Designer: Dennis Gassner
Original Music: Carter Burwell
Casting: Donna Isaacson, John Lyons
Cast: Tim Robbins (Norville Barnes), Jennifer Jason Leigh (Amy Archer),
Paul Newman (Sidney J. Mussburger), Charles Durning (Waring
Hudsucker), John Mahoney (Chief Editor Manhattan Argus), Jim True
(Buzz the Elevator Operator)
35 mm, color
111 minutes

1996
FARGO
Director: **Joel Coen**
Writers: **Joel Coen, Ethan Coen**
Producer: **Ethan Coen**
Director of Photography: Roger Deakins
Editors: **Roderick Jaynes**, Tricia Cooke
Production Designer: Rick Heinrichs
Original Music: Carter Burwell
Casting: John Lyons
Cast: Frances McDormand (Marge Gunderson), Steve Buscemi (Carl Showalter), William H. Macy (Jerry Lundegaard), Peter Stormare (Gaear Grimsrud), Harve Presnell (Wade Gustafson), John Carroll Lynch (Norm Gunderson), Kristin Rudrüd (Jean Lundegaard), Steven Reevis (Shep Proudfoot)
35 mm, color
97 minutes

1998
THE BIG LEBOWSKI
Director: **Joel Coen**
Writers: **Joel Coen, Ethan Coen**
Producers: **Ethan Coen**, John Cameron
Director of Photography: Roger Deakins
Editors: **Roderick Jaynes**, Tricia Cooke
Production Designer: Rick Heinrichs
Original Music: Carter Burwell
Casting: John Lyons
Cast: Jeff Bridges (Jeff Lebowski, The Dude), John Goodman (Walter Sobchak), Julianne Moore (Maude Lebowski), Steve Buscemi (Donny), David Huddleston (Jeffrey Lebowski, The Big Lebowski), Philip Seymour Hoffman (Brandt), Tara Reid (Bunny Lebowski)
35 mm, color
127 minutes

2000
O BROTHER, WHERE ART THOU?
Director: **Joel Coen**

Writers: **Ethan Coen, Joel Coen**, Homer (from his poem the *Odyssey*)
Producer: **Ethan Coen**
Director of Photography: Roger Deakins
Editors: **Roderick Jaynes**, Tricia Cooke
Production Designer: Dennis Gassner
Music: Carter Burwell, T-Bone Burnett
Cast: George Clooney (Ulysses Everett McGill), Tim Blake Nelson (Pete), John Turturro (Delmar), John Goodman (Big Dan Teague), Michael Badalucco (George Nelson), Chris Thomas King (Tommy Johnson), Jerry Douglas, III (Dobro player), Wayne Duvall (Homer Stokes), Holly Hunter (Penny), Mia Tate (siren), Christy Taylor (siren), Musetta Vander (siren)
35 mm, color
102 minutes

2001
THE MAN WHO WASN'T THERE
Director: **Joel Coen**
Writers: **Joel Coen, Ethan Coen**
Producer: **Ethan Coen**
Director of Photography: Roger Deakins
Production Designer: Dennis Gassner
Music: Carter Burwell
Editor: Tricia Cooke
Casting: Ellen Chenoweth
Cast: Billy Bob Thornton (Ed Crane), Frances McDormand (Doris Crane), Michael Badalucco (Frank), James Gandolfini (Dave "Big Dave" Brewster), Katherine Borowitz (Ann Nirdlinger), Jon Polito (Creighton Tolliver), Scarlett Johansson (Rachel "Birdy" Abundas), Richard Jenkins (Walter Abundas), Tony Shalhoub (Freddy Riedenschneider)
35 mm, black and white
116 minutes

2003
INTOLERABLE CRUELTY
Director: **Joel Coen**
Story: Robert Ramsey, Matthew Stone, John Romano

Screenplay: Robert Ramsey, Matthew Stone, **Ethan Coen**, **Joel Coen**
Producer: **Ethan Coen**, Brian Grazer
Director of Photography: Roger Deakins
Production Designer: Leslie McDonald
Music: Carter Burwell
Editor: **Roderick Jaynes**
Casting: Ellen Chenoweth
Cast: George Clooney (Miles Massey), Catherine Zeta-Jones (Marylin Rexroth), Geoffrey Rush (Donovan Donaly), Cedric the Entertainer (Gus Petch), Edward Herrmann (Rex Rexroth), Paul Adelstein (Wrigley), Richard Jenkins (Freddy Bender), Billy Bob Thornton (Howard D. Doyle)
35 mm, color
100 minutes

2004
THE LADYKILLERS
Director: **Joel Coen, Ethan Coen**
Writers: William Rose (writer of the original version of *The Ladykillers,* 1955), **Joel Coen, Ethan Coen** (writers of the remake of *The Ladykillers*)
Producers: **Ethan Coen, Joel Coen**, Tom Jacobson, Barry Josephson, Barry Sonnenfield
Director of Photography: Roger Deakins
Production Designer: Dennis Gassner
Original Music: Carter Burwell
Editor: **Roderick Jaynes**
Casting: Ellen Chenoweth
Cast: Tom Hanks (Professor G. H. Dorr), Irma P. Hall (Marva Munson), Marlon Wayans (Gawain Mac Sam), J. K. Simmons (Garth Pancake), Tzi Ma (The General), Ryan Hurst (Lump Hudson), George Wallace (Sheriff Wyner), George Anthony Bell (Preacher)
35 mm, color
104 minutes

# THE COEN BROTHERS

## INTERVIEWS

# Bloodlines

HAL HINSON/1985

IN HIS NOVEL *Red Harvest*, Dashiell Hammett wrote that after a person kills somebody, he goes soft in the head—"blood simple." You can't help it. Your brains turn to mush. All of a sudden, the blonde angel whose husband you just buried starts getting strange phone calls. You reach into your pocket for your cigarette lighter—the silver-plated one the Elks gave you with your name spelled out in rope on the front—and it's not there. Your lover limps in early one morning with blood on his shirt and a .38, *your* .38, stuffed in his jeans and announces, "I've taken care of it. All we have to do now is keep our heads." Yeah. That's all. Just keep your heads. Might as well go ahead and call the cops.

For the characters in the stylish new thriller *Blood Simple*, passion, guilt, and the sight of blood on their hands causes the world to warp and distort just as Hammett said it would, like the nightmare reflection in a fun-house mirror. The movie, which was put together on a shoe-string by Joel and Ethan Coen, a couple of movie-mad brothers from Minneapolis, has its own lurid, fun-house atmosphere. The camera swoops and pirouettes as if in a Vincente Minnelli musical; at times it scuttles just inches above the ground, at shoe-top level, crawls under tables, or bounces down hallways. Always some part of the frame is energized by an odd detail or incongruous fillip of color. Composed in phosphorescent pastels, in neon pinks and greens that stand out against the khaki-colored Texas landscapes, the movie has a kind of tawdry flamboyance that draws attention to itself, like a barfly adjusting

From *Film Comment*, March/April 1985.

her makeup by the light of the jukebox. *Blood Simple* is only the Coens' first movie—their contributions overlap, with Joel credited as writer-director and Ethan as writer-producer—but already they have an agile sense of visual storytelling and a playfully expressive camera style. They don't make movies like beginners.

If anything, the Coens' technique in *Blood Simple* is too brightly polished, too tightly screwed down. But their excesses come from an over-eagerness to impress, to put their talents on display. *Blood Simple* looks like a movie made by guys who spent most of their lives watching movies, indiscriminately, both in theaters and on TV, and for whom, almost through osmosis, the vocabulary and grammar of film has become a kind of instinctive second language. Made up of equal parts film noir and Texas gothic, but with a hyperbolic B-movie veneer, it's a grab-bag of movie styles and references, an eclectic mixture of Hitchcock and Bertolucci, of splatter flicks and Fritz Lang and Orson Welles.

On the face of it, *Blood Simple* may appear to be more about other movies than anything else, and there is an element of movie-movie formalism in their work. But the Coens aren't interested in just recycling old movie formulas. In *Blood Simple*, the filmmakers assume that the audience grew up on the same movies they did, and that we share their sophisticated awareness of conventional movie mechanics. But the Coens don't play their quotations from old movie thrillers straight; they use our shared knowledge of movie conventions for comedy. The movie has a wicked, satirical edge—there's a devilish audacity in the way these young filmmakers use their film smarts to lure us into the movie's system of thinking, and then spring their trap, knocking us off-balance in a way that's both shocking and funny.

The basic geometry of the film is a James M. Cain triangle: husband, wife, lover. The husband, Julian Marty (Dan Hedaya), is a brooding Greek with a militant brow and a puckered chin who owns a gaudy roadside night-spot called the Neon Boot. One look at Marty, who looks like he was born to catch lead, and it's clear why his wife Abby (Frances McDormand) thinks she'd better hightail it before she uses the pearl-handled revolver he gave her as an anniversary present on him. Ray (John Getz), a drawling bartender who works for Marty, becomes involved with Abby innocently enough when she asks him to help her move out. Almost inevitably, Abby and Ray fall into the nearest motel room where a fourth figure, a slob detective named Visser (M. Emmet Walsh), catches them *in flagrante* and delivers his photographic evidence to Marty ("I know where you can get these framed"), along with his own leering account of the evening's bedroom activities, setting the film's tragic spiral of events in motion.

Much of the pleasure in *Blood Simple* comes from watching the film-makers run their intricately worked-out plot through its paces. The film's narrative is never merely functional in the usual murder-mystery fashion; things don't happen in this movie just to push the plot along. Everything plugs into the film's basic idea: that we are dependent in our judgments upon what our senses tell us, and that our senses lie— that in life we never really know what's going on. The Coens have created a world in which nothing is exactly as it seems. When Marty sees Visser's picture of Abby and Ray nestled together in bloody sheets, we assume, as Marty does, that the hired killer has done his job and the lovers are dead. It's not until the next scene, when Ray saunters into the bar and finds Marty's body, that we discover the photo was doctored. In this movie, a corpse is not always a corpse.

All the characters in *Blood Simple* are able to see only part of the whole picture. Each character has his own point of view in the film, his own version of what has happened and why. And based on the evidence before them, each one behaves appropriately. But each one is limited by his own perspective and it's what they don't know, what they *can't* see from where they stand, that keeps getting them into trouble. Only the audience is given the whole picture. But the Coens never let us relax. Just as we think we're in synch with the film, they shove our assumptions back in our faces. Like their characters, we're making a mistake by believing what we see.

It's this layering of points of view, the interweaving of four versions of the same events, each one complicating and contradicting the other, that distinguishes *Blood Simple* from Lawrence Kasdan's *Body Heat* and other film noir re-treads. It's been some time since a low-budget thriller has had this kind of narrative richness. And if at times the Coens are a little too much in love with their own cleverness, occasionally bogging the movie down with self-conscious arty flourishes, they are saved by their drive to provide low-down thrills, to surprise and delight their audience. *Blood Simple* suggests that the Coens are an anomaly on the independent film scene. They don't see a conflict between film art and film entertainment. Nor, in *Blood Simple*, do they break new aesthetic ground. First and foremost, they are entertainers.

Some critics have used this aspect of their work to dismiss *Blood Simple* either as an independent film with a conventional Hollywood heart or as just another schlocky exploitation picture with a glossy, high-art finish. They use the film's accessibility as a club to beat it over the head with, as if to imply that the things that make the movie fun to watch, that satisfy an audience, are precisely the things that compromise its artistic purity. According to this logic, *Blood Simple* is little more than an audition piece, a stepping stone to the world of big-budget studio financing.

But it's the Coens' showmanship, their desire to give the audience a cracking good ride, that gives *Blood Simple* its freshness and originality. The film is most effective when it plays as a comedy. The Coens have a sharp eye for the oddball details of the sleazy Texas milieu they've created. Their humor is droll and understated; their characters spout a kind of terse, prairie vernacular that's dead-on authentic but with a twist, like Horton Foote with a rock in his shoe.

As the scuzzy detective slithering through the movie in a beat-up VW bug, M. Emmet Walsh is a redneck variation on all the bad cops and corrupt gumshoes in the hard-boiled genre. Dressed in a canary-yellow leisure suit, his belly sagging over his western-style belt buckle, Visser is the kind of half-witted vermin who likes to torture puppies in his spare time. Walsh gives his character a mangy amorality; one look at this guy and you know he's for sale at bargain-basement prices. His performance sets a new standard for scumbag character acting.

Dan Hedaya, who plays Marty, does something that even Walsh isn't able to pull off: he shows us what a slime the guy is and still makes us feel almost sorry for what happens to him. Marty is the perpetual outsider, the one who's always put upon and misunderstood. He doesn't even talk like the others. Instead of speaking in a lazy Texas drawl, he spits his words out quickly in a tight Northeastern accent that's clenched like a fist. With his dark, swarthy looks, gold chains, and European-cut shirts, he's on the opposite end of the sleaze scale from Walsh's Visser, but their scenes together are the best in the film.

The Coens aren't as successful with their main characters: John Getz and Frances McDormand are bland and uninteresting as Ray and Abby.

In *The Postman Always Rings Twice*, Frank and Cora were so hot for each other that sparks seemed to arc between them; their passion was so volatile that it almost *had* to erupt into violence. There are no comparable sexual fireworks between the lovers in *Blood Simple*; it's a tepid affair, and neither character has enough vitality to engage us. It may be that the Coens have a natural talent for creating lively villains. In any case, in *Blood Simple*, the sympathetic lovers are upstaged by their loathsome adversaries. Their low-watt rapport leaves a dark, empty space at the center of the film.

The most remarkable thing about *Blood Simple* is that it's satisfying both as a comedy *and* a thriller. What the Coens have learned from Hitchcock, whose spirit hovers over the film as it does in Brian De Palma's movies, is that murder can be simultaneously tragic and comic. The moment in *Blood Simple* when the two lovers confront one another, each one convinced of the other's guilt, and from out of nowhere a rolled-up newspaper arches into the frame, hitting the screen door between them with a sickening smack, is so startlingly unexpected and yet so right, that for a moment you're not sure you actually saw it. Watching *Blood Simple*, you begin to feel uncertain even of the ground beneath your feet. They have that kind of skill.

This interview took place with Joel and Ethan Coen, and their cinematographer Barry Sonnenfeld, in an apartment on the Upper East Side of Manhattan on the afternoon of *Blood Simple*'s commercial opening in New York. All three were casually dressed and, at the beginning of the session, excitedly talking, not about their opening night, but about their upcoming lunch at the Russian Tea Room, about superagent Sam Cohn ("Does he really eat Kleenex?") and the politics of who sits where. During the interview, the Coens chain-smoked Camels out of the same pack, passing it back and forth across the glass tabletop in front of them.

Q:   *Let's start with the basics. You were both born and raised in Minneapolis?*

JOEL COEN:   Yeah. We both grew up in Minneapolis, but have lived in New York, on and off, for about ten years. I moved here to go to school at NYU and haven't really lived in Minneapolis since then, except for about a year when we were raising money for the movie. We raised a lot of the money there, although some of it came from here and New Jersey and Texas.

ETHAN COEN:    I left Minneapolis to go to school at Princeton—I studied philosophy—and after that came to New York.

Q:    *How did you become interested in filmmaking?*

JOEL:    There were two things really. We made a lot of Super 8 movies when we were kids.

ETHAN:    They were incredibly cheesy, even by Super 8 standards.

JOEL:    We remade a lot of bad Hollywood movies that we'd seen on television. The two that were most successful were remakes of *The Naked Prey* and *Advise and Consent*—movies that never should have been made in the first place. At that time, we didn't really understand the most basic concepts of filmmaking—we didn't know that you could physically edit film—so we'd run around with the camera, editing it all in the camera. We'd actually have parallel editing for chase scenes. We'd shoot in one place, then run over to the other and shoot that, then run back and shoot at the first spot again.

Q:    *Did these films have titles?*

JOEL:    Yeah. The remake of *The Naked Prey* was called *Zeimers in Zambia*—the guy who played the Cornel Wilde part was nicknamed Zeimers. We had very weird special effects in that film. We actually had a parachute drop—a shot of an airplane going overhead, then a miniature, then cut to a close-up of the guy against a white sheet hitting the ground.

ETHAN:    It was hell waiting for the airplane to fly by. We were nowhere near a flight path.

Q:    *This sounds amazingly sophisticated.*

JOEL:    It wasn't, really. They were just hacked together. *Advise and Consent* was interesting, though, because at the time we made it we hadn't seen the original film *or* read the book. We just heard the story from a friend of ours and it sounded good, so we remade it without going back to any of the source material.

Q:   *When you finally saw the original, which did you like better, your version or theirs?*

ETHAN:   Well, we're big Don Murray fans, so I like the original.

JOEL:   Yeah, guys like Don Murray and the early Disney stars, you know, Dean Jones and Jim Hutton, are big favorites. Kurt Russell, too.

Q:   *Sounds like you watched a lot of movies on TV.*

ETHAN:   Yeah, we saw a lot of Tarzan movies and Steve Reeves muscle movies. What was that Tarzan rip-off with Johnny Sheffield?

JOEL:   *Bomba the Jungle Boy.* What's-his-name used to introduce those.

ETHAN:   Andy Devine.

JOEL:   Yeah, he had a thing called "Andy's Gang" . . .

ETHAN:   But that wasn't *Bomba*, that was a serial set in India called *Ramar*. Did you ever see *Tarzan's New York Adventure*? That's one of the greatest. And the sixties Tarzans were kind of weird.

JOEL:   A movie like *Boeing Boeing* was big with us. And we were into movies like *That Touch of Mink, A Global Affair*, Bob Hope movies, Jerry Lewis movies, anything with Tony Curtis, *Pillow Talk*. We tried to see everything with Doris Day. Those were important movies for us. I saw *Pillow Talk* again recently. It's incredibly surreal.

ETHAN:   It's a very weird, wooden aesthetic that nobody's interested in anymore. *The Chapman Report* is great that way too.

JOEL:   What's happened is that those movies have now become TV fodder.

Q:   *Did the look of those movies have anything to do with your decision to shoot Blood Simple in color? It's kind of film noir, which is usually done in black and white.*

JOEL:   There was a big practical consideration. Since we were doing the movie independently, and without a distributor, we were a little leery of making a black and white movie. But we never really considered that a sacrifice. We wanted to keep the movie dark, and we didn't want it to be colorful in the . . .

ETHAN:   . . . the *That Touch of Mink* sort of way.

JOEL:   Right. What we talked about early on was having the elements of color in frame be sources of light, at least as much as possible, like with the neon and the Bud lights, so that the rest of the frame would be dark. That way it would be colorful, but not garish.

BARRY SONNENFELD:    I think we were afraid that to shoot the film in black and white would make it look too "independent," too low-budget.

ETHAN:    Yeah. We wanted to trick people into thinking we'd made a real movie.

Q:    *The film has been criticized for that reason.*

JOEL:    Yeah, one critic said it had "the heart of a Bloomingdale's window and the soul of a resume," I loved that review.

ETHAN:    The movie is a no-bones-about-it entertainment. If you want something other than that, then you probably have a legitimate complaint.

JOEL:    But you can't get any more independent than *Blood Simple*. We did it entirely outside of Hollywood. To take it a step further, we did it outside of any established movie company anywhere. It can't be accused of not being an independent film. It was done by people who have had no experience with feature films, Hollywood or otherwise.

BARRY:    What this writer means by independent, though, is arty or artistic. It wasn't our intention to make an art film, but to make an entertaining B movie.

Q:    *Do you consider yourself linked in any way with other independent filmmakers and what they're doing?*

ETHAN:    The independent movies that we see aren't really avant-garde. John Sayles is an independent filmmaker who I like. Although I haven't seen his new film, I like what Alan Rudolph does. He'll make a movie for a studio, like *Roadie* or *Endangered Species*, and then go off on his own to make a movie just for himself for $800,000.

JOEL:    Also, I like low-budget horror movies that are made independently. They're mass-audience pictures, but they're done independently. I've worked with a lot of people who've done that stuff, like Sam Raimi. Those are the kind of independent filmmakers that we feel closer to than, say, the more avant-garde artists. I liked *Stranger than Paradise*, though, which I suppose is closer to being avant-garde than we are.

ETHAN:    I think there's room for all kinds of independent movies. And whenever anyone makes a successful one, no matter what kind it is, it's good for everybody.

Q:    *I think the distinction that's being made is between art and entertainment.*
JOEL:    That's a distinction that I've never understood. If somebody goes out to make a movie that isn't designed primarily to entertain people, then I don't know what the fuck they're doing. I can't understand it. It doesn't make sense to me. What's the Raymond Chandler line? "All good art is entertainment and anyone who says differently is a stuffed shirt and juvenile at the art of living."

Q:    *Some people see* Blood Simple *as a shrewd maneuver to establish your-selves on the scene in order to launch your careers as mainstream filmmakers.*
ETHAN:    They're wrong. We made the movie because we wanted to make it, not as a stepping stone to anything else. And we prefer to keep on making this kind of movie, independently.
JOEL:    Someone in *Film Comment* said *Blood Simple* was "aggressively New Hollywood." We wanted to make this movie, and the way we did it was the only way we could have done it. The main consideration from the start was that we wanted to be left alone, without anyone telling us what to do. The way we financed the movie gave us that right.

Q:    *When you were both still in school, you wrote a few feature scripts together. What were they like?*
JOEL:    The first one was called *Coast to Coast.* We never really did any-thing with it. It was sort of a screwball comedy.
ETHAN:    It had twenty-eight Einsteins in it. The Red Chinese were cloning Albert Einstein.
JOEL:    After that we were hired by a producer to write a script from a treatment he had. That was never produced. Then Sam Raimi, whom I worked with on *The Evil Dead,* hired us to write something with him called *The XYZ Murders.* It's just been finished. And we're writing some-thing with him now that Ethan and I are going to do.

Q:    *What movies had you worked on before* Blood Simple?
JOEL:    I was assistant editor on a few low-budget horror films, like *Fear No Evil.* There was another one that I actually got fired from called *Nightmare,* which had a small release here in New York. And *The Evil Dead.* Those are the only three features I've worked on. *Evil Dead* was the most fun. A lot of the stuff in our film, like the camera running

up on the front lawn, is attributable to Raimi, who does a lot of
shaky-cam stuff.

Q:    *How do you two collaborate when you're writing?*
JOEL:    He does all the typing. We just sit down together and work it
out from beginning to end. We don't break it up and each do scenes.
We talk the whole thing through together.
BARRY:    They pace a lot. And there's a lot of cigarette smoking.

Q:    *How was it determined that Joel would direct and Ethan produce?*
ETHAN:    We had a thoin coss . . . I mean a coin toss.
JOEL:    The standard answer is that I'm bigger than he is—that I can
beat him up so I get to direct.
ETHAN:    It's those critical three inches in reach that make the
difference.
JOEL:    To tell you the truth, the credits on the movie don't reflect the
extent of the collaboration. I did a lot of things on the production side,
and Ethan did a lot of directorial stuff. The line wasn't clearly drawn. In
fact, the way we worked was incredibly fluid. I think we're both just
about equally responsible for everything in the movie.
ETHAN:    Although, on the set, Joel is definitely the director. He's the
one in charge.
JOEL:    Yeah, I did work with the actors and all that. But as far as the
script and the realization, down to the tiniest details and including all
the major aesthetic decisions, that's a mutual thing.

Q:    *Who sets up the shots?*
JOEL:    This is where it gets really fuzzy. When we're writing a script,
we're already starting to interpret the script directorially. As to how we
want the movie to look, even down to specific shots and the kind of
coverage we want, that's worked into the writing of the script. Also,
before production, Ethan, Barry, and I storyboarded the movie together.
ETHAN:    Also, at the beginning of every day, the three of us and the
assistant director would have breakfast at Denny's—the Grand Slam
special—and go through the day's shots and talk about the lighting.
JOEL:    On the set, we'd put it together and look through the
viewfinder. Barry might have an idea, or Ethan would come up with

something different, and we'd try it. We had the freedom to do that, because we'd done so much advance work.

BARRY:    Also, on the set, we'd try to torture each other. For example, I didn't allow smoking . . .

ETHAN:    "It degrades the image." [Laughs.]

BARRY:    . . . which meant that only one of them would be on the set at any time, because the other one was off having a cigarette.

Q:    *The atmosphere of the film shows the influence of hard-boiled detective fiction. Have you read a lot of that stuff?*

JOEL:    We read all of Cain six or seven years ago when they reissued his books in paperback. Chandler and Hammett, too. We've also poured through a lot of Cain arcana.

ETHAN:    Cain is more to the point for this story than Chandler or Hammett. They wrote mysteries, whodunits.

JOEL:    We've always thought that up at Low Library at Columbia University, where the names are chiselled up there above the columns in stone—Aristotle, Herodotus, Virgil—that the fourth one should be Cain.

ETHAN:    Cain usually dealt in his work with three great themes: opera, the Greek diner business, and the insurance business.

JOEL:    Which we felt were the three great themes of twentieth century literature.

Q:    *Marty, the cuckold, seems to be lifted directly out of Cain.*

ETHAN:    He is, but a little less cheerful and fun-loving.

JOEL:    They're usually greasy, guitar-strumming yahoos, which of course Marty isn't. But yeah, that's where he comes from.

Q:    *Why did you set the film in Texas?*

JOEL:    The weather's good. And it just seemed like the right setting for a passion murder story. And people have strong feelings about Texas, which we thought we could play off of.

ETHAN:    And again, your classic film noir has a real urban feel, and we wanted something different.

Q:    *Did you set out to create a film noir atmosphere?*

JOEL:    Not really. We didn't want to make a Venetian-blind movie.

ETHAN:    When people call *Blood Simple* a film noir, they're correct to the extent that we like the same kind of stories that the people who made those movies liked. We tried to emulate the source that those movies came from rather than the movies themselves.

JOEL:    *Blood Simple* utilizes movie conventions to tell the story. In that sense it's about other movies—but no more so than any other film that uses the medium in a way that's aware that there's a history of movies behind it.

Q:    *How were you able to maintain such a delicate balance between the comic and the thriller elements in the story?*

JOEL:    I think that gets back to Chandler and Hammett and Cain. The subject matter was grim but the tone was upbeat. They move along at a very fast pace. They're funny . . .

ETHAN:    . . . they're insanely eupeptic . . .

JOEL:    . . . and that keeps the stories from being grim. We didn't want this to be a grim movie. There's a lot of graphic violence and a lot of blood, but I don't think the movie's grim.

ETHAN:    We didn't have an equation for how to balance the blood and the gags. But there is a counterpoint between the story itself and the narrator's attitude toward the story.

JOEL:    To us it was amusing to frame the whole movie with this red-neck detective's views on life. We thought it was funny, but it also relates directly to the story. It's not a one-liner kind of funny.

ETHAN:    It's easy to think that we set out to parody the film noir form because, on one hand, it is a thriller, and, on the other, it is funny. But certainly the film is supposed to work as a thriller and I don't think it would work as both at once.

JOEL:    Humorless thrillers—*Gorky Park* or *Against All Odds*—are dull, flat. They take themselves too seriously in a way that undercuts the fun of the movie. We didn't really think about making the situations in the film funny. Our thinking was more like, "Well, this will be scary," and "Wouldn't it be fun if the character were like this?"

Q:    *In preparing* Blood Simple, *did you look at other movies and use them as models?*

JOEL:    *The Conformist* is one of the movies we went with Barry to see before we started shooting in terms of deciding what we wanted the visual style of the movie to be, the lighting and all that. Also, we went to see *The Third Man.*

BARRY:    Which is funny because I read that Richard Kline [the cinematographer] and Larry Kasdan went to see the same two films before they shot *Body Heat.*

JOEL:    And came up with a completely different look. We wanted a real non-diffuse image which is the kind of image that Vittorio Storaro got in *The Conformist.* But in *Body Heat* they got this overexposed, halating image with light running through the windows. Maybe they saw a really bad print.

ETHAN:    We're also big fans of Robby Muller, particularly *The American Friend*, which we've all seen a number of times. So there are a lot of points of reference. Actually, we just wanted the movie to be in focus.

Q:    *Do you intend to continue your arrangement as it is at present, with Joel directing and Ethan producing, or do you want to switch it around next time?*

ETHAN:    We're going to continue the same way. [To Joel] We've got to do *Boeing Boeing* credits next time [in which, to calm top-billing egos, Jerry Lewis's and Tony Curtis's names revolved on an axis].

JOEL:    We're thinking that next time we'll have it say, "Ethan and Joel Coen's *Whatever.*"

ETHAN:    No, I like "Ethan Coen presents a film by his brother Joel."

Q:    *And you would like to continue working together?*

JOEL:    Oh yeah. In fact the three of us do. There are certain collaborations which are really fruitful. One of them is with Sam Raimi, which we hope continues on other movies in the future. Another is with Barry.

Q:    *As a result of the success you've had so far with* Blood Simple, *are the studios beating a path to your door with offers?*

JOEL:    We're getting a lot of talk, but we don't know what it means. You spend one week in Hollywood! [Laughs.] People have been calling. But we'd like to continue to work as independently as possible. Not independent necessarily of the Hollywood distribution apparatus, which is really the best if you want your movie to reach a mass market. But as far as production is concerned, there's a real trade-off involved. It's true that certain movies require more money to produce right than *Blood Simple* did. But the difference with us is, while we may need more money for the next one than we did for *Blood Simple*, we're still not talking about the kind of budgets that the studios are used to working with. We did this film for a million and a half, and, for me, three—four million dollars is an incredible amount of money to make a movie. And that's attainable without going to the studios.

ETHAN:    The bottom line is, even if *Blood Simple* does well, we're comfortable with the idea of making another low budget movie.

JOEL:    Right. We're not afraid of making movies for cheap.

# Invasion of the Baby Snatchers

## DAVID EDELSTEIN/1987

IF YOU'VE EVER LEFT SOMETHING on the roof of a car and then realized the goof several miles down the road, you'll get a kick out of a bit in *Raising Arizona*, Joel and Ethan Coen's farce about a babynapping and its aftermath. What's left on the car roof is an infant, and when the awful truth is discovered, the occupants—a pair of escaped convicts—make a squealing 180-degree turn and go barreling back to where the babe has presumably landed. Cut to the infant in his car-seat in the center of the blacktop, staring off screen with gurgling, Gerber-baby glee, while, behind him, the vehicle rushes in at ninety miles an hour, screeching to a halt about an inch from his little head. And the kid is still smiling.

This is how the guys behind the ghoulish *Blood Simple* invade the American mainstream: The kid is so *cuuute* and the gag so felicitous that you hardly register the perversity. In *Raising Arizona*, a young hayseed couple—excon H. I. "Hi" (Nicolas Cage) and police booking officer Edwina "Ed" (Holly Hunter)—learn they cannot have a child. (As narrator Hi puts it, "Her insides were a rocky place where my seed could find no purchase.") In desperate need of a baby to complete their blissful, suburban existence, they shanghai one of the newborn Arizona quintuplets, sons of Nathan Arizona (Trey Wilson), an unpainted-furniture baron.

In a world where moviemakers often inflate themselves and their motives, Joel and Ethan Coen—thirty-two and twenty-nine, respectively, both childless but presumably fertile—take the opposite approach: They talk coolly about craftsmanship and storytelling, and little else. With *Raising Arizona*, the Coens say, they wanted to make a film as different

---

From *American Film*, April 1987. Reprinted by permission of the author.

from *Blood Simple* as possible—galloping instead of languorous, sunny instead of lurid, genial and upbeat instead of murderous and cynical.

"It's not an emotional thing at all," says Barry Sonnenfeld, their cinematographer. "Given any topic, they could write an excellent script. Topics are incredibly unimportant to them—it's structure and style and words. If you ask them for their priorities, they'll tell you script, editing, coverage, and lighting."

When pressed for their attraction to the *subject*—babies, child-rearing, images of the family—the Coens squirm and smoke and do their best in the face of so irrelevant a question. We're in a small Greek coffee shop near Joel's Manhattan apartment, where, in less than half an hour, they have smoked three cigarettes apiece; the air in the room has grown so foggy that we seem to have drifted out to sea.

Finally, out of the cloud, Joel speaks: "You have a scene in a movie when someone gets shot, right? Bang! And the squib goes off and the blood runs down and you get a reaction, right? It's movie fodder, you know what I mean? And in a really different way, a baby's face is movie fodder. You just wanna take elements that are good fodder and do something different with them." He laughs—a reassuring laugh, like old bedsprings—and turns to his brother. "Wouldn't you say that's basically it?"

"Yeah," says Ethan, deadpan, "it's like a real cheap and shameless bid at making a commercial movie. We decided to sell out and that was the first decision."

If the Coens are tightlipped and ironic with interviewers, perhaps it's because they themselves can't account for the warmth and integrity of their movie. "That's your job," suggests Ethan, helpfully.

They don't make it easy. Few journalists are allowed on the *Raising Arizona* set, and when I arrive, there isn't a lot to see. It's the end of a thirteen-week shoot, and all I get to watch is part of a chase scene in a supermarket: There's no dialogue, the shots have been meticulously storyboarded, and the only real challenges are those facing the special effects people. (I spend a lot of time watching them blow popcorn and cereal out of an air cannon.)

But I'm lucky to be there at all, and it's hard to blame the Coens for their wariness of the press. No one paid any attention to them when they made *Blood Simple* on $1.5 million—money they raised themselves from private investors, most in the vicinity of their hometown, Minneapolis. Sometimes their crew consisted of one person, Barry Sonnenfeld. *Raising Arizona*, while no biblical epic, cost four times as much, sports a full roster of production assistants, and is being released by a major studio, Twentieth Century Fox.

"The attitude on *Blood Simple*," says Sonnenfeld, "was 'Just go for it, 'cause if we screw it up, no one will know about it, it'll be just one more unreleased movie.' I still take chances, but there's no question we're more scared."

By this point in the shoot, however, Joel and Ethan seem anything but antsy. (The Coens cowrote the script; Joel is nominally the director, Ethan the coproducer with Mark Silverman.) Although I have agreed in advance not to waylay them, they're happy to make small talk—or, in this case, baby talk.

"The babies were great," says Ethan, of the most potentially problem-ridden scene, in which Hi swipes Nathan, Jr. (T. J. Kuhn), from the nursery and accidentally liberates the other infants.

"We kept firing babies when they wouldn't behave," says Joel. "And they didn't even know they were being fired, that's what was so pathetic about it."

What gets a baby fired?

"Some of them took their first steps on the set," says Joel. "Ordinarily, you'd be pretty happy about something like that, but in this case it got them fired."

"They'd make the walk of shame," intones Ethan.

"The parents were horrified. One mother actually put her baby's shoes on backward so he wouldn't walk."

We're in a supermarket in Tempe, Arizona, in the middle of a long, flat stretch of shopping centers outside Phoenix. In keeping with the movie's visual motif of aggressive bad taste, the female extras shop with curlers in their hair and let out sustained shrieks; as Hi dodges their carts, a red-faced manager pulls out a shotgun and starts blasting. No babies are involved, but a pack of dogs have chased Hi into the super-market. Early on, it's clear that if you're ever pursued by angry dogs, the absolute best move would be ducking into a supermarket—the animals don't have much traction on those shiny floors and get easily traumatized.

"This is worse than when we had babies," says Ethan. "At least with babies, you could smack them around. People are afraid to hit dogs."

The Coens remain calm, laid-back. Joel, the taller, has nearly shoulder length hair and dangling arms; ten or fifteen years ago, the look was vintage pot-head. Ethan, unshaven, lighter, and more compact, divides his gaze between the action and the floor, pacing between shots and grinding out cigarettes. Synchronicity is the key: Sonnenfeld has compared them to a two-man ecosystem; and while they do communicate through tiny signals and monosyllables, they seem to be the recipients of what Mr. Spock would term a "Vulcan mind meld."

Jim Jacks, executive producer, narrates their trademark *pas de deux*: "You watch Ethan walk in a circle this way and Joel walk in a circle that way; each knows exactly where the other is and when they'll meet. Then they go to Barry."

This is also how the Coens write; they don't make films so much as pace them out. (Asked where the confidence to make movies comes from, Ethan replies, "Every little step considered one at a time is not terribly daunting.") Ethan, the more silent and cryptic of the two, majored in philosophy at Princeton, and the contrast between his placid demeanor and the nicotine-fuelled churnings of his brain gives pause. The computer in his head seems to try out hundreds of moves before it ever lets him *do* anything.

Between setups, the brothers take turns on a decent game of Ms. Pac-Man. They're going a little stir-crazy by now; Scottsdale, where they've been settled for the last few months, seems (as actress Frances McDormand puts it) like a big golf course; and the nearby desert, though magnificent, is not reliably soul-quenching.

Nicolas Cage sits in silence next to the book rack, idly flipping through magazines. On his canvas chair, a Band Aid separates "Nic" from "olas," the offending "h" obscured. Cage is touchy about misspellings of his first name, and, in a soothing (and poetic) gesture, Ethan ministered to the hurt. That's what producers are for.

Reluctant to discuss his methods, Cage is clear about his goals. He arrives on the set with a ton of ideas; even in the uncomplicated supermarket chase, he proposes a glance at his watch during a tiny lull. Joel politely shakes off the suggestion. Their relationship has been bumpy but respectful. Cage praises the brilliant script and the Coens' professionalism, but he's clearly miffed that he couldn't bring more to the party. "Joel and Ethan have a very strong vision," he says, "and I've learned how difficult it is for them to accept another artist's vision. They have an autocratic nature."

A few minutes after the interview, Cage summons me back. "Ah, what I said about Joel and Ethan . . . with relatively new directors, that's when you find that insecurity. The more movies they make, the more they'll lighten up. The important thing is not to discourage an actor's creative flow."

Not all the actors feel their flow was dammed, however. Holly Hunter, a friend of Joel and Ethan's (inspired by her ramrod Southern tenacity, they wrote the part of Ed for her), insists she always held the reins, but could rely on Joel as a safety net. "Joel and Ethan function without their egos," she says. Then, thinking it over, she amends, "Or maybe their egos are so big they're completely secure with anybody who disagrees with them."

That sounds more like it. "You can convince Joel and Ethan of things," says Sonnenfeld. "I find the best thing to do is bring up your point, drop it, and wait a couple of days."

The Coens radiate confidence, and you can bet their young, non-union crew picks up on it. The set ("remarkably sex and drug free," I'm told) behaves like a winning clubhouse—kids just up from the minors who know they'll top the standings by season's end. The tone is relaxed but super efficient. In return for artistic control, the Coens are determined to stay on schedule. "They worry more about going over budget than we do," says Ben Barenholtz, who signed both to a four-picture deal with Circle Releasing Company (producers of *Blood Simple*). Fox has left them alone; the day after I arrive, executive vice-president Scott Rudin flies in to see his first set of dailies.

To say the Coens come prepared to shoot is to understate the case. The script has been rubbed and buffed, the shots storyboarded. On the set they rarely improvise. Joel insists that when you make a movie for so little money, you can't afford to mess around. It's strange then, to hear him rhapsodize about Francis Coppola, a director who can't seem to work without a crisis, hammering out scenes and shots on the spot. "I have no idea how you can go into a movie without a finished script," Joel admits.

Sitting with Joel, Ethan, and Sonnenfeld in a Scottsdale Denny's before the next evening's shoot, the mood is as comfortable as one of those all-night bull sessions in *Diner*. The Coens aren't limo types, and it takes very little to make them happy—a pack of cigarettes, coffee, a warm Denny's. "When they're in work mode, creature comforts become minimal," says Frances McDormand, who played the heroine of *Blood Simple* and has lived with Joel for the past couple of years. (She was Holly Hunter's roommate before that, and has a brazen cameo in *Raising Arizona*.)

"They love the performance part of their job, like the minute you walk on a stage or the camera starts rolling. For them, the writing is one part of it, the budgeting and preproduction another, but it's all building toward the shoot. And then in postproduction, that's when they get to lead the artistic life: They get to stay up late and get circles under their eyes and smoke too much and not eat enough and be focused entirely on creating something. And then it starts again."

Truly, a design for living.

Joel and Ethan Coen grew up in a Jewish suburb of Minneapolis, the sons of two college professors—a father in economics, a mother in art history. (They have a sister, now a doctor.) Despite their ties to academia, they're almost perversely anti-intellectual about what they do; in fact, they insist that their home was short on high culture. Recalls Joel, "My mother once wrote an article, 'How to Take Children to an Art Museum,' but I don't recall her ever taking us."

Instead, the children were left to their own devices, and weaned on pop culture and television; they set James M. Cain beside Aristotle, and among their most favorite film experiences, cite fifties and sixties sex comedies like *Boeing Boeing* and *Pillow Talk*. (For the record, they also love good movies.)

From the age of eight, Joel made films—remakes of pictures like *Advise and Consent*—and eventually went off to study filmmaking at New York University, where he's remembered for sitting in the back of the class and making snotty remarks. He says he learned almost nothing, but welcomed his parents' subsidy to make movies. (In his thirty-minute thesis film, *Soundings*, a woman makes love to her deaf boyfriend while verbally fantasizing about his buddy in the next room.) At Princeton, Ethan was equally out of step. After neglecting to notify the college that he planned to return from a term off, he tried to cut through the red tape with a phony doctor's excuse (from a surgeon at "Our Lady of the Eye, Ear, Nose, and Throat") that claimed he'd lost an arm in a hunting accident in his brother-in law's living room. The school ordered him to see a shrink.

After film school, Joel worked as an editor on Sam Raimi's *The Evil Dead*—the *Don Giovanni* of hack-'em-ups—and quickly struck up a friendship with Raimi, for whom he and Ethan wrote a script called *The XYZ Murders*. It was mangled and discarded by its studio, Embassy (and had a limited Columbia release as *Crimewave*), a disaster that made the Coens more wary of dealing with major studios. "We've always let Sam make those mistakes for us," explains Joel. " 'Sam,' we tell him, 'you go do a movie at a studio and tell us what happens.' "

The Coens are pranksters, but colleagues also describe them as affable and generous, not to mention quick studies: They're fond of quoting entire scenes from other movies, along with lines from bad reviews. Their geniality doesn't come through in the rigid, Q & A format of interviews, though, and while promoting *Blood Simple*, their anarchic impulses came out. In their press conference at the 1985 New York Film Festival, for which *Blood Simple* had been selected, Ethan summed up their aesthetic by quoting Raimi: "The innocent must suffer, the guilty must be punished, you must drink blood to be a man."

"That's the great thing about Joel and Ethan," says Sonnenfeld. "They don't wanna be on the *Today* show. They don't wanna be in *People*. They don't give a shit. They wanna have a good time."

My formal interviews with the Coens are, in some respects, exercises in futility—me talking and Joel and Ethan smoking, their faces evoking Redford's response to Newman in *Butch Cassidy and the Sundance Kid*: "You just keep thinkin', Butch. That's what you're good at." Maybe the questions are dumb, or maybe (as they insist) they're just dull guys, movies being their one step out. Perhaps they learned a lesson from their *Blood Simple* interviews. "We wince when we read ourselves in print," says Joel.

Like their movies, the Coens seem suspended between high and low impulses. Ethan studied philosophy, of course, but only "for fun"; there's something absurd, he implies, about being an intellectual in a culture this junky. Like Preston Sturges—one of their models for *Raising*

*Arizona*—the Coens debunk all notions of aesthetic responsibility. Their movies poke fun at ideas, and their characters suffer from tunnel vision, each gripped by an obsession he or she can't be bothered to explain (nor, for that matter, can the Coens).

Perhaps they'd rather just listen. "Their favorite midtown lunch spot is the counter at Woolworth's," says editor Michael Miller. "They go to hear dialogue that will find its way into a script. The opening of *Blood Simple*—many of those lines they'd overheard. Their attention is never more riveted than when they're in the back seat of a taxi. I've seen Joel draw out taxi drivers in a way he doesn't draw out his friends. Once, on the way home from the airport, the driver had a ball game on—the Mets were playing someone and it was in the heat of the pennant drive—and Joel said, 'What's the game?' and the cabdriver said, 'Baseball, I think.' They loved that."

Found objects constitute much of the Coens' work. "It's not meant to be condescending," says Joel. "If the characters talk in clichés, it's because we *like* clichés. You start with things that are incredibly recognizable in one form, and you play with them."

# Interview with Joel and Ethan Coen

## MICHEL CIMENT AND HUBERT NIOGRET/1987

Q:  *Both your films belong to genres: one crime, the other comedy. Do you prefer to work in a genre framework?*

JOEL COEN:   We were more conscious of working in a genre with *Blood Simple* than with *Raising Arizona*. *Arizona* seems more absurd, an amalgam of genres. In *Blood Simple* the genre was, in a basic way, guiding the movie we were making.

ETHAN COEN:   With *Arizona* we didn't begin by thinking of diving into a genre. We'd wanted to broadly make a comedy with two main characters. We concentrated on them, more than the movie in a general sense.

Q:  *Did you first draw the characters, and then the setting?*

JOEL:   With *Arizona*, yes. The story was a way of talking about the characters. For *Blood Simple*, we started with a situation, a general plot. The characters went from there. So, the reverse.

Q:  *Why the Southwest with both, Texas, Arizona? You're from Minnesota . . .*

ETHAN:   Perhaps partly because we're *not* from the Southwest, which appears nearly as exotic to us as it is for you. It's like an attraction for us. For the second film, that type of desert landscape seemed the right place.

From *Positif*, July/August 1987. Reprinted by permission of *Positif* and the authors. Translated by Paul Buck and Catherine Petit.

JOEL:    Once again, *Blood Simple* had been conceived in a more planned way, more conscious. By not taking Texas as it really is, but as something preserved in legend, a collection of histories and myths . . . The subject is "deadly passion." If you associate that with a region of the USA, Texas is the most logical place. There are so many identical cases that have occurred in Texas that it's grown in the public imagination. So it was the logical place to construct our story. That situation was important for our dramatic bearings, because the film was supposed to be a slice of life, but still a fiction contrived to fit into an exotic place.

ETHAN:    My whole association with Minnesota, where we grew up, was very dull. The movie had to be shot anywhere but in Minnesota.

Q:    *The "folk tales" have some importance to* Raising Arizona, *like that of Davy Crockett?*

ETHAN:    We decided definitely to have a bond with the imaginary, that the movie wouldn't be a slice of life.

JOEL:    When we'd spoken with the cinematographer, Barry Sonnenfeld, regarding the look of the movie, we talked about opening it like a book of stories, with colors that had a certain vibration. That was part of the visual style.

Q:    *Your influences are more literary than cinematic?*

JOEL:    For a movie like *Raising Arizona*, I guess you can detect our admiration for Southern writers like William Faulkner and Flannery O'Connor.

ETHAN:    Even if we don't share her [O'Connor's] interest in Catholicism! But she has a true knowledge of Southern psychology that you don't find with many other writers. She also has a great sense of eccentric character. For *Blood Simple* the influence was more from crime writers like James Cain.

Q:    *What you say about Flannery O'Connor is especially striking, because of the director one thinks about after seeing* Raising Arizona: *John Huston. I'm reminded of sequences from his* The Life and Times of Judge Roy Bean, *or from* Wise Blood, *adapted from the novel by Flannery O'Connor.*

ETHAN:    Yeah, like the fantastic Stacy Keach character in *The Life and Times of Judge Roy Bean*!

JOEL:    As far as O'Connor is concerned, our characters haven't the same mystical obsessions as hers. Ours are terrestrial!

Q:    *One also thinks about Chuck Jones cartoons when viewing* Raising Arizona, *as in the supermarket scene.*
ETHAN:    We thought about these characters who rebound, and collide, and simply their speed of movement. We tried to refine the spirit of animation you find in pinball machines.
JOEL:    It's funny that you mention Chuck Jones, because we hadn't thought consciously about him for this film. On the other hand, his *Roadrunner* inspired us for *Blood Simple*, for the long scene where Ray [John Getz] tries to kill Julian Marty [Dan Hedaya], then bury him. There's a Hitchcockian side, but there's also Chuck Jones.

Q:    *What was the starting point for* Raising Arizona? *The idea of quintuplets?*
ETHAN:    Not really. Essentially, after having finished *Blood Simple*, we wanted to make something completely different. We didn't know what, but we wanted it to be funny, with a quicker rhythm. We also wanted to employ Holly Hunter, a long-standing friend. This isn't really the story of the origin of the project but Holly Hunter, her personality and, by extension, the character we conceived for her. On the other hand, *Blood Simple* started from an idea for a script.
JOEL:    The idea of kidnapping the baby was really secondary. We weren't that interested either in the problem of sterility or the desire for having a child, but by the idea of a character who has that desire and at the same time feels outside the law. This conflict allowed us to develop the story, that aspiration to a stable family life, and at the same time a taste for unusual experiences.
ETHAN:    Yeah, that tension in the character of Hi was our motive for the movie.

Q:    *How did the other characters develop? For example, the two halfwit brothers?*
JOEL:    We like those two guys a lot, they're like Laurel and Hardy. They're there to shake up the story, the other characters, everything. It's

like an old idea by Dashiell Hammett: an external character intervenes in a situation and we observe the reactions he provokes.

ETHAN:    At some point we said to ourselves: let's make two rough characters enter the story and watch what effect it'll have on the relationship between the heroes.

Q:    *Was your script very precise or did you leave yourselves some freedom for shooting?*

JOEL:    We work on the script till we're satisfied, but during shooting we're very faithful on the whole. There's very little improvisation in the dialogue. What changes a lot by contrast is the visual idea of the movie once the actors enter the set. During the retakes, we can think of other ways of "covering" the scene with the camera. That happens mainly in the dialogue scenes. By contrast, for action scenes, they're drawn beforehand and we follow the storyboard exactly. In fact, it's not a matter of referring to the storyboard during shooting, it serves us psychologically. We know what the visual idea of the shot is, we have it on paper and it's reassuring.

ETHAN:    Sometimes we look in the camera and discover the shot drawn on the storyboard doesn't work.

JOEL:    For various reasons. For instance, the location can pose problems you don't anticipate. And even if we wanted to improvise while shooting we couldn't because our budgets have been very low. *Blood Simple* was made for $800,000 and *Raising Arizona* for a little more than five million, which for Hollywood is very low. To obtain the maximum from that money, the movie has to be meticulously prepared.

Q:    *Do the actors induce you to change aspects of their characters during shooting?*

JOEL:    Absolutely. Particularly with Nicolas Cage and Holly Hunter. Nic's a really imaginative actor. He arrives with piles of ideas that we hadn't thought about while writing the script, but his contribution is always in line with the character we'd imagined. He extrapolated from what was written. The same with Holly. Even if she surprised us less because we had her in mind when we wrote her part, and we've known her a long time.

Q:     *Can you give us examples of the participation by the actors in their roles?*
JOEL:     We'd spoken at length with Nicolas Cage about his moustache and side burns. We wondered if he had to keep them throughout the movie or lose them at some point.
ETHAN:     He was also obsessed by his hair, like Woody Woodpecker. The more depressed the character was, the more flamboyant the tuft became. There was a curious capillary rapport!

Q:     *And the clothes?*
JOEL:     That, no, it wasn't in the script, the Hawaiian shirts.
ETHAN:     That's clichéd clothing on criminals in the Southwest, that style of flashy dressing.

Q:     *The character of the motorcyclist comes from a dream . . .*
JOEL:     We tried to imagine a character who didn't correspond specifically to *our* image of an "Evil One" or a nightmare become reality, but rather to the image that Hi would have. Being from the Southwest, he'd see him in the form of a Hell's Angel.
ETHAN:     We also tried to connect the characters through the music. Holly sings a lullaby in the movie and we asked the composer to introduce it into the musical theme that accompanies the bounty hunter, that also blends Richard Wayne and country music!

Q:     *Where did you find the interpreter for Randall "Tex" Cobb?*
JOEL:     He's not really an actor. He's a former boxing champion. He's been in a few movies. In the beginning he was more someone who brawled in the streets in Texas, then who tried without real success to make a career in boxing. He's less an actor than a force of nature. Not really someone it's easy to work with, and I don't know if I'd rush headlong into employing him for a future film. He played his role well in *Raising Arizona*, but he posed problems.

Q:     *What kind of language did you want for the characters? It seems like a very stylized argot.*
JOEL:     It's a mixture of local dialect and a vocabulary we imagined from the likely reading material of the characters: the Bible, magazines.

The voice-over was one of the starting points for the story. What we wrote first was the ten minutes preceding the credits.

Q:    *You established right from the start of the film this mixture of sentimentalism, concerning the baby, and the distancing irony.*
JOEL:    There are people who find the conclusion too sentimental. Once again, that doesn't reflect our own attitude to life. For us it's written in the context of the character, it fits with his ideas about life, what he dreams of accomplishing in the future
ETHAN:    We hide behind the main character! We hadn't really measured out the quantity of feelings we wanted to inject into that story, the characters guided us.

Q:    *Both films are visualized very inventively. Did certain images impose themselves on you before writing the script?*
JOEL:    In some cases, yes. Anyhow, it's different from writing a script for someone else. In that instance, the director generally doesn't want the script telling him the visual elements. Working for ourselves, on the other hand, we allow those elements to be introduced into the script. Sometimes, however, we write the scene and then we ask ourselves what's the best way to express the information, to make the public participate emotionally or to accelerate the rhythm. It's then that we think of the images. But, in fact, it's all very tied together, it's the two faces of the same coin. While writing the script, we knew we'd shoot on a wider plane and with more depth of field than in *Blood Simple*, which was more claustrophobic.
ETHAN:    I remember a specific image which pleased us when we wrote the script: to see Holly in uniform hurling orders at the prisoners. It might appear secondary, but that image had great importance in setting the writing in motion.
JOEL:    For instance, the first shot with that horizontal line and the character rushing into it was written like that in the script.

Q:    *How do you share the work?*
JOEL:    We write together without parting company. We lock ourselves in a room and write the script from A to Z. *Raising Arizona* took three and a half months. On the set it's basically a continuation of the

writing. We're always there, both of us, and we consult each other continually. The credits indicate a division of labor more rigid than what really happens. For effectiveness, and to avoid confusion, I speak to the actors and communicate most of the time with the technical crew, but for the directing decisions it's a mutual responsibility. Ethan, for his part, is busier taking care of the production.

ETHAN:    The same with the editing and mixing, it's a total collaboration.

Q:    *And the image of the two prisoners who come out of the mud?*
JOEL:    That sort of primitive birth! We asked ourselves how to introduce those two brutes who'd escaped from prison. That vision came to mind—it appeared to be an appropriate introduction.

Q:    *It's curious you've mentioned James M. Cain as having influenced* Blood Simple, *because one thinks more readily of Jim Thompson.*
JOEL:    In fact, at that time, we hadn't read him. After *Blood Simple* was released, the novels were republished in paperback in the United States and we started to discover him.

Q:    *Watching* Raising Arizona *one sometimes thinks of Preston Sturges.*
ETHAN:    We're mad about his films. We adore *The Palm Beach Story.*

Q:    *How did you get along when you were children?*
JOEL:    There's three years difference in age and that's important when you're a child. It was only after leaving school that we really got to know each other.
ETHAN:    Yeah, above all by writing together. Joel studied cinema at university. Me, I followed a philosophy course, God knows why. Joel then worked as an editor.
JOEL:    On horror films. Then we began to write scripts for others, and finally we wrote *Blood Simple.* When we were kids, we made films on Super 8. They were abstract and surreal. In winter, Minnesota, where we were born, resembles a frozen wasteland. There were fields covered with snow and the scenery was very abstract. We also shot remakes of films we saw on television, like *The Naked Prey* by Cornel Wilde that we made in our garden. And also *Advise and Consent.* That had a more epic dimension, we even had to construct the set inside the living room. We

saw many films, those of the fifties and from the beginning of the sixties with Doris Day and Rock Hudson, the worst period of Hollywood.

Q:    *Where did you study cinema?*
JOEL:    At New York University. Our professors weren't famous directors, they'd made a career essentially in teaching. I studied for four
years from 1972.

Q:    *And philosophy?*
ETHAN:    I mainly studied the history of philosophy. I wrote a thesis on
Wittgenstein. I don't see too many connections with my future work as
a filmmaker.

Q:    *You worked as an assistant director?*
JOEL:    No, I worked as an assistant editor on *The Evil Dead* where I
edited between a third and a half of the movie. At that time there was a
trend in horror films, low budget, produced independently, like *Fear No
Evil*. You always had to put "Evil" on the table . . .

Q:    *In* Arizona *there's some superb montage effects, particularly with the
motorcyclist on the road . . .*
JOEL:    Those cuts were specified in the script.

Q:    *You like popular culture, and at the same time you're ironical.*
JOEL:    Yes, we have that relationship with American popular culture.
ETHAN:    We have an attitude, a commentary with regard to the mate-
rial. We make jokes with it . . .

Q:    *The characters are very different in* Blood Simple *to* Arizona.
JOEL:    In *Arizona*, the characters were certainly supposed to be sympathetic. We got a lot of pleasure out of writing them. The character of Ed
has a restrained sympathy, which is very interesting, something very
mature. What's not easy is when a character's very wicked, and at the
same time you feel sympathy for him.

Q:    *There is a dark side with you, and a comic side. You don't seek realism.*
JOEL:    Some people have been offended by the characters in *Arizona*.
ETHAN:    For me, it's a very wild film.

Q:   *How was the idea of your first film born—why did you choose a typical film noir?*

ETHAN:   We've liked that type of story for a long while: James Cain, Dashiell Hammett, Raymond Chandler. It's a genre that really gives us pleasure. And we also chose it for very practical reasons. We knew we weren't going to have much money. Financing wouldn't permit other things. We could depend on that type of genre, on that kind of basic force.

JOEL:   The story called for special effects, exotic locations. And we knew we could realize a certain number of things for very little money. You can limit the number of characters, distribute them around a confined space. There's no need to spread out on an enormous scale, shoot things that create expenses. It was a pragmatic decision to choose that style of film.

Q:   *Barry Sonnenfeld, the cameraman, has shot both films.*

JOEL:   Yes, he's an old friend, from way before the movie. The collaboration is very close. Well before we began to shoot he saw the sets. We spoke about the movie, the way we were going to shoot certain places. He was involved very early, which once again, from a practical point of view, helps you work more efficiently. At the moment you begin to shoot, you can't suddenly start spending loosely. Everything has to be discussed beforehand.

Q:   *In* Blood Simple, *there are shots with astonishing effects, like the revolver firing through the wall, when one sees the hits via the light which comes through . . .*

JOEL:   When you speak about scenes constructed from images, that's a good example, because the image determined the situation there, which was then elaborated to integrate into the context of the story.

Q:   *How was your first film financed? With many partners? Independently?*

ETHAN:   We'd never made a movie before. We had no references. It was difficult to find a production company who trusted us, who would give us money to make a movie. So we spoke to private investors, large numbers of them. For the second film, that was incredibly easy. We went to see the American distributor of *Blood Simple*, Circle Films, who were interested in us producing another film. They liked our script. They said "yes."

Q:    *What's your ideal mode of production: to be independent or work with a "studio"?*
ETHAN:    We produced independently because of circumstances, particularly on the first one.
JOEL:    For the second, there was a path of least resistance. We could've sought the money elsewhere, perhaps from a studio. Because of *Blood Simple* we knew Circle Films. We trusted them, it was natural to work with them. There was no ideology behind those choices. As long as we could maintain the type of control we want, we could accept the financing of a studio.
ETHAN:    The problem is to get the money.
JOEL:    The problem is all the ties attached. The whole idea with regard to independent production is that it helps you to make the movie you want to make, and in the way you want to make it. If the studio permits the same thing, then that's all well and good. Some do it and manage very well, even with movies that don't correspond to the "Hollywood formula." Some directors are very successful in that system, making movies they want to make.

Q:    *What's been the shooting time for each of your films?*
JOEL:    Eight weeks for *Blood Simple*, ten for *Arizona*.

Q:    *Your film appears at the same time as* True Stories, *which is very different. But there's a common irony, pop-cultural roots, and a very modern visual approach.* True Stories *is more static while your film is more dynamic.*
JOEL:    It's coincidence. As is the fact that John Goodman [the larger of the two escapees in *Arizona*] acts in both movies. We chose him before *True Stories* was shot, and he came to film with us directly from shooting David Byrne's movie.

Q:    *How do you make the distinction between Arizona and Texas? The people? The feelings?*
JOEL:    Arizona doesn't carry all the baggage of Texas for an American audience. Texas is associated with many things, which isn't the case with Arizona.

ETHAN:    Arizona is now like so many towns in the Midwest and Southwest spread. The stores are the same as everywhere.
JOEL:    Once again, Arizona for us was one of the rare states where you can find that type of landscape. That type of desert only really exists in Arizona, closer to Mexico too . . .

Q:    *What American filmmakers of the last twenty years do you feel closest to? Not those you prefer!*
JOEL:    That question's much more difficult than those you admire! It's much easier to say the ones you like.

Q:    *Who do you like?*
JOEL:    Scorsese, Coppola, David Lynch.

Q:    *Kubrick?*
JOEL:    Yes.

Q:    *Kubrick's black humor?*
JOEL:    Yes, Dr. Strangelove.
ETHAN:    I like Walter Hill a lot, he's done some very interesting things.

Q:    *And Bob Altman?*
JOEL:    I like some of his movies. He did a great job of adapting Chandler with *The Long Goodbye*.
ETHAN:    Yeah, it's a very good movie. But I read somewhere it's the one he likes least. I can't understand why . . .

Q:    *No, he likes it a lot.*
ETHAN:    Ah! That's okay then.

# Shot by Shot

## STEVEN LEVY/1990

ONCE JOEL AND ETHAN COEN decided to do a gangster movie, it was inevitable that something like the Thompson jitterbug would find its way onscreen. The New York–based brothers, creators of *Blood Simple* and *Raising Arizona*, are known for infusing their intricately plotted screenplays with uniquely macabre twists. Their new film, *Miller's Crossing*, does not abandon this tradition.

Quite simply, the Thompson jitterbug—thus named by its wisecracking creators—refers to a gruesome dance performed involuntarily by a hood who's being riddled with bullets while his dead fingers continue to squeeze the trigger of a Thompson submachine gun. Though the antics are improbable, presumably the combination of shells pumped into him from below and the recoil of the still-firing tommy gun holds the dead man aloft, jerking him up and down as the bullets tear apart the room. In one scene of twenty-two quick cuts in this Thompson jitterbug, we see him shoot his toes off.

And another thing: all the while, the soundtrack blares an Irish tenor singing "Danny Boy."

Presumably a throwaway moment in the midst of the movie's key sequence, it is prime Coen: a borderline-tasteless, bloodstained piece of slapstick that results from blending the sensibilities of Stephen King and Samuel Beckett. "It isn't intended to be riotously funny, but there's something . . . *fun* about it," says producer Ethan Coen, an amiable

From *Premiere*, March 1990. Reprinted by permission of Sll/Sterling Lord Literistic, Inc. Copyright by Steven Levy.

fellow in his early thirties who looks mildly preppy with his short brown hair and polo shirt. "It's a Big Death, you know?"

Director Joel Coen, who in contrast to his younger brother has long dark hair and work clothes (a vaguely Neil Young-ish look), is mildly surprised that the jitterbug has been raised as an issue: "We didn't set out to make *Scenes from a Marriage*," he explains.

They did set out to make something different. The Coen brothers—self-described as "poky"—work on one project at a time and try not to repeat themselves. "We didn't want to do another out-and-out comedy, like *Raising Arizona*," says Joel. "We wanted to do something that was a little bit morbid. Less of a comedy, more of a drama. We've always liked gangster movies, so it was what we started to think about when we did another script."

They initially intended to explore the conflict between Irish and Italian gangs, a power struggle between second-generation immigrant groups. Eventually, a plot emerged, centering on the local mob boss, an Irishman named Leo, and his cagey lieutenant, Tom. The delicate ecosystem of their Prohibition-era town is upset when Leo falls for Verna, the sister of a Jewish bookie, and foolishly protects her brother from the Italian mobsters who hold a grudge against him. The crooked cops and politicians formerly in Leo's employ wait to see who prevails. Meanwhile, Tom is also having an affair with Verna and has some demons of his own to fight. Trying to play all the angles, he winds up in a nightmarish situation in the wooded area that lends its name to the film.

The Coens changed the concept somewhat as the cast filled out. The darkly Celtic Gabriel Byrne was cast as Tom. The part of Leo was written specifically for Trey Wilson, the irascible Nathan Arizona in the Coens' previous film. But two days before *Miller's Crossing* was to begin shooting, Wilson died of a cerebral hemorrhage. Stuck with the task of finding an immediate replacement, the Coens got lucky: Albert Finney, whom they greatly admire, was available. With Byrne and Finney in hand—and with Byrne reading his lines in a heavy brogue—the ruling gang members now represented a less-assimilated stripe of Irishman, and the Coens beefed up the ethnic character of the movie.

"We got mugged by the Irish," explains Ethan.

Then there was the task of re-creating a dirty industrial town, circa 1929. Normally, they would have considered such beefy towns as Chicago or Albany. But they didn't want to deal with cold or snow, and this was a winter shoot. "We looked around San Francisco, but you know what that looks like: period but upscale—*faux* period," says Ethan. Then someone suggested New Orleans, parts of which surprisingly fit the bill. Outside of the distinctive French Quarter, there were plenty of places that could pass for a generic Anytown in the late 1920s. "New Orleans is sort of a depressed city; it hasn't been gentrified," says Ethan. "There's a lot of architecture that hasn't been touched, storefront windows that haven't been replaced in the past sixty years."

The centerpiece of *Miller's Crossing* is the explosive assassination attempt that occurs when the Italian family sends its gunsels to rub out Leo. On one level, the Coens see the sequence as a tonic to what they consider a perilous amount of dialogue in the film thus far: "It's about time at that point to shed a little blood," says Ethan. "The movie's in danger of becoming tasteful, you know?"

On another level, the failed rubout is central to the audience's understanding of Leo's character: by fending off four would-be assassins with spectacular nonchalance, Leo shows us that his vulnerability as a boss might be overestimated. "This is Leo as the boss, Leo as the guy in control of the situation, as opposed to situations in the movie where he seems a bit naive," says Joel. "This is Leo in his element."

The scene also represents the Coens in *their* element: tour de force filmmaking. The rubout scene is an elaborate, explosive montage. But it also drips with irony, primarily because behind the gangster-movie images—blazing machine guns, body parts jerking from direct hits, a house burning down, and a car crash—we hear a soppy rendition of "Danny Boy," ostensibly the song playing on Leo's Victrola.

The scene begins with a long tracking shot in which we see Leo's just-killed bodyguard slumped over, his cigarette igniting a newspaper. The killer lets an accomplice into the parlor, and the pair climb the stairs to Leo's bedroom. Leo, meanwhile, has noticed smoke coming from beneath the floorboards—he's already stubbed out his cigar and grabbed his revolver. As the gunmen burst in, he's ready for them, rolling under the bed and shooting one in the ankles, then in the head. Then, appropriating the victim's machine gun, he dives out a window, dropping to street level outside the burning house. He dispatches the second gunman (Monte Starr), who is still in the bedroom—the jitterbug; ducks bullets from a speeding car full of more assailants; and then, patiently walking up the tree-lined street, keeps firing the tommy gun until his bullets reach the auto, which spins into a tree and explodes.

Needless to say, the logistics were considerable. Because the sequence was shot in various locations, ranging from studio interiors and a residential street in suburban Metairie to a house near the French Quarter to a vacant house (now occupied by novelist Anne Rice) in the Garden District, the tightly edited montage was filmed over a period of several weeks. Exactly which part was filmed when is hard to remember—with one exception. "We burned down the house the night of the Academy Awards," says Joel.

Perhaps the hardest shot to get right was the one in which Leo rolls under the bed to shoot. The Coens used an elevated set, about three feet off the ground, so the cameras would be level with the bed. The challenge was to coordinate the action with the technology—Finney had to shoot while the muzzle of the gunman's Thompson blazed, squibs in the mattress above him exploded, and an air gun shot feathers downward from the mattress. Eventually, the Coens were satisfied, but when the footage reached the editing room, they found that the first gunman's death was insufficiently vivid—the squib didn't "read" (it didn't explode properly and jerk the hood's head) when Finney shot him. So they reshot that part.

More edifying was the fate of the second gunman, the unwitting performer of the Thompson jitterbug. Not one but two men played the poor victim, whose extended dance of death still evokes silent mirth as the Coens review it in the editing room months afterward. Starr stood in for the head-on shots, but the reverse shots required the hardy stunt coordinator Jerry Hewitt.

"Thompsons are not light guns," explains Joel Coen. "It's difficult to hold one while it's firing and bucking, and also with squibs going up your back."

"It's hard," agrees Ethan. "You have to sell all that body language, taking the bullet hits. What sells the hit is the dance."

Ah, the dance. "We always knew we wanted to do that," says Ethan.

"You keep thinking of things you want to add to the scene," says Joel. "He shoots up the chandelier, the paintings, his toes. All kinds of fun things. It was a lot of fun blowing the toes off. The only regret is that it goes by so fast, you almost kind of miss it. They're a highlight."

In the course of planning this scene, the Coen brothers became expert in the lore of Thompson guns, several of which they procured for the film. While they are enamored of the gun's output—given sufficient ammunition, the monster can choke out eight hundred rounds a minute—they had to accept its predisposition to jam, a drawback that forced innumerable retakes.

Overall, though, they considered the Thompson guns a big plus. "The gun is incredibly loud, and it does vibrate," says Joel fondly. "You can see it sort of jingle. The whole thing was a very satisfying experience."

Even Finney got into the Thompson mania. Toward the end of the segment, as Leo walks down the street firing the gun at the speeding getaway car, Finney had to maintain a cool demeanor while controlling the powerful weapon. As an added challenge, the Coens set up a bucket behind him to see how many expelled cartridges he could land in it. "He got a very high percentage," says Ethan, as Joel collapses in laughter. "Technically, he's a very good actor."

Finney's machine-gun virtuosity helps end the sequence with a flourish. But what really makes the scene is "Danny Boy." The Coens recruited Irish tenor Frank Patterson—he played the vocalist in John Huston's *The Dead*—to perform the song. After the scene was edited, Patterson went into the studio with an orchestra and watched the monitor so he could tailor the cadences of the song to the mounting body count. At the end, when Finney, cigar stub in his mouth, sighs in satisfaction as he watches his last assailants die in flames, the music swells in old-world mawkishness: ". . . and I will sleep in peace . . . until you come to . . . meeeeee!"—a deliciously droll commentary on the Thompson jitterbug that came before.

# A Hat Blown by the Wind

## JEAN-PIERRE COURSODON/1991

Q:   *One of your actors, questioned about your collaboration on the set,
explained that: "In reality, Joel is the director—and Ethan too!"*
JOEL COEN:    That's true, we codirect. The division of labor suggested by
the credits is pretty arbitrary.

Q:   *Are there sometimes conflicts between you two during shooting about the
best method of directing?*
ETHAN COEN:    No, we write the scene together, we imagine it the same
way. Everything happens in the most straightforward way.

Q:   *Do you make any changes during shooting to the script, and do you let
the actors themselves improvise or provide changes?*
JOEL:    In *Miller's Crossing* the actors didn't change one single word of
the dialogue. We follow the script very faithfully, and a large number of
the production elements are already included. That said, in the middle
of shooting we rewrote the whole second part of the script.

Q:   *Do you think that situation of two directors can sometimes unsettle
the actors?*
JOEL:    I don't think so. Like Ethan said, we're generally agreed on the
type of interpretation we want. We didn't have any surprises on the set

---

From *Positif*, February 1991. Reprinted by permission of *Positif*. Translated by Paul Buck
and Catherine Petit.

because we had a lot of rehearsals beforehand. When we auditioned the main actors, they read not just one scene or two but the whole script.

Q:    *Albert Finney is a last-minute choice . . .*
JOEL:    The part had been written for Trey Wilson, who died just before the beginning of shooting. We had to delay it for ten days. It just happened that Finney was available and could commit himself for a few months. We didn't rewrite the dialogue for him, but the result would undoubtedly have been very different with Trey.
ETHAN:    What's strange is that the part would never have been written without Trey in mind, whereas now it's impossible for us to imagine any other actor than Finney in the Leo role.

Q:    *Who had the idea of making Finney and Gabriel Byrne speak with a strong Irish accent?*
JOEL:    The characters are of Irish extraction, but their parts weren't planned to be spoken with an accent. When Gabriel read the script he thought it had a style, a rhythm that was authentically Irish, and he suggested trying the lines with his accent. We were sceptical at the start, but his reading convinced us. So Finney took on the accent too.

Q:    *The film is out at the same time as other gangster movies.*
JOEL:    It's a coincidence. It's very different from the others, in any case from Scorsese's *GoodFellas*, the only one I've seen. I love it but the story and the style are completely different, like day and night.
ETHAN:    When they describe all those movies as gangster movies, it suggests a wider community that doesn't really exist. It's the type of situation journalists like to exploit, because they always try to identify fashions, trends. It makes good copy but doesn't mean a lot. Anyway, *Miller's Crossing* is really closer to film noir than to the gangster movie.

Q:    *The film unfolds in New Orleans, a city one doesn't usually associate with the genre. What dictated your choice?*
JOEL:    We had to shoot in winter, and we didn't want snow for the exterior shots, so we had to choose a Southern city. New Orleans happens not to be very industrially developed and many districts have only slightly changed since the twenties.

ETHAN:    We took care not to show the picturesque or tourist aspects of the city. We didn't want the audience to recognize New Orleans. In the story the city's an anonymous one, the typical "corrupted town" of Hammett novels.

Q:    *In your interviews you always give the impression that you avoid the issue when asked about the symbolism of the images, the motivation of the characters, the social implications of the film, etc.*
ETHAN:    Apparently, nobody wants to be satisfied with the movie, as if they absolutely need explanations beyond the images, the story itself. That always surprises me. But if you don't comply, journalists get the impression that you're hiding something from them.

Q:    *In his* New York Times *review Vincent Canby complains that Gabriel Byrne is often hard to understand and also complains about the obscurities of the film: some characters are only names in the dialogue and what happens to them is not clear. Are you sensitive to that kind of criticism?*
JOEL:    Not really. It doesn't really concern me if the audience sometimes loses the thread of the plot. It's not that important to understand who killed the Rug Daniels character, for instance. It's far more important to feel the relationships between the characters. The question of intelligibility concerns me more, but, until now, I haven't received any bad reactions concerning that.

Q:    *The relationships between characters are rather obscure: Leo and Tom, for instance. It's a friendship that degenerates into rivalry.*
JOEL:    Because of Verna's character. It's the heterosexual triangle of the movie.

Q:    *You spoke in your press conference about a homosexual triangle—Bernie, Mink, Dane—balancing the other one. The homosexuality of those three characters is scarcely evident (except perhaps for Bernie) and their relationships even less. How important is that triangle?*
JOEL:    It's difficult to say what made us think of it. It's not very important, it's a pretty minor point but it's somehow satisfying to us, a kind of symmetry or counterpoint maybe. It introduces a certain variety, and the process seems legitimate to us insofar as we don't do violence to the story or the characters.

Q:    *Tom, the hero, cheats, lies, and manipulates throughout the entire film. Does he nevertheless have ethics?*

JOEL:    Yes, I think there's a certain purity in his intentions, but it manifests itself in a very twisted way. He has principles that are in conflict with themselves.

ETHAN:    It's everybody's problem, in fact. The movie is a gangster story because it's a genre we're attracted to—a literary rather than a cinematic genre, by the way—but the conflicts of the characters, the morality, have a more universal application.

Q:    *What got you started, a theme, the idea of a character, or an element of the plot?*

JOEL:    Certainly not a theme. In reality the starting point of the script was an image, or a series of images, the desire to make a movie whose characters would be dressed in a certain way—the hats, the long coats—and would be placed in certain settings that were unusual for the genre: the countryside, the forest . . .

Q:    *The hat is more than an accessory in the film, it's a recurrent theme as soon as the credits start, with that hat blown by the wind in the forest. What is the significance?*

JOEL:    Everybody asks us questions about that hat, and there isn't any answer really. It's not a symbol, it doesn't have any particular meaning . . .

ETHAN:    The hat doesn't "represent" anything, it's just a hat blown by the wind.

JOEL:    It's an image that came to us, that we liked, and it just implanted itself. It's a kind of practical guiding thread, but there's no need to look for deep meanings.

Q:    *In a sense, Tom himself puts us on our guard against interpretation when he recounts his dream: he specifies that the hat doesn't change into something else, it stays a hat.*

ETHAN:    Sure, you can take it like that. Verna wants to give a meaning to Tom's dream, and it's gratuitous. Tom remains objective.

Q:   *How long did you take to write the script?*
JOEL:   Much longer than for the two previous movies. All in all, eight months more or less, but we stopped to write the script of the next one, which took two months.

Q:   *Would you contemplate shooting somebody else's script?*
ETHAN:   No, I don't think so, we've grown so used to working like this since the beginning. For us, creation really starts with the script in all its stages; the shooting is only the conclusion. It'd be very difficult for us to direct a script written by a third person.

Q:   *You've changed designers for* Miller's Crossing.
JOEL:   We like to work with the same collaborators, but Jane Musky, the designer of our first two movies, wasn't available. David Gassner, who worked with Coppola, helped us a great deal in the choice of colors. The colors are more controlled than in the previous movies.
ETHAN:   David had the idea for the building columns, to have the architecture reflecting the trees in the forest . . . He was our designer again for the movie we just shot, *Barton Fink.*

Q:   *What is Gabriel Byrne's musical contribution?*
JOEL:   He suggested a certain number of traditional Irish songs. We'd already decided to use "Danny Boy," but the other song, on which Carter Burwell based the main theme, is an old ballad suggested by Gabriel.

Q:   *What relationship do you have with Circle Films?*
ETHAN:   As you know, it's the independent distribution company which distributed *Blood Simple* and which later produced *Raising Arizona.* Fox contributed to *Raising Arizona's* budget and were the distributors, as they are for *Miller's Crossing* and the next one, *Barton Fink,* but our relationship with Circle remains the same. Ben Barenholtz as a distributor has always been interested in independent cinema, American and foreign, he's always taken risks. We're on the same wavelength.

# A Rock on the Beach

## MICHEL CIMENT AND HUBERT NIOGRET/1991

Q:    Barton Fink *is about the artistic block of a scriptwriter. What brought you to write the screenplay?*
JOEL COEN:    It happened when we were midway through writing *Miller's Crossing*. It's not really that we were ourselves "blocked," but our rhythm was slowed up and we wanted to put ourselves at a certain distance. In order to get out of the problems we had with that story, we began to think about another one. This was *Barton Fink*, which has two points of origin. First we wanted to work again with John Turturro—who we know well—and to create a character he could play. Then, the idea of a huge neglected old hotel, which preceded even our decision to set the story in Hollywood.
ETHAN COEN:    We wrote the script very quickly, in three weeks, before returning to *Miller's Crossing* to finish that. It's one of the reasons why both movies are released so close together. When we finished shooting *Miller's Crossing*, we had the script ready to film.

Q:    *Why have you situated the action in 1941, a key era for writers in Hollywood? Fitzgerald and Nathaniel West died, Preston Sturges and John Huston, two popular scriptwriters, moved on to become directors . . .*
JOEL:    We hadn't thought of that. On the other hand, we liked the idea that the world outside the hotel was on the verge of the Apocalypse since, for America, 1941 was the dawn of the Second World

From *Positif*, September 1991. Reprinted by permission of *Positif* and the authors. Translated by Paul Buck and Catherine Petit.

War. That appeared to fit the story. The other reason—which hasn't really materialized in the movie—is that we thought of a hotel where only old people, eccentrics, and the physically handicapped resided, because all the others would've left for the war. The more the script developed, the more that theme withdrew, but it prompted us, at the start, to choose that period.

ETHAN:    Another reason was the main character: a serious playwright, honest, politically engaged and rather naïve. It seemed natural he came from Group Theatre and the thirties.

JOEL:    The character had a little of the same background as a writer like Clifford Odets, though the resemblance stops there. Both wrote the same type of plays on proletarian heroes, but their personalities are very different. Odets was much more open to the external world, a very sociable guy even for Hollywood, which isn't the case with Barton Fink! The man Odets was also very different from the writer Odets; he was more sophisticated than what he wrote. There was a lot of passion in him.

Q:    *Have you read the Odets diary that he kept during 1940?*

ETHAN:    John Turturro read it. But there's still a distance that separates Odets from Barton Fink.

JOEL:    Turturro was also interested in the acting style of Group Theatre. At the start of the movie, the voice you hear off-screen is Turturro, and at the end, when he's typing a section of his script at the machine, it resembles Odets.

Q:    *The character of W. P. Mayhew is directly inspired by Faulkner.*

ETHAN:    Yeah, the Southern alcoholic writer. It's obvious that we chose John Mahoney for that part because of his resemblance to Faulkner, but it was also because we were very keen to work with him. There again, it's a starting point and the parallel is superficial. In the details Mayhew is very different from Faulkner, he hasn't had the same experience in Hollywood at all.

JOEL:    It's obvious Faulkner had the same disdain as Mayhew for Hollywood, but his alcoholism didn't paralyze him and he continued to be productive.

Q:    *Was the character of Jack Lipnick, the producer, inspired by Louis B. Mayer?*

JOEL:    Michael Lerner resembles him a little, but Lipnick is more of a composite. The incident with the uniform, for instance, came from the life of Jack Warner, who enrolled in the army and asked his wardrobe department to make up a uniform. Lipnick also has the vulgar side of Harry Cohn.

ETHAN:    What's ironical is that that colonel uniform, which is one of the most surreal elements in the movie, is at the same time one of the few to have been drawn directly from Hollywood lore!

Q:    *One of the great qualities of your films, and of* Barton Fink *in particular, is the totally unforeseeable nature of their unfolding. How do you construct your screenplays?*

JOEL:    In this case we had the course of the movie in mind from the start. The structure was even looser than usual and we were conscious that, towards the middle, the narrative would take a turn. We wanted the start of the movie to have a certain rhythm and to take the audience on a kind of journey. When Barton awoke and discovered the corpse near him, we wanted it to be a surprise without clashing with what had gone before.

ETHAN:    We were conscious that the demarcation line was very tight. We needed to astonish the audience without alienating them from the movie. Because of the way the hotel is presented, his arrival in Hollywood is not seen as totally "normal." But it's obvious that this movie is less bound to the conventions of a cinematic genre than, say, *Miller's Crossing*, which belongs to the tradition of the gangster movie.

Q:    *At what stage did you think of the image of the woman on the beach that heralds the last sequence?*

JOEL:    That came as soon as we began to ask ourselves what would be in that room. We wanted it to be very sparsely decorated, the walls to be bare, and just that view from the window. In fact, we wanted the only opening onto the external world to be that image. It seemed important to create a feeling of isolation. We needed to establish from the start a state of dislocation in the main character.

ETHAN:    The image of the beach had to inspire a feeling of comfort. I don't know exactly why we struck to that detail, but it served to create even more oppression within the room itself.

Q:    *With the sequence where Barton flattens the mosquito, the film passes from social comedy into the fantastic.*

JOEL:    Some people have suggested the whole second part of the movie is only a nightmare. It certainly wasn't our intention to make it a literal bad dream, but it's true that we wanted an irrational logic. We wanted the climate of the movie to reflect the psychological state of its hero.

ETHAN:    We wanted the audience to share the interior life of Barton Fink, and his point of view. But there's no need to go further. It would've been silly if he woke at the end into a larger reality than that of the movie. In the sense that it's always artificial to speak of the "reality" of a fictional character, we didn't want people to think he was more "real" than the story.

JOEL:    There's another element that enters into play with that scene. You don't know who killed Audrey Taylor. We didn't want to exclude the possibility that it was him, though he proclaims his innocence repeatedly. It's one of the classic conventions of crime movies to create false trails for the audience for as long as possible. With that said, we wanted to remain ambiguous until the end. But what's suggested is that the crime has been committed by Charlie, the neighbor in the room next door.

Q:    *From that point of view, the choice of John Goodman to play Charlie Meadows is fundamental—given that he usually plays the "pleasant type." For that reason, the audience is with him in the first scenes.*

ETHAN:    That role was written for the actor, and we were obviously conscious of that warm, affable image the audience feels comfortable with. We exploited that expectation in order to finally turn it round. Yet, as soon as he presents himself, there's something menacing, disquieting about him.

Q:    *The fact that Barton Fink takes the proletariat as the subject of his plays also obliges him to appear friendly towards Meadows, otherwise he would feel full of bourgeois prejudice.*

JOEL:    That's partly true, but Charlie also gains sympathy simply through his friendly behavior at the start.

ETHAN:    Charlie is equally conscious of the role Barton Fink intends to make him play, in a perverse way.

Q:    *While shooting this film you didn't know you'd be in competition at Cannes, and were even less aware that Roman Polanski would be president of the jury. It's ironic he's had to judge a film where* The Tenant *out of* Cul-de-Sac *meets* Repulsion.

JOEL:    It's clear we've been influenced by his films, but, at this moment, we have too many scruples to speak about it because it'd give the impression we kissed his ass. The three films you mentioned influenced us, of course. *Barton Fink* doesn't belong to any genre, but, if it has a lineage, it's obviously one that begins with Polanski.

Q:    *One thinks also of* The Shining *as well as the world of Kafka, and the black humor of the Jewish culture of Central Europe.*

JOEL:    That's true, except *The Shining* belongs more to the international horror movie genre. Several critics have also mentioned Kafka and that surprises me, because, to tell the truth, I haven't read him since my university days when I devoured *The Metamorphosis*. Some of them have alluded to *The Castle* and *In the Penal Colony*, but I've never read them.

ETHAN:    With so many journalists wanting us to be inspired by *The Castle*, I've got a newfound desire to discover it for myself.

Q:    *How do you share the writing of the script?*

ETHAN:    It's very simple and very informal. We discuss each scene together in detail without ever allotting the writing of such or such scene to either of us. But finally it's me who types. As we've said, *Barton Fink* was particularly quick to write, while *Miller's Crossing* was longer, almost nine months.

JOEL:    Usually we spend four months on the first draft that we then show to our friends, before dedicating two more months to polishing.

Q:    *How did you write* Barton Fink *so rapidly?*

ETHAN:    Perhaps we owe it to the feeling of relief after the difficulties of *Miller's Crossing*. Anyway, it was very easy.

JOEL:    It's strange but some movies present themselves almost entirely formed in your head. You know how they'll be visually and without perhaps knowing the end exactly, you have an intuition of the kind of emotion that'll manifest itself. Other scripts, on the other hand, are a little like slowly progressing journeys where you don't really know

where you're going. For this movie, we practically knew what state
Barton Fink would be in at the end. Likewise, at the very start we wrote
the ultimate tirade of Charlie, where he explains himself and says that
Barton was only a tourist in town. It makes things much easier knowing
in advance where you're leading your characters.

ETHAN:    We had the impression of knowing them really well, perhaps
because we're very close to the two actors, and that made writing their
roles very easy.

Q:    Miller's Crossing *is also a film where many characters and places and
different plots intersect.*
JOEL:    It's true that *Barton Fink* is much more contained. The story of
*Miller's Crossing* is so complex that we had a tendency to get lost while
we were writing it!
ETHAN:    *Barton Fink* is more the development of an idea, rather than all
the narrative intricacies that made up *Miller's Crossing*.

Q:    *How did that name come to mind?*
JOEL:    We found it at the start of working on the script, but we don't
know where it came from. It seemed to arrive just like that, by pure
chance.

Q:    *There's much humor in the film, from the wallpaper that falls from the
walls to the two police detectives. More of a duality of drama/comedy than in
your previous films.*
JOEL:    That's right. The movie's neither really a comedy nor a drama.
*Miller's Crossing* tended more towards drama and *Raising Arizona*
towards comedy.
ETHAN:    It seems we're incapable of writing a movie which, in one way
or another, doesn't get contaminated by comic elements.
JOEL:    It's funny, because at the beginning I saw *Miller's Crossing* more as a
comedy, while *Barton Fink* appeared to me as humor of the blackest kind.
ETHAN:    But unlike in *Miller's Crossing*, here we torment the main character for comic effect.

Q:    *Jon Polito has a role similar to the one in* Miller's Crossing. *In both
cases he's humiliated.*

ETHAN:    Except that in *Barton Fink* he's oppressed for twenty years. He
finally got used to it.

Q:    *The first image one sees of Hollywood is unexpected in this type of film:*
*a rock on a beach.*
ETHAN:    It's funny you mention that because we filmed other shots to
create a more conventional transition, but we decided not to use them.
All we needed was a rock on the beach, which also ushers in the end.

Q:    *It's the second time you've worked with the designer Dennis Gassner.*
JOEL:    We shot at least three weeks in that hotel where half the movie
takes place. We wanted an art-deco style and a place that was falling to
pieces, having known better days. The hotel had to be organically
linked to the movie—it had to be the externalization of the character
played by John Goodman. Sweat falls from his brow like wallpaper falls
from the walls. At the end, when Goodman says he's prisoner of his
own mental state, that it's like a hell, the hotel has already taken on
that infernal appearance.
ETHAN:    We used a lot of green and yellow to suggest a feeling of
putrefaction.
JOEL:    Ethan always described the hotel as a ghost ship set adrift,
where you get indications of the presence of other passengers without
ever seeing them. The only clue would be the shoes in the corridors.
You can imagine it peopled with traveling salesmen who've had no success, with their sad sex lives, crying alone in their rooms.

Q:    *You look at the Hollywood of fifty years ago, but in another way you're*
*confronted by the same problems. Do artists still meet philistines like Jack*
*Lipnick?*
JOEL:    Very probably. But *Barton Fink* is really very far from our own experience. Our professional life in Hollywood has been particularly easy, which
I'm sure is very unusual and very unfair. It isn't a personal comment in any
way. We financed our first movie *Blood Simple* ourselves, and the three that
followed have been produced by Circle Films in Washington. Each time
we've presented them with a script, which they've liked, then agreed on
the budget. We have no rejected scripts in our drawers. There are, of course,

projects on which we've begun work but haven't finished writing for one reason or another, because there were artistic problems we couldn't resolve or because their cost became prohibitive.

Q:   *Is there an unfinished project that was particularly dear to you?*
JOEL:   No, because finally you're taken by another movie which seduces you and which becomes your main preoccupation. We'd still like to realize one or two shorts we've written, but it's very difficult to produce them in America because there's no market.

Q:   *Why have you called in Roger Deakins this time?*
JOEL:   Our usual cameraman Barry Sonnenfeld wasn't free, and as we'd liked Deakins's work we asked him to work for us. He seemed suitable for the project.
ETHAN:   We very much liked his night shots and interiors in *Stormy Monday*. We'd also seen *Sid and Nancy* and *Pascali's Island*.

Q:   *Have you made a storyboard as with your previous films?*
ETHAN:   Yes, in some detail. But, of course, many changes happen when we're on the set, though we still arrived with each shot prepared. This was a simpler movie to make than *Miller's Crossing*, and the budget was a third less, as was the shooting time: eight weeks instead of twelve.

Q:   *Did you shoot sequences that were removed in the editing?*
JOEL:   For *Miller's Crossing* entire sequences were shot which didn't find their way into the movie. That wasn't the case with *Barton Fink*, nearly everything was used. I remember some shots of studio life in Hollywood we decided not to keep: they were pretty banal.

Q:   *Compared to your previous films, which had scenes like the night shooting in* Miller's Crossing, Barton Fink *has a much more rigorous style.*
JOEL:   That wasn't intentional. It's probably because *Miller's Crossing* had so much dialogue that, at a certain stage, we wanted to give the viewers some visual punches. The gangster genre also permits those grand action scenes. But for *Barton Fink* that style of thing didn't seem appropriate. Big spectacle would've upset the balance.

Q:    *The "writer victim" of Hollywood is part of the legend of cinema.*
ETHAN:    Yeah, it's almost a cliché. On top of that, we give them the dignity of victim status that they probably don't deserve, because Barton Fink is probably not a great artist and Mayhew is no longer capable of writing.

Q:    *Do you feel close to some of your contemporaries in American cinema?*
JOEL:    There are quite a lot of things we like, but we don't see affinities with our work. The American film industry is in pretty good health today; a good number of directors are getting their ideas successfully onto the screen, either in the factory products from the big companies—which are mostly formulaic, though there are exceptions—or the independent cinema.

Q:    *Your style of cinema contrasts strongly with most of the Hollywood films of today. For example, you begin all your films right in the middle of a scene without setting up the context, as in* Miller's Crossing.
JOEL:    At the beginning of *Miller's Crossing,* we have two shots: the first is of a glass with ice, then a close-up of [Jon] Polito. We didn't want to show straightaway who was holding the glass. You saw someone with the glass, heard the tinkle of ice, but the person is blurred in the shot; then, you see Polito, hear his monologue. The ice is a crucial element in the shot. Then you see Albert Finney, but you still don't know who's holding the glass, and finally, you arrive at Gabriel Byrne in the background. All of that was prepared in the storyboard.
ETHAN:    We wanted to create a mystery around the character who was going to become the movie's hero.
JOEL:    Polito's important in that scene because he gives the information, he begins to recount the story.
ETHAN:    We held back Gabriel's entrance in the conversation. He's the last to speak, five minutes after the movie has begun.

Q:    *How do you explain the relative commercial failure of* Miller's Crossing, *despite positive worldwide critical reception?*
ETHAN:    It's always difficult to speculate. Maybe the story is too complicated to follow.
JOEL:    After all, the plot of *The Big Sleep* was pretty hard to understand, too! It's difficult to analyze why it failed, but it was still a disappointment to us.

# That Barton Fink Feeling:
# An Interview with the Brothers Coen

JIM EMERSON/1991

JOEL AND ETHAN COEN'S MOVIES are kind of hard to describe. And god bless 'em for that.

The brothers' first feature, 1984's *Blood Simple*, can fairly be tagged as a noir-ish thriller—but that doesn't adequately convey the movie's absurdist tone or its morbid sense of humor.

And 1987's *Raising Arizona* is definitely a comedy, but there's a screwball sense of dread and hysteria running through it that isn't *just* funny ha-ha.

Likewise, 1991's extraordinary *Miller's Crossing* can be accurately labeled a gangster picture, but that doesn't begin to describe the uniquely stylized netherworld in which it takes place.

And then came *Barton Fink*, fresh from an unprecedented sweep of the major awards (picture, director, actor) at the Cannes Film Festival. And this creepy-funny tale of an ambitious New York playwright who comes to Hollywood in the early '40s to write a screenplay is the Coen brothers' most deliciously, provocatively indescribable picture yet.

"Well, the danger of describing it as a comedy," says director/co-writer Joel, thirty-six, "is in setting up an expectation that it's going to be . . ."

"It's a buddy movie," interjects producer/co-writer Ethan, thirty-three.

From *Jeem's Cinepad* website http://www.cinepad.com/home.html, no date. Reprinted by permission of the author.

JOEL:    "Yeah, Ethan likes to call it a buddy movie for the '90s. I'm not sure what you would call it. John Turturro (who plays the title character) thinks it's a sort of coming-of-age story. It's like a sort of black comedy, I guess."

ETHAN:    "Well, there is a certain sort of somber quality to it that you wouldn't associate with a comedy. And people might be sort of put off by it if they think they're going to see a straight comedy. Yeah, it's hard to describe, generically. . . ."

Well, whatever. Let it suffice to say that *Barton Fink* does a tantalizing job of confounding an audience's expectations. On one level it's a pungent satire of Hollywood in the '40s; on another it's a comic character study of a callow and arrogant intellectual; on yet another it's a sort of allegorical horror film. And when Barton is alone in his seedy room at the Hotel Earle, it resembles nothing so much as Roman Polanski's moody and demented 1976 psychological shocker, *The Tenant*.

ETHAN:    "Yeah, it's kind of ironic that Polanski was . . ."

JOEL:    ". . . the head of the jury at Cannes" (where *Barton Fink* walked away with so many prizes).

ETHAN:    "Well, wait. I mean, if you had to describe (*Barton Fink*) generically, you couldn't do better—not that this is a genre—but it's kind of a Polanski movie. It's closer to that than anything else."

JOEL:    "It's true. And *The Tenant* is a movie that we're both familiar with and like."

ETHAN:    "It's also like the 'Person Alone in the Room' genre."

JOEL:    "Yeah, (Polanski's) *Repulsion* is sort of like that. There are definitely influences from Polanski, I'm sure."

ETHAN:    "That was kind of cool, meeting him at Cannes."

JOEL:    "He's got his own sense of humor and it's present in all of his movies, even though you wouldn't call his movies comedies, exactly."

Exactly. Not unlike the films of the Brothers Coen. Although Joel is credited as director and Ethan as producer on all Coen movies, their collaboration—like their conversation—involves much more give and take than the separate titles would imply.

JOEL:    "In Cannes, we took a codirecting credit, because it more accurately reflects what actually happens. For us, here, the fact that we separate the two credits is fairly arbitrary to a certain extent . . ."

ETHAN:    "Well, not totally arbitrary. I mean, Joel talks to the actors more than I do and I probably do production stuff a little more than he does. But it's largely overlapping."

JOEL:    "It also sort of stakes out the territory we want to keep exclusively ours by, in a sense, assigning it to each of us individually. Psychologically, it's sort of important to us to realize that Ethan produces the movie and I direct, so, in a sense, we don't want another producer—or another director. That's sort of why we keep it separate that way, but it doesn't really reflect what happens on the set."

Although there are a number of idiosyncratic filmmakers out there, few get to have their visions released intact by major studios. Even David Lynch has made *Blue Velvet* and *Wild at Heart* (and in 1997, *Lost Highway*) for smaller independent companies. But Twentieth Century Fox (under studio president Joe Roth) released *Raising Arizona, Miller's Crossing*, and *Barton Fink*, through an arrangement with the Washington, D.C., company Circle Films. Circle has financed all of the Coens' pictures ever since releasing their independently made first feature, *Blood Simple.*

ETHAN:    "We don't have to convince everybody that the story should go like this and not like that. We haven't had to defend anything to anybody. We have a really good relationship with Circle Films, who've produced the last three movies. We just give them the finished script and the budget and they go, 'Yeah, OK. Fine.'"

JOEL:    "We've been remarkably lucky in that we've been free to make the movies we've wanted to make the way we've wanted to make them. They've all been made for a price. They've all been low-budget by Hollywood standards. But that's part of why we've been able to do it that way—or mostly why. *Miller's Crossing* was the most expensive one: about $11 million. *Barton Fink* was considerably less."

Some critics and audiences have found the uncategorizable weirdness of *Barton Fink* frustratingly off-putting and insular, as if the Coens were attempting to be strange and obscure just for the sake of being strange and obscure. But the brothers say it isn't so.

JOEL:    "It's not a conscious decision to be, uh . . ."
ETHAN:    "I think the movie's really entertaining. We tried to make it that way . . ." He laughs. "Was there any whining there?"

JOEL:    "Well, to be fair, we knew that it wasn't. . . . What's the best way to say this? It's like, we knew that it wasn't going to be *Terminator 2*, you know? So, we weren't surprised that we're not in twenty-two hundred theaters. But I also don't think it's as difficult as some people think it is. I mean, some people come out going, 'I don't get it.' And I don't quite know what they're trying to 'get,' what they're struggling for."
ETHAN:    "It's a weird story, but it's a fairly straightforward story that I think can be enjoyed on its own terms . . . *Barton Fink* does end up telling you what's going on to the extent that it's important to know— you know what I mean? What isn't crystal clear isn't intended to become crystal clear, and it's fine to leave it at that."
JOEL:    "But we have had the reaction where people leave the movie sort of uncomfortable and befuddled because of that. Although that wasn't our intention to do that. I was going to say that maybe our telling of the story wasn't as clear as it should have been, but I don't think that's true. In terms of understanding the story, it comes across. The question is: Where would it get you if something that's a little bit ambiguous in the movie is made clear? It doesn't get you anywhere."

Like The Box, for example? Most filmmakers would feel they *had* to reveal what's in the box that Charlie leaves with Barton. But, of course, this is a movie about how much Barton does *not understand* ("Empathy requires understanding," Judy Davis drawls to him), so it's much more fun to leave the box unopened. Indeed, the fact that Barton doesn't open it may be seen as a sign of a slight maturation on his part.

JOEL:    "It's almost like a genre rule: Don't Open The Box."

The ending may be enigmatic, but it's undeniably right. Barton sits by the sea when suddenly a pelican dives into the frame and drops into the water in front of him: Plop! The screen goes black. It's a moment that makes you laugh with delight and gives you shivers, for reasons it may not be possible (or desirable) to describe. The Coens say it's just part of the way they make movies.

JOEL:    "We have an uncanny ability to make birds do what we want them to do. In *Blood Simple* there's a shot from the bumper of a car and it's going up this road and a huge flock of birds takes off at the perfect moment and crosses (the car's trajectory). And then a second later, their shadows sweep across the road."

So, once again, the birds cooperated with the Coens—and so did the mosquitoes that inhabit Barton's hot and sticky room at the Hotel Earle. And if you think the movie flirts with absurdity, well . . .

JOEL:    "We got a letter from the ASPCA on this movie, or some animal thing. They'd gotten hold of a copy of the script and wanted to know how we were going to treat the mosquitoes. I'm not kidding. It's true."

*Barton Fink*, which deals with the subject of Barton's writer's block as he's attempting to write a wrestling picture for Wallace Beery, was written when the Coens themselves were stymied during the writing of the intricately plotted *Miller's Crossing*.

ETHAN:    "It was just going really slowly. It took us a really long time. I guess because the plot was so involved; we just got sick of it at a certain point. And we decided to take a vacation from it in the form of writing something else, which turned out to be this."

JOEL:    "We were about halfway through and . . . It's not exactly writer's block, but sometimes you hit a wall in terms of thinking about the plot or something and it just becomes easier, when we'd get together to write, to think about something else. That's how *Barton Fink* happened. And it actually got written very quickly, in about three weeks. I don't know what that means. It's not an enormously complicated movie from the point of view of, like, the sequence of the plot, the sequence of events or anything like that. . . ."

ETHAN:    "*Miller's Crossing* got sort of intricate and this one, for whatever reason, we just never got hung up."

So, did they know where *Barton Fink* was headed when they started writing?

JOEL:    "Roughly, but not exactly."

ETHAN:    "We sort of knew about the turn that happens two-thirds of the way through."

JOEL:    "We had a fairly good idea, early on in the writing, what the resolution of the main part of the story—the Charlie and Barton part—would be.

Did they steep themselves in Hollywood lore to come up with the hilarious scenes at the mythical studio, Capitol Pictures?

ETHAN:    "We didn't do any research, actually, at all. Maybe one of the things that contributed to the writing of the script was that we'd previously read some stuff. There's a really good book called *City of Nets*, about German expatriates here (in Los Angeles in the '40s)."

JOEL:    "It's a book not exclusively about the movie colony. It's also about the musicians and the writers who came here. It was a sort of interesting picture of Hollywood in that period. It was one of the things that started us thinking about Hollywood as a setting. But we didn't go out and do research beyond it."

The Coens describe their writing technique as, well, fairly non-structured.

JOEL:    "He does most of the typing."

ETHAN:    "Yeah, I usually type, because I type better. It's incredibly informal. I mean, us writing is basically just us sitting around in a room, moping for hours.

JOEL:    "With an occasional burping out of some pages."

ETHAN:    "Sort of like our interviews."

Each of the Coens' films has created a world of its own, only tangentially related to reality as most of us are familiar with it.

And although certain characters in *Barton Fink* appear to be modeled on historical figures—studio boss Jack Lipnick (Michael Lerner) after Louis B. Mayer; Southern novelist/screenwriter W. P. Mayhew (John Mahoney) after William Faulkner; and Barton Fink himself after playwright Clifford Odets—the similarities are only superficial.

"(John Mahoney) really does resemble Faulkner, physically," Joel says. "Although, the character in *Barton Fink*, obviously—outside of the physical resemblance and the fact that he's an alcoholic—he really doesn't resemble Faulkner very much in any other respect. Barton *is* based on Clifford Odets (*Awake and Sing!*) from the point of view of his background, but it's not really supposed to be . . . Odets had a much more successful career in Hollywood than Barton."

The two main roles, of Barton and his intrusive next-door neighbor Charlie Meadows, were written with John Turturro and John Goodman in mind. Both actors had worked with the Coens previously—Turturro on *Miller's Crossing* and Goodman on *Raising Arizona*. (And both actors later appeared in *The Big Lebowski*, in parts written for them.)

The Coens say they came up with the idea of Barton's Wallace Beery wrestling picture because they thought it was funny—only to find that Beery had indeed made such a movie for director John Ford in 1932, called *Flesh*.

"We thought it was like a joke," says Ethan. "It kind of goes past people: 'Oh yeah, wrestling picture.' We were sort of disappointed that there actually was such a thing. It makes it a little more pedestrian that it really exists."

# Inside the Coen Heads

## TAD FRIEND/1994

SUSAN SARANDON CREPT up to the magnificent double doors. It was February 1993, in Wilmington, North Carolina, and she was visiting her longtime companion, Tim Robbins, who was filming *The Hudsucker Proxy.* The set's lavish scale clearly took her aback. Was this a Coen Brothers film? Weren't they supposed to be small-budget, art-house, seat-of-the-pants productions peopled with little-known character actors? She poked her head through the doorway to survey the scene: the gargantuan office, massive art deco fixtures, terrazzo-marbleized walls—and there, behind a huge desk, wearing a gray suit, smoking a fine cigar, and looking serenely iconic, Paul Newman.

Sarandon turned to the movie's director. "It's gorgeous!"

Joel Coen nodded, almost. Unshaven, ponytailed, fingering a cigarette lighter like a rosary, he has a perpetual up-all-night-for-the-French-lit-exam look. His brother, Ethan, unshaven, curly-haired, and shorter, wandered out of Newman's office trailing a hand along the wall, like a kid counting his footsteps. Ethan is nominally the producer, but the brothers write and film their movies together, behaving as one brain. "Can we make the second hand go faster?" Ethan asked the special-effects gang boss, referring to the huge Hudsucker Industries clock outside Newman's window.

"Like, a hair?"

"Two hairs," Ethan said, with no change of expression. "Two hairs and a tidge." The scene depends on a certain mechanized

From *Vogue* 184, April 1994. Reprinted by permission of International Creative Management, Inc. Copyright © 1994 by Tad Friend.

exactitude: the synchronized movements of a ticker-tape machine, a Newton's Cradle ball-bearing game, and the clock hand. (Later, in post-production, the Coens will have an animator paint in better, more foreboding clock-hand shadows.)

*The Hudsucker Proxy*, set in 1958, is a comedy about Norville Barnes (Tim Robbins), a nice cluck from Muncie, Indiana, who comes to New York and is chewed up by the relentless engines of the city— emblematized by that sweeping clock hand. He is played for a patsy both at work and in his affair with hard-bitten reporter Amy Archer (Jennifer Jason Leigh). He triumphs by inventing the Hula-Hoop, is dragged down to the point of suicide, then triumphs again.

The assistant director shouts the ritual "Lock it up!" and everyone quiets for a take. (Ethan has been trying to get the AD to shout instead, "All aboard for hilarity!" with only mixed success.) In this scene, Norville, working in the Hudsucker mail-room, enters with a letter for the movie's villain, Sid Mussburger (Newman). Mussburger is looking to install a moron as president (thus, "proxy") so the company's stock will fall and the board can acquire a controlling interest. Norville's haplessness—he ends up rolling around trying to extricate his foot from a burning trash can—catches Mussburger's eye.

As Robbins comes in, Newman is telling an underling over the phone, "Either you get me a grade A dingdong or you can tender your key to the executive washroom." The quirky, precise language is a Coen trademark: Words like *rumpus* and *nonce* leap from their screenplays. Nicolas Cage's doleful metaphor for his wife's barrenness in *Raising Arizona*—"the doctor explained that her insides were a rocky place where my seed could find no purchase"—is classic Coens, as is the chiming consonance of *Barton Fink's* "You're a sick fuck, Fink."

That wised-up ear is one reason Joel and Ethan have been everyone's favorite auteurs since *Blood Simple*, the film noir they shot in 1982 for a mere $855,000, and released to great acclaim in 1984. Another reason is astonishing technique: They flaunted their talents early in *Blood Simple*, when the camera glides assuredly along a bar top, approaches a sleeping drunk—and bumps up and over his head before resuming its prowl.

The Coens have since made *Raising Arizona*, a hyperactive comedy about a baby-napping; the 1930s-ish gangster film *Miller's Crossing*; and *Barton Fink*, in which a Clifford Odets–like playwright goes to

Hollywood, suffers from severe writer's block, and gets entangled with a serial killer. Each is funny, weird, and masterful, yet utterly individual in tone. In an industry rife with overbudgeted disasters and studio interference, the Coens are also legendary for storyboarding their scenes down to the minutest sound effect, for adhering to the budget, for not having been spoiled by critical success, and for having always preserved the contractual right to make the movie's final cut—a right that many filmmakers work decades to achieve.

Between camera setups, I asked Joel how it felt to be filming here, at the corner of the Carolco lot's Kassar Boulevard and Rambo Drive—a round-about way of inquiring whether he has any concerns about selling out. None of their previous movies cost more than $9 million; *Hudsucker* is a $25 million film executive-produced by the flashy action-film maven Joel Silver (*Die Hard, Lethal Weapon*). It's their first movie with stars, their first movie with potential for real commercial success. Coen's eyes fluttered skyward at my question. "Oh . . . well . . . in the Disney lot they have Mickey Drive. . . ." The next shade of apparent boredom would be a coma.

He and Ethan went off to murmur to the actors: Joel leaning over Robbins, and Ethan sleepily lying across Newman's desk. "It was never some angst-ridden, torturous process of self-examination," Robbins said later of these discussions. "Mostly it was 'Let's do it again . . . but funnier.' "

But though low-key and seemingly open to suggestion, the Coens know exactly what they want: actors who serve the story and say the lines as written. Nicolas Cage, the star of *Raising Arizona*, called them "autocratic." "It's difficult to convey to an actor that he is just supposed to be the bad guy in a melodrama, and not, as is natural, seek to go beyond it," Joel would say later about *Hudsucker*.

That bad guy, Paul Newman, says Joel and Ethan "are musicians with a great sense of verbal rhythm. I'd say, 'What do you want, Stravinsky or Bach?' They usually wanted *The Rite of Spring*." Deeper questions of theme or intent were off-limits. "They call this an 'industrial comedy,' " Newman notes with amiable perplexity. "What the fuck an industrial comedy is, I have no idea."

Joel and Ethan are known to all as "the boys." They finish mumbling each other's sentences, have similar problem hair, always wear jeans and sneakers, have quick, thievish minds, and love to exchange movie dialogue (like the "You fuckin' my wife?" scene between Joe Pesci and Robert De Niro in *Raging Bull*).

They supposedly grew up in a suburb of Minneapolis with an older sister, Debbie, and two college-professor parents, and spent a lot of time with a Super 8 camera making movies like "Froggy Went A' Courtin'," which featured road-killed frogs and toads. Both brothers are said to have married within the past year, each for the second time (Joel to Frances McDormand, star of *Blood Simple,* and Ethan to Tricia Cooke, an editor who has worked on Coen films).

Yet it's hard to imagine Joel and Ethan in a domestic context; they comprise their own private biosphere. They often seem like extremely precocious kids with an Erector set, refusing to explain to the adults just what it is that they're building. They talk in a private shorthand: a "Miles" is the faint squawk of the person at the other end of the on-screen telephone; an "ambassador" is a gesture, look, or remark that introduces you to a character's motivations; and "hubcaps" are the diminishing sounds after a big aural effect—the clatter of an ashtray after someone slams a fist on a desk. While filming *Miller's Crossing* they called the A camera "Elvis" and the viewfinder "Little Elvis," Elvis's reputed nickname for his penis. Instead of saying "that's a wrap," they'd announce "Ladies and gentlemen, Elvis has left the building."

And the Coens are a legendarily tough interview. Bored by recounting the truth, they are by turns gnomic and absurd. They told one reporter that Jennifer Jason Leigh was actually "bald as a cue ball" and wore a wig throughout filming, and that she showed no embarrassment about taking out her false teeth and swishing them around in a glass.

I first spoke with them at length in their ground-floor office on Manhattan's Upper West Side. Joel, thirty-nine, slouched on the couch smoking Camel Lights while Ethan, thirty-six, paced in distracted loops and circles, chewing a toothpick. He would make six or seven small loops near the dour photo of Kurosawa on the wall, then a long circle out of sight through the kitchen. Eventually he'd reappear and resume his tight loops, the orbiting electron to Joel's collapsed neutron.

Friends of theirs had said that Joel puts key objects in the left side of the frame, whereas Ethan favors the right, and that Joel worries more about camera angles while Ethan focuses more on the dialogue. Surely there were other, more interesting differences?

There was an excruciating silence. "No . . . nah . . . no, no, no . . . not really," Ethan finally said. "It's a terrible question, a terrible thing to do. . . ." Joel mumbled. "It's like you're on *The Dating Game*," Ethan said. "Yeah," Joel said. "You're going to find a real resistance to talking about ourselves as opposed to talking about the movies."

OK: Tim Robbins said to ask about the European critics' interpretation of the buzzing mosquito in *Barton Fink*, and how it epitomizes people overinterpreting your movies.

A longer silence. "That's another thorny thing . . ." Ethan finally said. "You're getting to the nub," Joel said, as Ethan started to snicker. "On the one hand, we want to talk about the movies . . ." "But the movies speak for themselves," Ethan concluded.

I tried asking them about an idea proposed by Sam Raimi—their co-screenwriter on *Hudsucker*, the man who gave Joel his first break after NYU film school as the assistant editor of Raimi's movie *The Evil Dead*, and their close friend. Raimi had remarked that the Coens have several thematic rules: The innocent must suffer; the guilty must be punished; you must taste blood to be a man. "Joel and Ethan are playing with an additional one," he'd added. "The dead must walk."

Joel and Ethan shrugged, separately. "That really applies more to *The Evil Dead* than anything else," Joel said. "I guess they applied to *Blood Simple*," Ethan allowed. And to *Raising Arizona, Miller's Crossing, Barton Fink,* and *The Hudsucker Proxy*, I pointed out. "Yeah . . ." Joel said. "Yeah, yeah, yeah, yeah, yeah, yeah," Ethan said, gnawing a fingernail. Ethan had actually quoted Raimi's formulation to explain their own work at the New York Film Festival in 1984; now they both had deflective amnesia.

Finally, after they'd evaded the last of my questions, I said, "Well, what *should* I be asking you? This is something of a disaster."

"I thought it was going really well," said Ethan, genuinely surprised.

"Yeah," Joel said, shaking his head as if the whole thing were out of his control. "There was a picture of us in the *New York Times*, taken by a friend of ours, where we were sitting there glumly looking like we'd just ax-murdered our mother, and when my wife Fran looked at it, she said, 'Jesus, what a couple of assholes.' "

"We could never figure out how to end the movie," says Sam Raimi, who wrote *Hudsucker* with Joel and Ethan beginning in 1984, when they all shared a house in Los Angeles. "We left it two scenes from the end, with Norville up on the ledge about to jump." Raimi had always wanted to have a definite ending in mind, but Joel and Ethan were happy working without that safety net, improvising, disagreeing, letting it all hang out. (Their closed-ranks cohesion kicks in later, when they start to film.)

"I would actually throw firecrackers or ladyfingers at the boys to get them moving, to spark an idea," Raimi said. "Sometimes when Ethan was pacing, I'd move some of the objects in the room. He'd come up to these obstacles and make a hoarse barking noise—'Hunhh!' I'd like to think I was jogging him to a higher plane. When I'd suggest something they considered absurdly wrong, they'd just laugh and laugh and say 'No, no, no—you can't, because . . . because you just *can't.*' I suggested that Mussburger might turn out to be a nice guy who'd been led astray. When they broke into laughter I realized it's a film of broad strokes, of blacks and whites, and that changing Mussburger would diminish Norville's plight. But they accused me of trying to malign the film, kill them, destroy art."

Finally with a definite ending, ten years later, *The Hudsucker Proxy* is a very funny movie. When Norville says "You have a very charming wife, Sid," Mussburger replies absently, "So they tell me." (Raimi says the Coens wanted Mussburger's wife to be Jack Lemmon in drag; they settled for an actual woman.) Amy Archer says of the Hula-Hoop, "Finally there would be a thing that brought everybody in America together— even if it kept them apart, spatially." A great many stock characters turn up like old friends: haughty society wives, persnickety executive secretaries, Germanic scientists, Germanic psychiatrists, even asylum attendants carrying butterfly nets. It's not parody, exactly. The Coens use these classic totems to emphasize Norville's predicament. He's surrounded by people behaving like caricatures, like subhumans. They also use them as a flat-out gag. "Part of the fun of all those stock characters," Ethan says, "is just its stupidity."

Recognizable visual or thematic influences on *Hudsucker* include *His Girl Friday*, *The Front Page*, *Mr. Deeds Goes to Town*, *The Court Jester*, *The Fountainhead*, and *The Big Clock*, among many others. "We agreed that *Citizen Kane* had the scale and perspective we wanted," says production designer Dennis Gassner, "but we wanted to do it much better than they did it, do it the Coen way, not the Welles way." Adds Leigh, "Making the movie really brought me back to all those childhood sick days when I was home with the stomach flu. I would watch those great screwball comedies by Cukor, Sturges, and Capra and laugh and laugh until it was the next time to throw up."

The Coens pureed all these referents in their cranial Cuisinarts, then spiced in most of the recurrent Coen motifs: "howling fat men, blustery titans, violence, vomiting, and peculiar haircuts," as their friend William Preston Robertson puts it. (There is, alas, no vomiting in *Hudsucker*.) The movie has showy camera pans up the side of a building and, later, into a screaming woman's mouth (the Coen "Glottis Shot"). It has hyperrealistic sound effects, like the foreboding scrape-scrape of a sign painter as he scratches the former president's name from his office door.

It has a tour-de-force wordless montage of the Hula-Hoop being readied for production and then catching on across America, choreographed to characteristically unexpected music, in this case Khatchaturian's "Sabre Dance." This, Joel and Ethan's favorite part of the movie, is reminiscent of their other great wordless montages: the fifteen-minute section of *Blood Simple* in which the bartender buries his boss alive in an open field; the gunfight in *Miller's Crossing* that features a gangster being shot to pieces as his twitching finger continues firing his own Thompson submachine gun while "Danny Boy" floats lyrically into our ears.

What *Hudsucker* doesn't have is signposts to help the audience root for the characters. There is one appealing balcony love scene, but in their detachment the Coens seem to be laughing up their sleeves at Norville and his romance. "It's almost axiomatic that a movie's principal characters have to be sympathetic, and that the movie has to supply moral uplift," Joel said. "People like it. But it's not interesting to us. You're not supposed to sympathize with Gabriel Byrne in *Miller's Crossing*, or with Barton Fink. John Turturro used to say that Fink is the guy who if you're invited to a party, everyone asks—" Joel adopted a tone of suspicion— "'Is Barton going to be there?' And you only sympathize with Norville in a certain way—he's an outsider, and with good reason. He's not just misunderstood." Coen gave an Arnold Horshack laugh. "People feel Jennifer is too tough in the movie, but I don't feel that at all—that's the way the movie works. People do find that distance chilly, or cold around the edges."

Other film staples the Coens find uninteresting: "A theme song sung by a pop singer just for the movie," Joel said. "A journey to self-awareness," Ethan suggested, "where you open the script and a character says, 'I thought you were feeling that I . . .' " "A tearjerker about a cancer patient," Joel said. Any story involving a triumph of the human spirit, I suggested. "Yeah, yeah," Joel said, and Ethan snorted and chuckled. The film behind their eyes dropped away, briefly.

This aloofness from the viewer's sympathy is why the Coens have remained highbrow darlings and box-office lepers. Joel Silver couldn't contain the sneer in his voice when he said of *Barton Fink*, which won the Palme d'Or at the 1991 Cannes Film Festival, "I don't think it made $5 million, and it cost $9 million to make. They've had a reputation for being weird, off-center, inaccessible. They were having trouble getting the money for this $25 million script—people were stymied by the fact that Joel and Ethan's name was on it."

Silver, surprisingly, was a huge Coens fan, so he got involved to line up the money after the Coens had written the last two scenes and begun shopping the script in 1991. Even stranger, the Silver-Coen collaboration has gone well. At least until now. The problem, Silver said bluntly, is that "if they intend to continue making mainstream, higher-budget films, this film is going to have to deliver asses on seats." When the movie premiered at the Sundance Film Festival in late January, Silver, concerned that *Hudsucker* would "be perceived as a festival film" (i.e., an arty head-scratcher), kept telling the Coens, Robbins, and Leigh that they had to stress at the press conference that it was an accessible, straight-ahead comedy. They did so, but only dutifully.

"The pressures are very visible and very legitimate," Ethan acknowledged. "It's all money: Making more money makes it easier to get money for your next film." Joel added, "But as far as being perceived as mainstream movie-makers—that's not particularly important to us. It's not like we're doing this so we can now go do . . ." he casts about, "*Beethoven III.*"

What saves the Coens from social autism is their engaging ironic distance on their own ironic distance. The introduction to the forthcoming book version of the *Hudsucker* screenplay is a Q and A between Joel Silver and one "Dennis Jacobson, professor of cinema studies at the University of Iowa." In fact, it was written by Joel and Ethan, who always use the introductions to their published screenplays to mock themselves.

The pseudo-Silver reveals that the Coens whined a lot, seemed happiest playing with their storyboards, and hadn't wanted Paul Newman in the picture. "Their attitude, it was funny. Like it's a sin to use a movie star. God forbid somebody should actually be enticed into the theatre to see one of their movies. 'No, he's too iconic.' And Tim Robbins, that whole thing—forget about it."

DJ:    Tim Robbins was not their choice either? And yet he's very good.

JS:    This—I found this unbelievable at the time, but this—Ethan wanted to play the part. . . . He says only he understands the character fully. . . . It was absurd, but I let him test.

DJ:    How was it?

JS:    What do you think how was it? It was goddamned embarrassing. It's—it was like the early days of talkies. Ethan is lumbering around on this pathetic little set they've mocked up, with his flat Midwestern voice, chopping the air with his hands, these stiff gestures, I mean, Richard Nixon doing a love scene. Stiffo.

And so forth. "The intros to screenplays are always some screenwriter gassing on with self-congratulation or some sort of foggy analysis of what they've just done," Joel says. "We'd rather do something that's fun to write." It's a few days later. He is sitting alone in his office with no lights on. Cigarette smoke curls up dimly through the dark afternoon.

I start to ask whether there wouldn't be some value in a clear explanation of their tenets, and then catch myself. Stupid question. "If Preston Sturges could somehow be reanimated to write a clear explanation of his working principles, his trade secrets, wouldn't you want to read that?" I ask.

Joel looks uncomfortable. "It's interesting to know that Preston Sturges had a big dog on the set that frequently barked and ruined takes. That's more interesting to me than anything Sturges could tell me about his working methods." He's aware that he sounds willfully perverse.

"What if you won an Oscar and had to make an acceptance speech? Would you riff through that emotional moment, too?"

"We'd be so mortified at the thought of having to speak in public that I doubt we'd write anything," Joel says, and laughs. "We'd probably wing it. I'm always impressed, genuinely, by graceful acceptance speeches." A long pause. "I think that sort of thing is just beyond my capabilities."

"I can't watch our old movies—I'm overcome by a fog of boredom," Ethan says. He sits alone in an armchair, willing himself to stay in one place. "I saw *Blood Simple* on TV a while ago, and I enjoyed it because it was different: They had commercials. I think all black-and-white movies should be colorized and chopped up with commercials. If you had hooked my brain up with electrodes, you'd have seen a big spike of interest when the Ty-D-Bol Man came on."

So where is the pleasure in doing what you do? He thinks for a while, making an effort, then begins pacing again, to get the thoughts flowing. "Well, in *Raising Arizona*, we blow up a car. And to be incredibly crude about it, it's just so cool to sit there and watch a car blow up. That was a peak. It gave us a deep, warm feeling of inner satisfaction."

Joel is still puzzled by the imputation of chilliness in their movies. "You can put a five-year-old on the screen and make him cry—and that's the most cerebral, formulaic-bullshit corny manipulation, yet everyone will be crying their eyes out." He makes a "boo-hoo" sound.

"People have a problem dealing with the fact that our movies are not straight-ahead: They would prefer that the last half of *Barton Fink* just be about a screenwriter's writing-block problems and how they get resolved in the real world, or that *Raising Arizona* just be about a couple of schmoes in a trailer park who want to have a kid—the arrival of the bounty hunter from hell interrupts the comfort level people have with their world. But we feel a strong emotional connection to those characters, we're not laughing down at them."

So the end of *Raising Arizona*, when Hi has a vision of him and his wife "suffused in a warm, golden light" and in a land where "all parents are strong and wise and capable, and all children are happy and beloved," is totally serious?

Joel Coen snickers faintly, then gathers himself. "Absolutely."

# Closer to Life than the Conventions of Cinema

## MICHEL CIMENT AND HUBERT NIOGRET/1996

Q:    *Was* Fargo *inspired by a news item, as the press dossier claims, or have you invented a false trail?*
JOEL COEN:    Generally speaking the movie is based on a real event, but the details of the story and the characters are invented. It didn't interest us to make a documentary film, and we undertook no research on the nature or details of the murders. But, by telling the public that we took our inspiration from reality, we knew they wouldn't see the movie as just an ordinary thriller.

Q:    *Did that kidnapping (of a woman, organized by her husband) have many repercussions back in 1987?*
ETHAN COEN:    No. In fact, it's astonishing how things of that nature receive so little publicity. We heard about it through a friend who lived near to where the drama took place in Minnesota, which is also the state we originate from.

Q:    *Why have you called the film* Fargo *when the main action is situated in Brainerd, which is a town in Minnesota?*
JOEL:    *Fargo* seemed a more evocative title to us than Brainerd, that's the reason.

From *Positif*, September 1996. Reprinted by permission of *Positif* and the authors. Translated by Paul Buck and Catherine Petit.

ETHAN:    It's literally the sound of the word that we liked. There's no hidden meaning.

JOEL:    There's a Western connotation, with Wells Fargo, but we didn't intend that, it's just something people have picked up on.

Q:    *You return in a certain way to the territory of your first films,* Blood Simple *and* Raising Arizona.

JOEL:    There are resemblances, but important differences as well. These three movies are set on a small scale. They're about criminality and kidnapping and are very specific in their geographical location. Frances McDormand plays in both *Fargo* and *Blood Simple.* But we've always considered *Blood Simple* as belonging to the tradition of melo- dramatic novelists like James M. Cain, with an additional horror-movie influence. In *Fargo* we attempted a very different stylistic approach, tackling the subject in a very dry manner. We also wanted the camera to tell the story as an observer. The construction is tied to the original true story, but we allowed ourselves more meanders and digressions. Each incident didn't necessarily have to be at the service of the plot. We even took the liberty of not introducing the heroine, Inspector Gunderson, until the middle of the movie.

ETHAN:    It was also a way of telling the audience not to expect a genre movie. It's different from *Blood Simple.*

Q:    *What have you brought to the subject?*

JOEL:    There were two or three things that interested us in relation to that incident. First it happened within an era and a region we were familiar with, which we could explore. Then it concerned a kidnapping, a type of event which has always fascinated us. In fact, we have another very different script on a kidnapping that we'd like to film. And finally there was the possibility to shoot a criminal movie with characters far removed from the stereotypes of the genre.

ETHAN:    It's probably a subject we wouldn't have dealt with outside of that context. When we begin to write, we try to imagine very specifi- cally the world in which the story unfolds. The difference is that, up until now, these were purely fictional universes, while in *Fargo* we needed you to be able to smell the place. As we were from the region, it helped us to understand how it might play within that milieu.

Q:    *In the credits, was the function of "accent adviser" a joke?*
ETHAN:    No, not at all. Most of the actors came from the region and they had no need of advice, but Frances McDormand, Bill Macy, and Harve Presnell needed coaching so that their accents harmonized with the others.
JOEL:    The people there speak in a very economic way, if not monosyllabic. That seems as exotic to other Americans as it does to you in Europe! In fact, the Scandinavian influence on the culture of that region, the rhythm of the sentences, the accent, are not at all familiar to the rest of America: it might as well have happened on the moon! New Yorkers have a general conception of the Midwest, but they ignore all of those cultural "pockets," those microsocieties with their idiosyncrasies and peculiarities.
ETHAN:    When we were small, we weren't really conscious of that Scandinavian heritage that marked the region so strongly because we had no points of comparison. It was only on arrival in New York that we were astonished there weren't more, like Gustafsons or Sondergaards. All the exoticism and strangeness of that region comes from the Nordic character, from its politeness and reservation. There's something Japanese in that refusal to show the least emotion, in that resistance to saying no! One of the comic wellsprings of the story comes from the conflict between that constant avoidance of all confrontation and the murders gradually piling up.
JOEL:    We didn't have to do much research into that manner of speech, those expressions, the cadences were all familiar to us. Our parents still live in that region, so we go back there regularly and we know its culture. After all, it formed us as people. But not having lived there for a long time, we've the feeling of being half-divorced from the environment in which we grew up.

Q:    *The episode featuring Marge and her old friend from school is a digression from the very tight central narrative.*
ETHAN:    Someone pointed out that in that scene Frances plays very withdrawn, like an Oriental, while her Japanese friend is voluble and irrational like a "typical" American. By creating that digression we really wanted to draw a contrast.
JOEL:    We wanted to give another point of view of Frances's character without it being related to the police enquiry. That's also what happens in the scenes with her husband.

ETHAN:     Our intention was to show the story had a relationship to life rather than to fiction, setting us free to create a scene that had no relationship to the plot.

Q:     The Hudsucker Proxy *was without doubt your most "theatrical" film. This one, as a contrast, is probably the least.*
JOEL:     We wanted to make a new start from a stylistic point of view, to make something radically different from our previous movies. And the impetus was the previous movie, which was the most stylized of all. But, curiously, by starting from real events, we've arrived at another form of "stylization." The results are maybe not as different as we'd envisaged!

Q:     *A little like Kubrick with* Dr. Strangelove, *you begin with a quasi-documentary presentation, then gradually, with a cold humor, everything becomes dislocated and absurd.*
ETHAN:     That comes partly from the nature of the story itself. There's a shot composed at the beginning that's modified later in the film, as the characters lose control.
JOEL:     It's implicit in the construction of the narrative. When a character suggests to you, in the first scene, how things are going to happen, you know full well it's going to unfold very differently. The reference to Kubrick has been made before, but I understand it more now. There's a very formal side to his approach, as well as a steady progression from the commonplace towards the baroque.

Q:     *How do you manage not to fall into caricature, which could overwhelm your work at any time?*
JOEL:     I suppose it's partly intuition about the tone, and it particularly depends on the actors' capacity to know how far they can go. There is, for instance, with Frances a very authentic manner, very open in presenting her character. It prevents Marge from becoming a parody of herself. Frances was very conscious of the dangers of excess, with that mannerism of dragging out words at the very end of each sentence.
ETHAN:     It was a constant process of adjustment on set between the actors and us. They gave us a wide range of behavior and mannerisms that we constantly discussed throughout the shooting.

JOEL:    We work a lot with *feeling*. It's difficult to express through words why Marge, in the movie, is not a caricature but a real, three-dimensional person.

ETHAN:    All we know is that, when we wrote the script and when the actors interpreted their roles, none of us thought of the story as a comedy.

JOEL:    And that helped to make the characters comical and credible at the same time. The comedy wouldn't have worked if it had been played as comedy, rather than with sincerity.

Q:    *The relationship between Marge and her husband is also very strange.*

JOEL:    We were seduced during casting by the very direct acting and impassive face of John Caroll Lynch, who seemed to us perfectly suited to the tone of the movie.

ETHAN:    He totally personifies how undemonstrative people are in that place. The relationship with his wife is based on the unsaid, but they succeed in communicating somehow.

Q:    *The end resembles a pastiche of the classic Hollywood "happy ending," with the wife and husband in bed symbolizing a return to order and normality.*

JOEL:    It's true that it's a return to normality, but we didn't intend for it to be a parody! There was an article in the *New York Times*, where the journalist asked why the people of Minnesota didn't like the ending when it all turned out so well for them!

Q:    *The only question mark at the end concerns the money. But wasn't the money the main component of the plot?*

JOEL:    All the men in the movie are preoccupied by money.

ETHAN:    At the same time we didn't want to be too specific, for instance, concerning the nature of the debt contracted by Jerry. It was sufficient to understand that that character was trapped by engaging in something which turned out badly. Elsewhere, during the whole movie, Jerry is a poor lost soul who can't stop improvizing solutions to get out of the situations he's already gotten himself into. He never stops trying everything, brimming over with activity. He's almost admirable in that respect!

JOEL:   What interested us from the start in the William Macy character was his absolute incapacity, even for one minute, to project himself into the future and evaluate the consequences of his decisions. There's something fascinating in that total absence of perspective. He's one of those people who construct a pyramid without thinking for a moment that it could collapse.

Q:   *Did writing the script take much time?*
ETHAN:   We began it before shooting *The Hudsucker Proxy*, then returned to it; so it's difficult to evaluate the time it took us. Two years have passed. What's certain is that the writing was easy and relatively quick, particularly in comparison with other scripts like *Miller's Crossing*.

Q:   *Was it established from the start that the kidnapped woman wouldn't have any physical presence?*
JOEL:   Absolutely. And even at a certain point in the story, it was clear for us she would cease to be a person to those who'd kidnapped her. Besides, it was no longer the actress Kristin Rudrüd playing the part, but a double with a hood on her head. So, we weren't interested in the victim! And, it didn't seem at any point that the husband himself was at all preoccupied with what could happen to her! Carl, one of the kidnappers, didn't even know her name!

Q:   *Did you choose Steve Buscemi for the role before thinking of Peter Stormare as the other kidnapper?*
ETHAN:   In fact, we wrote both roles for those actors. Likewise for Marge played by Frances McDormand. Peter's an old friend of ours and it seemed interesting, given his Swedish origins, to give him this part. Of course, his character is an *outsider* in relation to the milieu, but at the same time he maintains ethnic bonds with it.

Q:   *How do you work with your musical composer Carter Burwell?*
JOEL:   He's been our collaborator since we started. Usually, he looks at the movie from the outset, from end to end, then he composes sketches on the synthesizer to give us an idea of the direction in which he intends to work. Before creating his score, he plays us bits on the piano,

and we reflect together on their relationship to certain sequences of the movie. Then he moves onto the next stage.

ETHAN:    In the case of this movie, the central theme is based on some popular Scandinavian music that Carter found for us.

JOEL:    We often work with him that way. For *Miller's Crossing* the music came from an Irish folk theme which he orchestrated and added to it bits of his own composition. For *Raising Arizona* he used American popular music, with Holly Hunter singing a tune. On the other hand, for *Blood Simple* and *Barton Fink* he wrote all the music, without external inspiration. With *The Hudsucker Proxy* it was different again, a mixture of original compositions by Carter and bits from Khachaturian.

ETHAN:    When he's orchestrated his score we go into the studio with him for the recording. For the last two movies, he conducted the orchestra himself. As the movie's projected while he works, he can modify the score as he goes along. Our entire collaboration lasts a maximum of two or three months.

Q:    *How long did the editing take you?*

JOEL:    Twelve weeks. Which is short for us because normally we take longer, as we don't begin editing while we're shooting.

Q:    *Did the photography pose any particular problems?*

JOEL:    It was simpler than for the other movies. We discussed it at length with Roger Deakins because we wanted to do a lot of shots without coverage. At the start we decided to have only fixed shots.

EHTAN:    Then we realized that "purist" attitude was a little stupid.

JOEL:    We made some adjustments by sometimes moving the camera, but in such a way that the audience doesn't notice. We didn't want to make the camerawork as stylized as we'd done in the past, because we didn't want to emphasize the action, to make it too dramatic or crazy.

ETHAN:    Roger Deakins worked with a camera operator whereas before he's mainly been his own cameraman, including on the two movies he photographed for us. This time he didn't take everything in hand, although he often took control of the framing. On *Fargo* we'd had problems with the weather because we needed the snow, but the winter when we shot was particularly soft and dry. We had to work in Minneapolis with artificial snow. Then, as the snow hadn't yet fallen, we went to North Dakota for the end of the shoot, the big exterior scenes. We had what we wanted there: a covered sky, no direct sunlight, no line on the horizon, and a light that was neutral, diffused.

JOEL:    These landscapes were really dramatic and oppressive. There were no mountains, no forests, only flat, desolate stretches of land. It's just what we wanted to convey on the screen.

Q:   *Do you often put your eye to the camera?*

JOEL:    On the first movie we made with Roger Deakins, *Barton Fink*, we constantly looked in the viewfinder. On *Hudsucker Proxy*, less. And even less on *Fargo*. That's undoubtedly due to the material and the different visual approach to each movie, but also to the growing affinity with our cinematographer. He understood our intentions more and more and we trusted him more and more. When we work regularly with a collaborator, a kind of telepathic language is established. I also think Roger enjoys working with people like us who have an active interest in lighting, rather than with filmmakers who rely entirely on him.

Q:   *There's a contradiction between the press package, which attributes the editing to you, and the credits, which list a certain Roderick Jaynes.*

JOEL:    When we assemble the movie ourselves, we use the pseudonym Roderick Jaynes. We prefer to lend a hand rather than be seated beside someone and tell them what to cut. It seems easier to us. Besides, we're both in the cutting room. When we work together we obviously don't get that feeling of isolation that others sometimes feel. On *Barton Fink* and *Blood Simple*, we were our own editor. On the other movies, we had an editor but we'd still be in the editing room whenever we could. If we've occasionally called in Tom Noble or Michael Miller, it's because the cutting had to begin during shooting.

Q:   *Your films take place in New Orleans, New York, Hollywood, in the West and Midwest. It seems you like to explore the geography of America.*

JOEL:    We'd like to shoot elsewhere, but, strangely, the subjects that come to mind are always situated in America. That's what seems to attract us.

ETHAN:    It always seems that the world in which our stories take place is connected to us, however remotely. In the case of *Fargo*, the bond was much tighter, of course.

JOEL:    We need an intimate knowledge of the subject or at least an emotional relationship with it; at the same time, it only interests us if it's kind of exotic in some way! Minnesota, for example, we know very well, but not the characters who people *Fargo* and their type of behavior. Or again, in the case of *Barton Fink* and *Miller's Crossing*, the exoticism comes from the temporal distance.

Q:    *What are your relationships with the characters in* Fargo *who, for the most part, are a little deficient?*
JOEL:    We like all of them, perhaps most of all the simple ones!
ETHAN:    One of the reasons for making them simple-minded was our desire to go against the Hollywood cliché of the bad guy as a super-professional who controls everything he does. In fact, in most cases criminals belong to the strata of society least equipped to face life, and that's the reason they're caught so often. In this sense too, our movie is closer to life than the conventions of cinema and genre movies.
JOEL:    We're often asked how we inject comedy into the material. But it seems to us that it's present in life. Look at those people who recently blew up the World Trade Center. They'd rented a van to prepare the explosion, and, once the job was finished, they returned to the rental agency to reclaim their deposit. The absurdity of that is, in itself, terribly funny.

Q:    *What are your current projects?*
ETHAN:    At this moment we're preparing two scripts without knowing which will be finished first, or which will be financed first.
JOEL:    One of them concerns another kidnapping, but in a very different manner. And the other's a kind of film noir about a barber in northern California at the end of the forties.

# This Is a True Story

DAVID BENNUN/1996

"THIS IS A TRUE STORY."

Thus the Coen Brothers introduce *Fargo* to the screen. It's a remarkable change for director/writer Joel and producer/writer Ethan. Having cut their teeth on Sam Raimi's inventive, grisly, and hugely enjoyable *Evil Dead*—their handiwork is clearly visible, in retrospect, as is Raimi's own influence on them—their own films made famous their high style, unlikely scripts, and kinetic camerawork. Now they have made a low-key, slow-paced picture which places its emphasis on narrative and character. These characters are not the expected misfits, grotesques, or eccentrics, but straightforward American mid-westerners who, even in the midst of villainy and violence, retain a kind of open-faced bewilderment. The only other Coen Brothers' film to which it bears any resemblance is *Blood Simple*, and then only in terms of its plot.

"What was interesting to us in the first place about doing this movie," explains Joel, "was the fact that from every point of view, stylistically, the architecture of the narrative, the way the characters came across, it was an attempt to do something very far from what we'd done before. It's more naturalistic generally in terms of everything. Unembellished sets, real locations. If they're told up front that it's true, the audience gives you permission to do things that they might not if they're essentially coming in expecting to watch a fictive thriller."

---

From *Melody Maker*, 1996. Copyright © 1996 by David Bennun. Reprinted by permission of the author.

The characters are actually very banal, in a curiously wonderful way. That's what makes their behavior so extraordinary, because they are—especially the hopeless criminal mastermind, Jerry—the least sinister people on earth. Did the Coens feel they were taking a risk, that banal characters might result in a banal movie?

"I would have put it in slightly different terms," Joel says. "It was more an attempt to bring both the villains and the hero down to a recognizable, ordinary scale. The hero [Marge] isn't a super-cop. she's a very real ordinary person with ordinary and mundane concerns. As Ethan says, they're banal in the evil sense, in terms of Jerry, and banal in a good way in terms of Marge. But not with any sort of pejorative connotation, just ordinary."

"Even Steve Buscemi's character," agrees Ethan, "violent as he is and heinous as the things he does are, you're right, you couldn't call him sinister."

The only thing that any of them really have in common with previous Coen characters is that dumb pig-headedness, that inability to recognize the reality of situations.

"Yes, in a way," says Joel, "but the people who do these kinds of crimes, generally, in reality, are not rocket scientists. There's a tendency in movies to make criminals much smarter than they are in real life. I mean, if you read about how these things usually happen, it's incredible stupidity that usually trips these people up. Marge, on the other hand, is easy to underestimate."

*Fargo* is set in Minnesota, where the brothers grew up. Is it an accurate representation?

"No," ponders Joel, "in a sense, it's kind of a distorted view of Minnesota. Distorted in its selection. In New York or L.A., people think we're putting them on with the accents."

Is the setting deliberately unusual?

"Yeah, definitely. I mean, it wasn't as if we were looking for a movie to do there, but this was immediately attractive to us for that reason. It's the juxtaposition of the politeness of the culture and the horrible stuff that's engendered by these crimes. Almost the opposite of *Blood Simple*: that was essentially an overheated melodrama. Americans especially associate Texas with crimes of passion."

And is the austere look a reaction to the commercial failure of the lavish *The Hudsucker Proxy*?

"It's a reaction to the self-conscious artifice of *Hudsucker*," replies Ethan, "in terms of wanting to do something different, not because the last film failed, although it did, but just because we always do."

Were you stung by the critical barbs aimed at *Hudsucker*? Do you take any notice of complaints about "style over substance"?

"People have been saying that about our movies since we started," Joel laughs, "so, no, not really—or we would have learned our lesson by now."

"If you took it to heart when they said a movie was really terrible," adds Ethan, "you'd have to take it to heart when they said it was really great. It gets very unhealthy in either direction."

*Fargo* is as good as anything the Coens have done, and that's saying something. One of its most effective traits is what Frances McDormand (coincidentally Mrs. Joel Coen), who plays Marge, calls the inclination of "rural mid-America to resist self-analysis." This makes it a far more effective psychological thriller than any of those stalked by the shadow of Freud. We never fully understand why the people in it do the things they do. Just like life, really.

# Making It Clear: The Coen Brothers

## GARY SUSMAN/1998

DON'T EXPECT TO FIND DEEP MEANING in the utterances of the Coen Brothers, any more than you would expect to find it in their films.

Sure, if you ask about the inspiration behind *The Big Lebowski*, Ethan will explain, "The narrative is suggested by Raymond Chandler's Philip Marlowe novels. It's this episodic narrative about a character who's not a private eye in this case, just a lay-about pothead who works his way through L.A. society trying to unravel this mystery."

And if you ask Joel why the characters are obsessed with bowling, he'll say, "We like the design aspects of bowling. The sort of retro aspects of it seemed like the right fit for the characters. One of the people this is loosely based on was in an amateur softball league in L.A. that really took up a lot of his time. We changed that to bowling because bowling seemed more compelling from a visual point of view." He adds, "It's the only thing that calls itself a sport where you can smoke and drink beer."

But mostly, the brothers (Joel is credited as director and Ethan as producer, but both direct, write, produce, and edit) have no trenchant explanation for any of their weirdness. Asked why they made Vietnam vet Walter (John Goodman) an observant Jew, Ethan replies, "What's the point of any of the characterization? It's a peg to hang a few gags on him. There's something about the incongruity of a Vietnam vet, gun

From *Boston Phoenix*, March 5–12, 1998. Reprinted by permission of the author.

buff, military fanatic being also a devout converted Jew that was appealing to us."

So you make a point of going for what will make the weirdest character? "Weird isn't the right word," says Ethan. "The most vivid character. Yeah, sure."

In fact, when asked at last month's film festival in Berlin whether the movie had any point at all, beyond laughing at German nihilists and Latino pederasts, Joel said, "I guess you hit the nail on the head."

Jeff Bridges, who plays the film's stoner hero, the Dude, insists that the movie does have a moral dimension, though he's hard pressed to explain it. "I think it's a film about grace, how amazing it is that we're all allowed to stay alive on this speck hurled out into space, being as screwed up as we all are. Like, *Fargo* had a moral resonance to it. This one, I think, does as well. It may not be apparent to most people at first. But working in it, kind of bathing in this thing, it rang for me. It's not a real clear thing that you can say, 'That's what it means.' It's a little different."

How did the Coens justify the film's quirks to him? "They kind of laughed. It's their style to have these weird things, like that Oriental guy in *Fargo* with that Fargo accent. Where does that go? It doesn't go anywhere. Or [in *Lebowski*] the dancing landlord. Why are you here? It's kind of lifelike. It rings true somehow."

Neither did the Coens explain much to Julianne Moore, who plays Maude, an aristocratic artist who mystifies and ensnares the Dude. "They don't really talk a lot, which I love. I don't like to talk a lot when I'm working. It gets in the way. They do seem to communicate in some symbiotic way. I really loved it because you have this duality that becomes the vision on the set. You get a larger breadth of artistic vision. There's always an eye there. Which I really enjoyed."

So if you have any questions, you can go to either one of them? "Yeah. Which I thought was extremely odd. I didn't discover that until the first day on the set, when Ethan came over, and the line was 'Jeffrey, tell me a little about yourself,' and Ethan said, 'Lose the "little,"' and he never told Joel, 'I told Julie to do this,' which would take obviously an incredible amount of time. That's when you realize that they just do that. But Joel will come over and say something, and they just balance it that way."

Moore, however, is a trouper who doesn't question the strangeness, whether she has to dance in a dream sequence in a Valkyrie costume with bowling-ball breastplates or swoop across a room, spattering paint onto a canvas on the floor, while suspended naked in a harness. "I had no idea what they were going to do," she says of that scene. "I assumed I was going to be upright. I didn't know I was going to be like Superman. That was terrifying. And I was pregnant, and it was three in the morning, and I was thirty feet in the air, and they had to bring me up really fast. It was really strange, but it was worth it in the end."

# The Coens Speak (Reluctantly)

DOUG STONE/1998

THE RASCALLY COEN BROTHERS have never been the best interview subjects, possibly because they rankle at the constant questions about their relationship with each other. (When asked by *Elle* magazine, "Do you guys ever fight?" Joel Coen replied, "That's not an interesting question.") So it can be a somewhat painful experience to see the brilliant siblings in a hotel hospitality suite being bombarded with questions from a dozen journalists about everything except their movies. Awkward silences, long pauses, and a couple of audible groans were among the responses to various questions.

But when the topic of conversation narrows to specific questions about their hilarious new film *The Big Lebowski* starring Jeff Bridges (as "The Dude," a doobie-smoking burn-out who gets mixed up in a wacky kidnapping scam), the boys open up (just a bit). The movie, which also stars John Goodman, Julianne Moore and includes an hysterical cameo from John Turturro, returns the Coens to the comic-genius territory of *Raising Arizona.*

INDIEWIRE: *You majored in philosophy at Princeton. What is your philosophy of filmmaking?*
ETHAN COEN: Oooh—I don't have one. I wouldn't even know how to begin. You've stumped me there. None that I've noticed. Drawing a blank on this one.

---

From *IndieWIRE*, http://www.indiewire.com, March 9, 1998. Reprinted by permission of *IndieWIRE* and the author.

IW:    *How much did* The Big Sleep *influence* The Big Lebowski*?*

JOEL COEN:    We wanted to do a Chandler kind of story—how it moves episodically, and deals with the characters trying to unravel a mystery. As well as having a hopelessly complex plot that's ultimately unimportant.

ETHAN:    And there was something attractive about having the main character not be a private eye, but just some pothead intuitively figuring out the ins and outs of an elaborate intrigue. And then there's Walter, whose instincts are always wrong.

IW:    *Why is kidnapping a favorite theme of yours?*

ETHAN:    It just turned out that way. I don't know why kidnapping has figured into three of our movies. Not because of any personal obsession.

IW:    *Did you ever run around with the kinds of Los Angeles bowling-dope-smoking types that are depicted in the film?*

JOEL:    To tell you the truth, we're still tourists in L.A. We have lived there for short periods of time, but we've always really lived in New York. But the character of the Dude is based on a member of an amateur softball league, but we changed it to bowling because it was more visually compelling, and it's the kind of sport you can do while you're drinking and smoking. And it's also very retro—just as the characters are products with an earlier time, it seems that there's so much associated with bowling in terms of design, and specifically in L.A.

IW:    *Is Jeff Dowd one of those types?*

JOEL:    Yeah, Jeff Dowd [an indie producer's rep and friend of the Coens] is certainly one of those types that the Dude is based on . . .

IW:    *What's the attraction of setting the film specifically in 1991?*

ETHAN:    Well, setting the film during the Gulf War was an opportunity to have Walter gas about something. . . .

JOEL:    That's the main reason.

ETHAN:    And it's more attractive to make something time specific than just present day, because. . . .

JOEL:    . . . because just what is present day?

IW:     *What will you do if you ever win an Oscar for editing? [The Coens edit their own films under the credited pseudonym Roderick Jaynes, a fictional British film editor who supposedly hates their work.]*
ETHAN:     We actually had a discussion with the Academy about that. Proxies can't accept anymore after Marlon Brando queered it for the rest of us.

IW:     *Did you set out on this movie to teach America what nihilism means?*
ETHAN:     [laughs] Nihilism strikes a terrible chord in Walter [John Goodman's character] who is particularly horrified by it.
JOEL:     [bitterly sarcastic] Everything's a lesson for America.

# Coen Job

RAY PRIDE / 1998

I CAUGHT A GLIMPSE of the Coen Brothers at a distributors'
party at Sundance this year. (There had been a tribute to Joel's wife,
Frances McDormand.) Joel had clamped on probably the best don't-fuck-
with-me scowl I'd ever seen as he piled through the room. Talking to the
two of them a few weeks later, their disingenuous finish-each-others'-sen-
tences, joined-at-the-quip, self-amused chuckle-monkey behavior is kind
of amusing, even when you play back the tape and find out just how little
they've actually said.

The Big Lebowski, set during the Gulf War, is a return to form for all
of those who admire the Coens at their most sarcastic, where large men
scream very loudly and jokes are pounded into the ground with vigor
and brio. Jeff Bridges plays The Dude, a.k.a. Jeff Lebowski, a Los Angeles
pot-smoking and White Russian–swilling seventies-style layabout mistaken for a millionaire of the same name. He'd rather be bowling with
his buddies Donny (Steve Buscemi, never allowed to finish a sentence)
and Walter (John Goodman, increasingly, indelibly insane as the story
progresses). They're characters whose behavior never shifts, as nuts as
cartoon characters come to life. Goodman's Walter is a bullet-headed,
barely contained titan of rage, running on the fumes of cracked beliefs
and fierce garble-gabble. The resemblance to Raymond Chandler's con-
voluted plots and view of L.A. melts away under the barrage of sple-
netic rage that the pig-ignorant characters unleash on one another.
(The bowling-fantasy musical number is another matter altogether.)

---

From Newcity, March 9, 1998. Reprinted by permission of the author.

"The Chandler stuff is accurate," says tall, dour Joel. "Even specifically accurate in terms of some of the details of the movie. But it's
much more of the case that we were thinking about Raymond Chandler
in general. We wanted to do a Chandler kind of story, both in terms
of how it moves, episodically, and dealing with the characters trying
to unravel a mystery. But also in terms of the movie being about
Los Angeles the way Chandler's are about L.A. I haven't read any
recently, but we both read a lot of Chandler when we were kids."

It would seem that part of the attraction would also be the convolu-
tion and the inscrutability of the storytelling in both Chandler and the
film, *The Big Sleep*. "Yeah, exactly," Joel says. "*The Big Sleep* was a hopelessly complicated plot, right. At bottom, the plots in Chandler are very
unimportant. Very complex but very unimportant."

Ethan, shorter, shaggy-haired, adds, "But also there's something
attractive about a main character who isn't a private eye but he's just
this pothead that Jeff plays. There's something attractive about having
him figure out intuitively the ins-and-outs of the elaborate intrigue."
Pretty much, The Dude and Walter and company are guys who've
learned about life from movies and TV. "Ahhhhhh. Yeah," Ethan ventures. "There's something about . . . right. The Dude smoked a lot of
dope and had a lot of input."

Joel cuts in: "It's more of a case of him being a sponge for, you know,
the culture that he inhabits in general, the things that he's heard, that
he regurgitates from previous scenes. That's filtered all through his sort
of reefer haze." Ethan grins. "That's the fun of putting him at the center
of the movie."

So is The Dude an archetypal Angeleno for the Bros? They swap
looks. "The Dude is based on several people, including a member of
an amateur softball league," Joel says, "but we changed it to bowling
because bowling seemed so much more visually compelling and it's
the kind of sport you can do while you're drinking and smoking. It's
also very retro. The characters are all the product of an earlier time,
and bowling in terms of design, particularly in L.A., and specifically
an earlier L.A."

Both *Fargo* and *The Big Lebowski* are set a few years back, almost-
period pieces. "In the case of this one," Ethan says, "setting it at the time
of the Gulf War is an opportunity to have Walter gas about something."

Joel says, "That's it, that's really the reason." But Ethan continues. "Also . . . well, in the case of both movies, *Fargo* is also set not present day, but almost present day, right, it's somehow almost more attractive to make the time specific somehow than just make it present day . . ."

"What *is* the present day?" Joel asks. Ethan says, "Yeah. It's completely unspecific."

Speaking of the recent past, I wondered if the Oscar has been a help or a nuisance. Ethan says, "Well, who knows? You know real specifically how it figured as a nuisance but you don't know specifically what it gained you, since you don't know how easy it would be to raise money for the next movie absent that, so . . ." The grin again. "Nuisance! We're sure it was a nuisance, the gain we're not so sure about." Joel adds, "Yeah, you know, I guess it's hard to tell." The tape degenerates into a volley of blurts and counter-blurts and a couple of giggles. Joel's voice rises from the din, "We were in the middle of this movie when all this stuff happened. It's a little bit distracting because everybody's breathing heavily about it while it's happening and it's strange when you're in the middle of making another movie and going to work every day. Beyond that?" They both shrug.

# The Brothers Grim

ANDY LOWE/1998

Q:   *How do you cope with dual interviews?*
ETHAN COEN:   Fine. But we're much happier with the anal, film-geek types. It's also a lot easier in Europe with you guys. In the States, the mainstream press tend to poke around for . . . something else. They're not really interested in the two-way brother thing.

Q:   *They want something scurrilous.*
ETHAN:   Yeah. Well, mostly, not even necessarily scurrilous. Something . . . warm and sweet normally makes them just as happy. But definitely something personal.

Q:   *I'll try to stick to anal, textual film questions, then.*
ETHAN:   Okay. Good.

Q:   *The bad guys in* The Big Lebowski *are rather feeble German nihilist-pornographers. Why German? Why nihilist?*
JOEL COEN:   Well, we're obviously not saying that all Germans are nihilists. We're saying that those particular Germans are nihilists. With John Goodman's character being so rabidly Jewish, it just sort of worked with that. And it also worked with the whole techno-pop thing. It was a function of the music we associated with the various characters. We are always looking to make characters geographically or sociologically or ethnically as specific as we possibly can. The more specific they are,

From *Total Film*, May 1998. Reprinted by permission of *Total Film*.

the easier it is to develop them and make them more interesting for ourselves and for the audience. But people miss that, and they sometimes mistakenly extrapolate it into some grand statement about that region.

Q:    *Your films do tend to get analyzed to death. I found a tortuous breakdown of* Barton Fink *on the Internet: the hotel represents Hell, John Goodman represents The Common Man, and the whole film is apparently a parable about the natural allure of fascism for The Common Man . . .*
ETHAN:    Yeah. It's a weird impulse when people feel the need to read things as code—and very specific code, at that.
JOEL:    We never, ever go into our films with anything like that in mind. There's never anything approaching that kind of specific intellectual breakdown. It's always a bunch of instinctive things that feel right, for whatever reason. A good example from *Barton Fink* is the two cops who come to interview Barton—if you watch it, one's kind of German and the other . . . well, we just wanted them to be representative of the Axis world powers at the time. It just seemed kind of amusing. It's a tease. All that stuff with Charlie—the "Heil Hitler!" business—sure, it's all there, but it's kind of a tease. We're definitely guilty of teasing.
ETHAN:    America is extremely sensitive to ethnicity. A lot of people picked us up on the head of the studio in *Barton Fink* being Jewish. But . . . most studio heads *are* Jewish! What's the problem?
JOEL:    There was a critic in the U.S. who complained about that scene in *Miller's Crossing* where Bernie [John Turturro] is taken out into the woods and shot. He said that it was much too reminiscent of the genocide of the Jews in Europe. Well . . . I guess that's the risk you run by being so specific with your characters.

Q:    *John Turturro can do them all, though. Italians, Jews, Mexicans . . .*
JOEL:    Yeah, John does get cast in a lot of those parts. He's very specifically ethnic, but it's very hard to tell . . . which one.

Q:    *You've made your Texas, New York, and Minnesota movies. Did you specifically want to make* The Big Lebowski *your L.A. movie?*
ETHAN:    Oh yeah. Definitely. It was conceived that way, in as much as all the characters are pretty much emblematic of Los Angeles—they're all types who seem like people you would meet there. But the L.A. thing

is also connected to the fact that very consciously a Raymond Chandler thing—a sort of wandering intrigue which explores different parts of the city, through the characters.

JOEL:   I've never had a chance to develop much of a relationship with L.A. I'm always a tourist there. Happily, it is possible to make movies and not live in L.A. But it was definitely Chandler's novels that inspired *The Big Lebowski*—in terms of its story and setting.

Q:   *How familiar are you with the kind of people who inhabit your films? The earthy inhabitants of* Fargo *are totally different from the more exotic characters who populate* The Big Lebowski.

ETHAN:   Well, a couple of the characters in *The Big Lebowski* are, very loosely, inspired by real people. We know a guy who's a middle-aged hippy pothead, and another who's a Vietnam vet who's totally defined by, and obsessed with, the time he spent in Vietnam. We find it interesting for our characters to be products of the sixties in some way, but set in the nineties.

Q:   *Did you have an urge to realize the cinematic potential of bowling?*

ETHAN:   Oh yeah. The guy who the Walter character is based on is an avid member of, and consequently obsessed with, an amateur softball league team in L.A. But we changed it to bowling, because it's more interesting, visually. All of the stuff associated with bowling—y'know, the architecture, the machines, it's all sort of retro to the fifties and sixties. Classic bowling design era—you see it all over L.A.

Q:   *There's also a pre-set character type associated with bowling.*

JOEL:   Yeah. That fitted in well with the layabout Dude guy.

ETHAN:   But you mean the slobby aspects of it, the male thing. Men getting together with their little leagues . . . and it is, in a strange way, kind of a buddy movie.

Q:   *The English equivalent would be darts.*

JOEL:   Yeah. It's the same thing, really—big guys with their stomachs hanging out, drinking.

ETHAN:   It's not really a physically taxing thing. You can be a slob and do it.

Q:    *You give the impression that most of humanity is either moronic or mad, and both types come up in the two main* Big Lebowski *characters.*
JOEL:    Well, it's one thing making up stories, and quite another having a conception of the human race. One doesn't necessarily have anything to do with the other. But it is true, most of the characters in our movies are pretty unpleasant—losers or lunkheads, or both. But we're also very fond of those characters, because you don't usually see movies based around those kind of people. We're not interested in burly superhero types.

Q:    *A big criticism that's been levelled at your pictures is that they're all technique and no heart.*
ETHAN:    Well, the process of writing a story is different from the business of how the characters behave or how they interact.
JOEL:    *Lebowski* is a good example. The story, if you reduced it to the plot, would seem rather ridiculous or uninteresting. And it's the same with a lot of Chandler—the plots are there to drive the characters.

Q:    *Why was* The Hudsucker Proxy *such a flop?*
JOEL:    I dunno, why was *Fargo* not a flop? Most people don't like *Hudsucker*, and I don't know the reason. It's as much of a mystery to me that people went to see *Fargo*, which was something we did thinking, ah, y'know, about three people will end up seeing it, but it'll be fun for us . . .

Q:    *How do you work together? Is it essential that you produce and direct your own scripts? Would you consider developing someone else's script?*
JOEL:    We both rewrite together, we're both out there on the set and in the editing room together. There are no creative tantrums. We just consider ourselves extremely lucky that, so far, we've been able to do our own scripts. It's not that we are philosophically opposed to the idea of working on someone else's material, but I think it would be difficult, because, for us, so much of the process starts with imagining the story. I think it would feel strange and very different to the modification process that we're used to. We just haven't found anything so far that's more interesting than what we've been writing or working on ourselves.

Q:   *You seem to be very interested in crass, venal men who spend most of their time sitting behind desks. Do you have a lot of personal experience of these people?*

JOEL:   Yeah. That's true! No, we haven't had a lot of experience of them, but it is absolutely true that we're interested in crass, venal men behind desks. There's Sidney Mussberger in *Hudsucker*, M. Emmet Walsh in *Blood Simple*, Jack Lipnick in *Barton Fink*, Arizona in *Raising Arizona . . .* I guess even Bill Macy in *Fargo . . .*

ETHAN:   Waring Hudsucker—maybe. Although you can't really call it a desk. Maybe a threshold.

Q:   *Is it true that you wait to make a film until your ideal cast is available?*

JOEL:   It was true with *Lebowski*, which was largely written before *Fargo*. We tried to get it together, and we held the Walter part for John Goodman until he'd finished with *Roseanne*. Jeff Bridges, too, although we didn't write only with him in mind. It varies. With *Fargo*, we wrote for Frances McDormand, Peter Stormare, and Steve Buscemi.

Q:   *What Hollywood films have you seen recently?*

ETHAN:   I liked *Starship Troopers*. Really funny. It was pretty bold that he went in on a $100 million movie with no stars.

JOEL:   *Bound* was good. A lot of people said it was a "Coen brothers kind of movie." I don't know about that, but it was fun, I liked it.

ETHAN:   *L.A. Confidential*. That was . . . okay.

Q:   *Is mainstream Hollywood all out of ideas?*

JOEL:   Well, I think a lot of good, interesting movies still get made. It's just like any other aspect of popular entertainment—the majority of the stuff isn't going to be particularly good. It's the same with music, books . . . most of it is naturally going to be dull. Movies—especially Hollywood movies—are an easy American whipping boy, because it is true that most of it is shit. But it's not surprising. It's more a natural by-product of a healthy, extremely productive industry.

Q:   *You took the Palme D'Or for* Barton Fink *and the two Oscars for* Fargo. *Does winning awards thrill you?*

JOEL:   Well, 1996 was kind of a flukey year.

ETHAN:    Yeah, they didn't have any other important movies to give the awards to that year.

JOEL:    We have an odd relationship with Hollywood. We've never really felt marginalized from them, except through our own choice—we don't live in L.A., we don't develop stuff through the studios. We've always had pretty cordial relationships with studios—y'know, they've distributed and financed our movies.

ETHAN:    But that's the nature of this business. Box-office success, awards—it's all very capricious, and never quite what you'd expect. But you tend to snatch your moment of favor.

Q:    *There was word of* Fargo *being adapted into a television show. Is that happening? Are you involved in any way?*

ETHAN:    Someone had the idea that it could be turned into a series of one-hour shows, and that Marge could solve a different case each episode. I think they filmed a pilot, directed by Kathy Bates.

JOEL:    We weren't really involved. I can't say that we weren't happy that it died.

Q:    *You're working on an Elmore Leonard novel—the Western,* Cuba Libre.

ETHAN:    Yeah. But only as a writing job, not to do the movie itself.

Q:    *You worked with Sam Raimi (director of the* Evil Dead *films) on* Crimewave *and* The Hudsucker Proxy. *Do you have any plans to work with him again?*

JOEL:    No plans, but I'm sure it'll happen one day. Last I heard, Sam was making a movie in Minnesota. Hmm . . .

Q:    *What's the atmosphere like on a Coen Brothers movie set? How are you to work for?*

ETHAN:    As with all movie sets, the atmosphere is mostly incredibly tedious. Elementally chaotic, maybe, but, to an observer, it would seem like nothing was going on. And, mostly, they'd be right. There's a lot of time spent doing really exciting things like setting up lighting.

JOEL:    When the camera's running, you have to be very quiet and well-behaved. After the camera stops, you become a dictator. I think we're good to work for. It's more of a collegial kind of atmosphere. As you can imagine, given the fact that we do this together, we're essentially collaborative. We're just more comfortable working with people we're used to working with.

Q:   *Can you think of a genre that you'll never get round to tackling? Sci-fi, perhaps?*
JOEL:   I'd like to do a Western.
ETHAN:   I don't know much about sci-fi, so . . . I think outer space is maybe a little too sterilized, even for us. We thought of doing an American version of the *Odyssey*, with a guy escaping from a chain gang, finding his way home.
JOEL:   That would be generically closer to what we've done a lot of. Y'know—a southern hayseed movie.

Q:   *So what's coming up next?*
ETHAN:   Our big thing at the moment is something set in California in the late forties—we're working on the script now. It's basically the Bob Crane story. Bob Crane was the guy who played Hogan in *Hogan's Heroes*, which was a sitcom about American prisoners of war in Germany. Bob Crane was a guy who enjoyed playing the drums in topless bars, and watching and appearing in porn movies. He was murdered in Arizona years later, while being interviewed there by a guy who had installed lots of secret video equipment in order to tape himself in . . . certain sexual situations [Crane was bludgeoned repeatedly with a camera tripod and a video cable was tied round his neck]. I think it would be an interesting cautionary tale about Hollywood, sort of a companion piece to *Barton Fink*.

# The Logic of Soft Drugs

MICHEL CIMENT AND
HUBERT NIOGRET/1998

Q:   *Since* Raising Arizona, *we've seen lots of twisted and eccentric characters in your films, but probably never in such great number as in* The Big Lebowski!

ETHAN COEN:   That's true, you have the feeling you're attending a congress of misfits! Of all the participants, [John] Turturro is undoubtedly the strangest. I was just talking about that relationship with *Raising Arizona* with Joel yesterday. Perhaps it comes from all those secondary and tangential characters who drift in and out of the movie and are all bizarre in their own way.

Q:   *One also has the idea that* The Big Lebowski *is made in opposition to* Fargo: *an almost anarchic freedom facing a logical rigor, the heat of California after the coldness of Minnesota. You appear to take the same starting point situation, a kidnapping, then reshuffle the cards.*

ETHAN:   For us it was above and beyond all else a Californian story. We even drew loose inspiration from a Chandler plot outline. All his novels, or almost all, are situated in Los Angeles. We have to admit we like to do variations on a dramatic situation like kidnapping, which you can also find in *Raising Arizona*. You could also say that there's a certain logic in *The Big Lebowski*, but it'd be the logic induced by soft drugs!

---

From *Positif*, May 1998. Reprinted by permission of *Positif* and the authors.
Translated by Paul Buck and Catherine Petit.

JOEL COEN:    The logic here is more episodic—like in a Chandler novel, the hero sets out to clear up a mystery and while doing so visits a lot of odd characters who spring up like Jack-in-the-boxes.

Q:    *How did you construct that world populated with bizarre people?*
ETHAN:    We bore in mind Chandler's pattern, a story like *The Big Sleep*. We had a millionaire in Pasadena and, as so often with his novels, a mature and sophisticated woman, Maude, played by Julianne Moore, and a licentious and depraved girl, Bunny, played by Tara Reid. The main character is often involved in a romantic sub-plot with the first type of woman.
JOEL:    But, of course, it's not a private eye movie. We wanted to use those conventions, but without being too literal.
ETHAN:    We took models when they were convenient. For instance, in Chandler there are suave night-club owners like Jackie Treehorn, played by Ben Gazzara. He looks like Norris in *The Big Sleep*.
JOEL:    Of course, one of the gags of the movie is that Jeff Bridges is involved in a private eye adventure, while he's the antithesis of that. His character, by the way, like John Goodman's, is loosely inspired by real people. One is known by us, the other we heard about. Walter Sobchak [Goodman] is more of a composite of different people.

Q:    *It's your second film set in Los Angeles. The first,* Barton Fink, *evoked Hollywood, while this one has as its background a different kind of L.A.*
JOEL:    We live in New York and we like L.A., but we always feel like *outsiders* there. It's a fascinating enough place to entice us to shoot two movies there. In *The Big Lebowski* it's a more marginal Los Angeles— Venice Beach, the Valley, Pasadena—which, in people's minds, isn't really part of the city. The cultures in Los Angeles are more isolated from each other than in New York because of that huge surface spread. All of those sub-cultures are juxtaposed without really communicating. But, in fact, there's as much diversity as in New York.
ETHAN:    The main difference lies in the characters. You wouldn't expect to meet the Dude or Walter in New York. First, they wear shorts! It's a totally informal city. You don't see the chief of police at any point, but he's probably wearing shorts too! The scene in the house with the guy

who's a television scriptwriter, who's been inspired by a real-life event, couldn't be transported to a New York suburb and still stay in tune.

JOEL: The idle, laid-back, jobless character played by Jeff Bridges, who seems to live in slow motion, just seems typical to us of that local culture.

Q: *Bowling is in itself a subculture.*

JOEL: It's pretty much an accident that it gained an important place in the story. One of the people who inspired Walter's character was part of an amateur softball team. We chose to make him into a bowling fanatic since that offered us more visual possibilities. The bowling culture was also important in reflecting that period at the end of the fifties and the beginning of the sixties. That suited the retro side of the movie, slightly anachronistic, which sent us back to a not-so-far away era, but one that was well and truly gone nevertheless. The action itself takes place at the beginning of the nineties, but all the characters refer to the culture of thirty years ago, they are its aftermath and its mirror. Jeff Bridges is an aging hippie, John Goodman is defined by his Vietnam experience, while Maude (Julianne Moore) has for her blueprints the sixties New York Fluxus artists like Yoko Ono before she met John Lennon, or Carol Schneeman, who literally threw herself into her projects for physical support. Maude owes her a lot! Ben Gazzara also echoes people like Hugh Hefner from that period. The difference from *Boogie Nights*, which represents the seventies, or the new movie Todd Haynes has just shot, *Velvet Goldmine*, on rock stars like David Bowie in that same period, is that *The Big Lebowski* doesn't really take place in the past. It's contemporary movie about what's become of people who were formed and defined by that earlier period.

Q: *The voice-over of a character who we only see much later—which will also conclude the movie—is reminiscent of hearing popular legends of the Old West, as the narrator has a cowboy style.*

ETHAN: In that specific case, I don't remember how the idea came to us. But we've always liked to create a certain distance that takes us away from reality by enclosing the story in a frame.

JOEL: The Stranger (Sam Elliott) is a little bit of an audience substitute. In the movie adaptations of Chandler it's the main character that speaks offscreen, but we didn't want to reproduce that though it obviously has echoes. It's as if someone was commenting on the plot from an all-seeing point of view. And at the same time rediscovering the old earthiness of a Mark Twain.

Q:    *There's also a reference to* Fargo *via the girl with a Scandinavian name, Knudsen, who comes from Minnesota!*
ETHAN:    In fact, we'd more or less written that script before shooting *Fargo*. If there's a reference, it would actually be in reverse order, at least chronologically. We didn't specifically want to refer to *Fargo*, but it's true we'd been in Minnesota to check out the remote places that girl on the run might have come from.

Q:    *Walter mirrors quite a few American archetypes: his memories of Vietnam, his violence, his relationship to women, his know-it-all claims . . .*
ETHAN:    And he's always right! That tough guy character presented great comic possibilities, above all if he was associated with the character of Jeff Bridges. They are obviously each other's stooges. Steve Buscemi wondered why his cretinous character made up a trio with those two! We thought about that: perhaps he's only there because he's the only one who can bowl well. For Walter, our model was one of our friends, a Vietnam veteran whose conversation always comes back to that war. There's also a bit of John Milius in that character: he's a great story-teller, but also a macho show-off, with the same concerns and the same obsessions.

Q:    *Was the Dude the first protagonist you had in mind before writing the script?*
ETHAN:    The movie was conceived as pivoting around that relationship between the Dude and Walter. The idea sprang from the scenes between Barton Fink and Charlie Meadows, who was played by John Goodman. That's the reason why the bowling seemed an appropriate context: it's not that the sport isn't played by women, but they have their own teams. In bowling, there's a real segregation of the sexes. In *The Big Lebowski* you spend time exclusively in the company of men. The worlds of the private eye and the Western, which we refer to at the end of the movie, are also very masculine.

JOEL:    The two women of the movie, Maude and Bunny, are minor characters and don't have big roles. This story is, in fact, that of a marriage, an odd couple formed by Jeff and John, their fluctuating relationship. There's often a *slow burn* in their confrontations, until John Goodman blows up.

Q:    *The bowling scenes are very choreographed.*
JOEL:    The idea was to shoot those bowling rituals almost in slow motion. The credits sequence was conceived to make you enter that world and understand the importance of bowling to the movie.

Q:    *There's a whole surrealist aspect in the visual ideas: the flying carpet, the naked man covered only with oak leaves, the beach party . . .*
JOEL:    The dreamlike sequences echo in one sense the hallucinations of the private eye in Chandler's novels. It's also to do with the marijuana consumption of the hero! For me that corresponds to Los Angeles, which is a more surreal place than New York. There's an Oriental side, a *1001 Arabian Nights* aspect to that city. You can't be more remote from a New York sensibility than in that beach party given by the pornographer. It's the world of the drugs consumer. And the sound of the bowling is also a narcotic for the Dude. In people's minds the hallucinatory psychedelic culture is associated with Southern California and San Francisco.

Q:    *An image like that of the three red devils with their giant scissors, was it suggested by specific reminiscences?*
JOEL:    In a way we foreshadow that image with the picture showing scissors in a red field which hangs in Maude's loft.
ETHAN:    We don't know specifically where we found our inspiration, but we knew the background had to be black. Nothing in particular influenced us. It was a synthesis of several ideas, including that of our costume designer Mary Zaphres. And, well, maybe Ingmar Bergman had something to do with it!

Q:    *The choreography refers to Busby Berkeley.*
JOEL:    We always wanted to pay tribute to him, he's one of our heroes. He was an incredible choreographer who never worried about justifying

his extravagance. His audacity and sense of freedom fascinate us. Frankly, it's very difficult to remake that mixture of surprise and precision. We've even more admiration for him now after trying to imitate him!

ETHAN:   Nobody can equal him because that would cost too much money. He had an abundance of resources and considerable rehearsal time to reach that state of perfection. We had thirty-five girls where he had 350.

Q:   *Did you use a storyboard?*

ETHAN:   We were forced to for some shots that had to be composed on a computer, in particular where the Dude [Bridges] passes his head between the dancer's legs. It was very rigorous work.

Q:   *The three nihilists are Germans. Do you think your movie could also be qualified as nihilistic? What is its moral point of view?*

JOEL:   Certainly not. For us, the nihilists are the bad guys, and, if there's a preferred moral position, it'd be that of Jeff Bridges, though it's difficult to define! In a curious way, you could say he has the moral code of the private eye. But, in his case, it's very fluid! What you can say with certainty is that the movie leads to a reconciliation between the Dude and Walter despite their difficult relationship. In a detective movie, there's a line of clear conduct, a much more solid spine, even if it's never explicit. That's not the case with the Dude.

ETHAN:   It's also due to the fact that it's a comedy. In the detective movie, the protagonist leads a crusade after the death of his partner, for example, and he seeks the truth. He is a knight errant. The Dude wavers more at the surface of things. It's Walter who pushes him to undertake the venture, only to jeopardize it later.

Q:   *As in a number of your films, the protagonist is like a prisoner in a revolving door from which he can't get out, and his life becomes a nightmare. But it's the first time you play on the confusion of identity where someone is mistaken for someone else.*

ETHAN:   That's not treated seriously, but it's true we were attracted by the idea that those two characters, the Dude and the Big Lebowski, who are so different, have meeting points.

JOEL:    Here again, that nabob has been inspired by Chandler. You find him in *The Big Sleep*, and also in *The High Window*. He's a recurrent character, the domineering, all-powerful figure who becomes a catalyst. Chandler's novels cut across all the social classes of Los Angeles, and this character is at the top of the ladder. He represents Money. He appears in *Chinatown*, he's contributed to the town's construction. He symbolizes an old order, which, in the end, you discover is all a sham.

Q:    *You often mention Chandler. Are there any other crime writers you're attracted to?*
JOEL:    *Miller's Crossing* was certainly born from our desire to tell a story the Hammett way. But we also like James Cain a lot.

Q:    *You add Jewish humor. But it's the first time you have had fun so openly with a Jewish character, Walter Sobchak.*
ETHAN:    It's true we've created Jewish characters before but we didn't make their Jewishness into a comic element.
JOEL:    Our grandpa was very orthodox. He didn't drive his car on the Sabbath. I remember, as a child, that I found it weird he didn't want to light the cooker. That didn't seem such a big job to me! Our parents were religious, but not excessively so. When Grandpa paid us a visit during the Sabbath, my mother used subterfuges to make him believe we were obeying the law and refusing to do all that was forbidden. That's how we learned about acting!

Q:    *The style of the photography in* Fargo *is very clear-cut. How did you discuss the visual ideas for* The Big Lebowski *with Roger Deakins?*
JOEL:    That's exactly the question Roger never stopped asking us, and I don't think we ever succeeded in answering it exactly! The difficulty for Roger was to juxtapose those stylized, dreamlike, abstract scenes with other very down-to-earth ones, like the place where the Dude lives, the scene at the end with the Stranger, not to mention the bowling alley. In that last case, the style of the photography was imposed by the fluorescent light on the ceiling. As always there's a link with the chromatic scheme and the design. Rick Heinrichs wanted very rich or very saturated colors, as you can see from the star-motifs on the far side of the bowling alley. The clothes also followed that style, as did Turturro's

tights. That brings the movie closer to a studio work, as distinct from *Fargo*. Again, you can find the L.A. spirit in the colors, whether saturated or pastel, from the blue of the ocean to the blue of the sky.

Q:    *The film opens on an aerial view of a landscape.*
JOEL:    We wanted to introduce the story with that panoramic view which goes hand in hand with the cowboy song, reminiscent of the pioneer spirit. The voice of the Stranger becomes a frame for the story. The original music, as with other elements of the movie, had to echo the retro sounds of the sixties and early seventies. There's a lot of tunes from that period. There's also older classical music, like Mozart's *Requiem,* or Mussorgsky's *Pictures at an Exhibition.* There are sequences that we wrote with the music already in our head, like the Latino song "Oye Como Va," for the sequence with Turturro.
ETHAN:    In that case, it's the music that defines the character. It's the same for the cowboy played by Sam Elliott. Dylan's "The Man in Me" was chosen at the time of writing. As was "Lujon" by Henri Mancini for Ben Gazzara's character. . . . The German nihilists are accompanied by techno-pop and Jeff Bridges by Creedence [Clearwater Revival]. So there's a musical signature for each of them.

Q:    *Why shoot the film after* Fargo, *when the script was written before?*
ETHAN:    Because John Goodman was busy elsewhere. On top of that, while we hadn't an actor in mind for the Dude role during the writing of the script, we decided later to offer it to Jeff Bridges who was already working, shooting *Wild Bill* for Walter Hill. So it was for scheduling reasons that we shot it after *Fargo.*

Q:    *Did the writing take longer than for other films?*
JOEL:    Not really. We write pretty fast, with the exception of *Miller's Crossing,* which took us much more time because we encountered difficulties in structuring the plot. Generally we work in stages. For instance, for *The Big Lebowski* we wrote forty pages then let it rest for a while before resuming writing. That's fairly normal for our way of working. We have a project for which we've written a few dozen pages almost two years ago, and we'll soon be finishing that. It's not that we particularly like to work like that, but that's how it often happens.

We encounter a problem at a certain stage, we pass to another project, then we come back to the first script. That way we've already accumulated pieces for several future movies.

Q:    *Do they always revolve around a kidnapping?*
ETHAN:    Not always, but it's true that it comes up frequently in what we write. A screenplay we've half-written takes its inspiration from the *Odyssey*, which is also one of our favorite plot outlines. It's the story of a prisoner in a convict camp in the southern states, during the Depression, who manages to escape and try to return home, going through different episodes in which he resorts to tricks like Ulysses. Curiously enough we've just finished a new script, commissioned this time for another director, which is an adaptation of an Elmore Leonard novel featuring a kidnapping!

# Ethan Coen, Joel Coen, and *The Big Lebowski*

## KAREN JAEHNE/1998

OTHER BROTHERS MAKE FILMS TOGETHER, but Joel and Ethan Coen stand out as the young hipsters. Only a decade ago, they embarked on a subversive path from independent filmmaking to low-budget Hollywood fare with a distinct intellectual edge. Beginning with *Blood Simple*, they helped launch the White Trash aesthetic that was picked up by others and continued with their own film, *Raising Arizona*. Their ironic experiments in genre have produced not only a smashing debut in *Blood Simple*, but also their gangster love story, *Miller's Crossing*, and their inside-Hollywood drama, *Barton Fink*. *Fargo* was their sweetest, truest, and most straightforward film in its portrayal of ordinary people capable of surprising us with extraordinary acts.

Interviewing them makes you feel like a bicycle built for two. One will start a sentence. Sometimes, the other will finish it—or not. They don't always finish sentences. In the following transcript, I've used the dots of an ellipsis (". . .") to denote a change of speaker from Joel to Ethan or back. It's hard to break out from a tape recording, but it should give you an idea of the way they think and express themselves.

Q:    *When did you conceive of* The Big Lebowski?
THE COENS:    These things are hard to pin down. We work on a script a bit, then work on a different one. We went back to this after making *Fargo*, but. . . . well, it had been there for a long time.

From *Filmscouts*, http://www.filmscouts.com. Reprinted by permission of *Filmscouts*.

Q:    *Why do you keep putting kidnapping episodes in your movies?*
COENS:    Well, kidnapping is a good device. . . . It presents a kind of urgency to the plot, a high-stakes kind of crime. . . . but we don't really think, gee, how can we put kidnapping into this movie? . . . no, we don't have an obsession with kidnapping, it's just. . . . one of those things. . . . It's our attempt to do one of those Chandler stories about L.A., you know, with the kidnapped heiress or. . . . those are all reasons we came up with after the fact . . . but when we're writing, we just follow the story wherever it leads us, and if it leads us to kidnapping, well there we are!

Q:    The Big Lebowski *strikes me as a rather brilliant, daring, and brave defense of a certain state of consciousness.*
COENS:    Yes . . . yeah, right-on. Well, we thought there was something appealing about this complicated and weird plot being unraveled by a pothead.

Q:    *Do you think marijuana should be legalized?*
COENS:    Uh . . . well . . . uh, you mean it's not? . . . Actually, the point of view is built into the character of the Dude. It's in the core, the core of the. . . . Yeah, it's about L.A., man.

Q:    *You couldn't make a pothead movie about a New Yorker?*
COENS:    It'd be a different thing. . . . Yeah, a really different thing, probably more violent . . . or not!

Q:    *What exactly is the relationship between Bunny Lebowski and the German gang?*
COENS:    Just the pornographic film they made. . . . yeah, just pornography.

Q:    *They're not in cahoots on the kidnapping?*
COENS:    Uh, are they? . . . uh, no, I don't think so . . . maybe? . . . No, I don't think so.

Q:    *The production design in* The Big Lebowski *is highly original in adapting kitsch and very, very funny, which is due, I guess, to Rick Heinrichs. How do you work together?*

COENS:    Very well, he's great. He loves to take design as far as it will go. He worked on *Fargo*, and that was really an unsung accomplishment, because we wanted no design. *Fargo* had absolutely nothing. We told him to find the most soul-deadening, flattened locations, and he'd find some dumpy cafe, and we'd say, no, it's too good. . . . Less color, less design, less kitsch. Now that can be hard. But one thing he actually made in *Fargo* was the big Paul Bunyan. For *The Big Lebowski*, he had lots to do. Everything was made over, the bowling alley. . . . everything!

Q:    *What's it like working with Roderick Jaynes?*
COENS:    [they finally laugh out loud—yuk-yuk-yuk] He's getting harder and harder to deal with! Roderick Jaynes is a pseudonym we use for doing the editing ourselves, because we cut our own movies . . . When we got an editing nomination, we were going to have a friend of Roderick Jaynes accept the award, but the Academy wouldn't let us do that, because of Brando.

Q:    *You mean they don't allow acceptances to be designated ever since Brando sent a Native American to accept his Oscar and give a political speech.*
COENS:    Something like that. . . . I guess . . .

Q:    *How much input do the actors have into the characters in your films?*
COENS:    Well, the characters are always the focus of the movie, and we develop them over months and months of talking about them and writing them. . . . We get them down on paper and then turn them over to the actors who are sometimes exactly the people we had in mind when we were working on them. . . . Let's just say, the characters are the result of two things—first, we elaborate them into fairly well-defined people through their dialogue, then they happen all over again, when the actor interprets them.

Q:    *Roughly how long does it take you to get the script to the point you like it?*
COENS:    That's really hard to say. . . . It depends on so many things, you never really stop working on it until you start shooting. . . . And

even then we do things as we think they're necessary. . . . We tried to do this a few years ago, but people weren't available and. . . . Then they were available and the script was virtually finished, so . . . you know, that's how it works with availability and why you have to have several things going on all the time . . . We're like everybody else in being kind of lazy and taking the path of least resistance and just making the movie that can be made. But you always want to do something basically different from the last thing you did.

Q:    *Your other movies seem to have a moral or a message at the end. What do you see as the message of* The Big Lebowski?
COENS:    None. . . . None of them have messages. . . . You see a moral in them? Do we have morals?

It wasn't really over, but that's all for now, folks!

# The Coen Brothers

DAVID BENNUN/1998

A CLOUD OF BEFUDDLEMENT passes over Ethan Coen's open, upturned face. He sets down his coffee cup, carefully. He looks faintly appalled.

"Have we ever *what*?" he asks.

Gotten tattooed. You know, had a sherry too many one night. Found yourself in a basement establishment. Wall charts covered in leaping tigers, coiled serpents, and hearts skewered by daggers. A heavyset individual leaning over you with a vibrating needle: "Let me get this straight buddy . . . You want a flaming cine camera and the scrolled legend, 'We're the Coen Brothers and you're not'?"

"Why," demands Joel Coen bullishly, "would we want to do that? I even think ear-piercing is weird. You know what the new thing is?" He turns to his brother. "Embedded jewellery. They stick it under the skin so all you can see is the bump underneath."

Ethan now looks aghast, but strangely pleased at this unprompted fashion report. He picks up his cup once more from the little table in the dainty Bayswater hotel suite and sips from it. "Maybe they missed out on acne when they were kids."

These two men wrote and directed their first movie in 1984. It was called *Blood Simple*, and it involved grisly murders both faked and real, knives stuck through hands, live burials, that kind of malarkey. Their next, *Raising Arizona*, was about half-bright rednecks getting caught up

---

From *Uncut* Magazine, 1998. Copyright © 1998 by David Bennun. Reprinted by permission of the author.

with baby-snatching, bank-robbing, and a bounty-hunting biker who bore more than a passing resemblence to Death. Since then they've done exploding Hollywood hotels, fat angels flapping through frozen time, a pregnant cop chasing killers in a blizzard, and a kidnapping mystery set around an amateur bowling team. They think ear-piercing is weird.

Joel and Ethan Coen are very, very normal, and they want you to know it. They are the siblings who invented the independent thriller. Who brought high style to the world of low budgets. Opened the betting on celluloid black humor. They probably go to fancy dress parties as themselves, in check shirts, jeans, and blazers. This pair would rather rub up against a brace of skunks than the glamour of the film industry.

"Independent movies? We were in at the start of all that bullshit," they cheerfully assert. Fourteen years and seven films on they have gained no more respect for the world they work in. Meanwhile indie flicks have become big business, with major studios bankrolling cheap movies—on the quiet, to avoid losing that all-important cachet. Everybody thinks they alone know what's going on, and nobody's really fooling anybody. It's all cack-handed subterfuge and preposterous lies. You can see why the Coens fit in so well. It's just like one of their scripts.

Cack-handed subterfuge and preposterous lies: a fair summary of *The Big Lebowski*, the Coens' latest release. *The Big Lebowski* may not be quite the film that its predecessor, *Fargo*, was—but few films are. And with the Coens you know that at the very least you're in for a laugh. *Fargo* made the dull Twin Cities of Minnesota and their bleak environs seem like one of the funniest places on God's own ludicrous planet. This time round, they've roped in Jeff Bridges to mosey through a meandering tale of modern L.A.—the only American city, reckons one commentator, stupider than Minneapolis.

Ethan is really tickled by that. "Yeah, L.A., as someone once said, 'Where even the Jews are dumb. I kind of like L.A. Dumb doesn't quite say it. But it's true about the Minneapolis part. L.A.'s got its share of dumbness, that's for sure. But yeah, the main guy, the Jeff Bridges guy, is supposed to be in a way emblematic of L.A. He's not dumb exactly, but he's a little foggy. A little slow. Very relaxed. Jeff can do those sorts of slow-metabolism characters without being boring. He's very funny, he works as the thread through the whole movie."

Bridges's character, self-styled The Dude, is a guileless, easy-going drugs casualty who wanders into a kidnapping plot after being mistaken for a millionaire who shares his surname, Lebowski. Buffeted about like a leaf on a breeze, all the hapless Dude wants out of life is to play on the same bowling team as John Goodman and Steve Buscemi. A fine ambition, and most of us would settle for less. But chance has other plans for The Dude, and whatever hope he has of steering an even course through the weirdness that envelops him like polka-dot fog is well and truly scuppered by his maniac mate Walter Sobchak (Goodman).

Walter, a survivalist type who runs his own security firm and acts as if he can't go down to the newsstand without a Bowie knife clenched between his molars, is obsessed with his past as a grunt in Vietnam. The fact that he never went to Vietnam is by the by. Through the judicious deployment of shotguns, tire irons, pistols, and rank idiocy, he succeeds in buggering up The Dude's progress at every halting step of the way. Bearing in mind Goodman's loose-cannon roles in *Raising Arizona* and *Barton Fink*, you have to wonder if the Coens don't take enormous pleasure in casting him as a variety of psychos.

"That's true," nods Joel, "we've done it at least twice. In *Barton Fink* truly he was a psycho. I guess you could argue here that he's just rather volatile. I mean, okay, he does trash that Corvette with a crowbar. And then there's the part where he throws the guy out of the wheelchair, but . . ." Joel pauses to stare evenly at Ethan, who has started to laugh like a drain. "But mainly he's just a volatile blowhard."

While Goodman's role is typically flammable and Steve Buscemi's uncommonly low-key, another Coen regular, the ever-excellent John Turturro, turns in what may be the most memorable (if least dignified) performance of both the movie and his career. Not bad going, seeing as he's only on screen for about three minutes.

". . . but he makes an impression," gurgles Ethan. "He goes to the core." By now he's emitting a strange, hiccupping laugh, as if the memory alone is too hilarious to handle. "Originally he was just like a good bowler, the nemesis bowler, but we thought, make him a Hispanic pederast, it'll give John something to get his teeth into." And sure enough, the sight of Turturro mincing up to Goodman in a pink jumpsuit and hissing, in a voice halfway between Speedy Gonzalez and Kaa the python, "If you try an' pull any of that pistol shit on me, I'm gonna jam that gun up your ass and pull the trigger until it goes *click*"—well, it's not one you're likely to forget in a hurry.

"There's not a lot of vamping with the dialogue," adds Ethan, "but John came up with touches like the hairnet and the little dance"—a minimal yet fantastically obscene gyration—"when he gets a strike. It's funny, you identify with his character after a while. We were thinking on set how that character could have his own TV series. It's a pity how you only see him for three minutes."

The Coens have a well-known liking for surrounding themselves with familiar faces, film after film, on both sides of the camera. Some cinema buffs have put this down to their unslakable thirst for control: once the brothers have found people who'll do exactly what they want, claim the cineastes, then they stick with them. This all seems a bit sinister and not a little hysterical. Certainly, the Coens make no secret of their technique, in which scripts are precision instruments and each showy take is carefully mapped out in advance.

"We've been accused ever since we started of placing style over substance," says Joel with a low chuckle, "and we've never taken any notice—or we would have learned our lesson by now." Control is obviously not just important to them but necessary, which makes it all the more curious that the film *The Big Lebowski* most closely resembles is *The Long Goodbye*, made by that most rambling and unsettled of great directors, Robert Altman.

"Yeah, that's the most important antecedent to the movie," agrees Ethan, "because it tends to update Raymond Chandler in a much more direct way than this. But also the Elliot Gould character is purposefully . . ."

"Anachronistic." Joel stamps the word onto the end of Ethan's sentence.

". . . anti-Marlowe," continues Ethan, undeterred. "Of the current time and yet not, wandering around L.A. in a suit. In *Lebowski*, all the characters were supposed to be throwbacks to or defined by experiences they had in another era. The Dude is obviously a classic sixties burnout case, but Goodman's character too identifies himself as a Vietnam vet. Julianne Moore is that kind of Fluxus artist who's kind of passé now. So they're all meant to be anachronistic in a way."

"There's ways in which it's very much similar to and influenced by *The Long Goodbye*," Joel puts in. "But it's also very different in that, it's true, we're very different kind of filmmakers, from a very simple craft point of view. It's more deliberately a stylistic mish-mash."

A mish-mash which very likely stretched to the limit the skills of the Coen's regular film editor, Roderick Jaynes. A tall, florid Englishman with a taste for Saville Row suits, Jaynes keeps a low profile and is little known outside the technical side of the movie industry. Or at least he was until last year, when he was nominated for an Academy Award for his work on *Fargo*, and the Coens were forced by Oscar protocol to admit that he doesn't exist. They edit their own movies.

"We had a long discussion with the academy," explains Ethan, "in the event that he won. We thought of sending an actor, but they won't let you accept by proxy any more, not after the Marlon Brando thing . . ."

In 1973, Marlon Brando refused to turn up to accept his Best Actor award for *The Godfather*, sending in his place an American Indian woman called Sacheen Littlefeather, to protest discrimination against Indians and the erosion of their fishing rights. In a twist worthy of Ethan and Joel, Brando's Indian turned out to be a little-known Californian actress by the name of Maria Cruz. It's not known whether her fishing rights had been molested at any point.

Couldn't the Coens have picked up the award themselves—perhaps with one standing on the other's shoulders, wearing a very long over-coat?

Even Joel finds the notion entertaining. Ethan, meanwhile, has all but dropped off his chair.

"We—could—always," he gasps, "have—dressed—up—like—a—pantomime—horse."

The pair's taste for jokes, lies, and concealments got them into more serious trouble when *Fargo*, announcing itself as a true story, was revealed by a diligent journalist as being 100 percent proof pure fiction, unsullied by even a hint of fact. Was that yet another Coen Brothers prank?

"Fargo wasn't a prank," protests Ethan. "It wasn't like *Sleepers*, where the writer said it was based on his own life and it turned out he probably invented it. We wanted to do one of those true-story type movies. It just so happened we didn't know any true stories that were interesting. So we made one up. We weren't trying to put one over on people, we just wanted that dispensation in the terms of the narrative. Once you've committed yourself in that way, it's like Richard Nixon, you know, you can't stop lying." "The Roderick Jaynes thing, that *was* more of a prank," allows Joel. "It was kind of like, how many times do you want to put your name on the credits?"

Looking at the two immaculately American-casual types sitting in front of me, it's hard to imagine that their own lives in any way resemble the films they make. Think of other left-field filmmakers and you can picture them in the same world as their movies. Abel Ferrara is by many accounts just as intense, twisted, and drugged-up as his own work. Quentin Tarantino makes films as an expression of what he would love to be, and often insists on acting out his fantasies in them. But as for the Coens—"Oh Lord, no, HEH HEH HEH HEH!" Joel is all but convulsed by the idea. "Can you imagine? No, neither of us, I don't think, connects their lives to the movies in one way or another. Our lives are like the movies only in the weird respect that when you make a movie about Minnesota, then you spend five months traipsing around looking for snow up there. And then you spend five months in bowling alleys in L.A. Your life starts to get segmented by the subject matter of the movies."

So, for instance, when The Dude gets knocked out not once but twice in *The Big Lebowski*, had the brothers done any hands-on research for the acid-flashback dreams he experiences?

"We were big pot smokers," says Joel. "We're not anymore. I mean, I used to be when I was a kid."

"Yeah," concurs Ethan. "We're not method writers, if there is such a thing. I smoked a lot of pot in high school. It's the kind of thing you're glad you did when you were young, so you got over it."

That would explain why both sequences in the film were closer to Busby Berkeley than, say, Peter Fonda's *The Trip*.

"Yeah," says Ethan. "A very rigid drug scene. Hahahahahaha."

That's the Coen Brothers, then. Very, very normal. And say what you like about that, but it seems to work for them. They've never made a boring film, and not even the bloke who directed *Nice Girls Suck Dick 3* can make that highfalutin boast. Here's to them, Mr. and Mr. Normal and their freakish imaginations. Cheers.

# Gates of Ethan

## NICHOLAS PATTERSON/1998

ETHAN AND JOEL COEN are the reigning heavy-weight champions of independent filmmaking. As the big Hollywood studios pump millions of dollars into mindless remakes, this producer-director-writer team has cranked out a line of intelligent, original, and relatively low-budget movies, from the early *Blood Simple* and *Miller's Crossing* to the more elaborate *Barton Fink* and *Fargo*, and their most recent film, *The Big Lebowski*.

Now Ethan Coen has released his first collection of short stories: *Gates of Eden*. The stories exhibit many Coen hallmarks: close attention to diction, a fine eye for ethnic conflict, and a taste for grotesque violence and deadpan humor. Coen, who jokingly describes himself in his bio as "the Samuel Gelbfisz Professor of English as a Second Language at the University of Colorado at Boulder," employs a bizarre cast of characters that includes a college-educated boxer trapped in a mob feud and a maverick weights-and-measures man.

Coen's knack for dialogue has made him popular with actors as well as audiences, and the vocal talent for the *Gates of Eden* audiobook includes Steve Buscemi, Matt Dillon, John Goodman, William H. Macy, Ben Stiller, and John Turturro. Coen himself, who spoke to us on the phone from New York, sounds eerily similar to Jeff Bridges's slow-talking, California-surfer-slang-slinging "Dude" in *The Big Lebowski*.

---

From *Boston Phoenix*, November 19–26, 1998.

Q:    *I didn't start reading your book till last night, but I didn't stop reading it until I finished it, around 5 a.m. this morning.*
A:    That's good.

Q:    *In your book and in your movies, you pay homage to gangsters, from bootleggers up through Godfather-esque Mafia types. But they're all vintage gangsters. What do you think of gang bangers today? Do you think they lack style? Creativity?*
A:    Ah, Jesus, man. Style and creativity? I don't know, it's more an alien style to me, you know. It's a different ethnicity now. Lack style? No. I'll tell you who has style: snowboarders have style. They have the shit, man. They got the wardrobe. Those are my current role models in terms of the culture. But there's not a lot of drama to be wrought from snowboarding.

Q:    *You could say the same thing about bowling, which you got a lot of drama out of in* The Big Lebowski.
A:    Bowling is more communal. You can have characters interacting, which is more difficult on snowboards.

Q:    *In* Miller's Crossing *you have Jewish, Italian, Irish, Danish gangsters. What's the appeal?*
A:    I don't know. Well, actually, I do know. *Miller's Crossing* is pretty much just a shameless rip-off of Dashiell Hammett, mostly his novel *The Glass Key*, but to a lesser extent *Red Harvest*. More than anything else, it was an enthusiasm for Hammett's writing that was the genesis of that movie. It's Hammett—in a word, that's what it is.

Q:    *Do you think some of the stories in the book are influenced by Hammett? When I think of "Destiny," the protagonist, Hector Berlioz, is trying to be a Dashiell Hammett–style detective but not quite succeeding. He wants to be a badass, but he doesn't really have his shit together in the way Sam Spade did.*
A:    Right, and he has the handicap of being a symphonic Romantic composer. Yeah, I mean [Hammett] is an influence—more than an influence. If Hammett hadn't written his books, then obviously those stories wouldn't exist, certainly not in anything like the form that they exist now.

Q:   *You're probably going to hear this question over and over, but what kind of differences do you find between writing a screenplay and writing these stories?*

A:   The main difference for me, the obvious one, is that I write movies with a collaborator—with my brother—and these I wrote by myself. They're different things. It's common that you see collaborations among scriptwriters, and probably to a lesser extent in drama. When you're writing fiction for print, you're finishing it to a higher polish. What you are writing is the finished product. So you get very fussy and try to perfect everything in a way that precludes working with somebody else. Whereas when you're writing a movie, the script is by no means the finished product. It's a little more slapdash—you're just sort of putting together a blueprint for what the finished product is going to be: to wit, the movie itself. Working alone is better and worse. It's different. That's why I like doing both. The liability is you don't have the immediate feedback, and you don't have anybody to share the burden of having to come up with ideas. The work is that much less cross-pollinated. The virtue of working alone is that you can sort of follow ideas a little bit without having to justify them. You can sort of work it all the way through, wherever it goes. You don't have to think "How can I make sense of this?" as you would have to in presenting an idea to somebody you were collaborating with.

Q:   *Does it give you more freedom?*

A:   In a way. But there's a different kind of freedom in having ideas come out of left field that you didn't have to have the onus of coming up with. There is something liberating about that as well.

Q:   *Why did you decide to write the book in the first place?*

A:   Well, I'd been writing these stories for quite a while. As we've been working on movies I've been writing stories. A couple of them, three of them, have been published in magazines, but the rest of them not. At a certain point I just had a sufficient number of them to peddle as a book. My agent circulated a manuscript consisting of eleven of the stories and a promise to write three more within a certain amount of time to sort of fill out the volume.

Q:   *Have you run into people saying, "Oh, your book only got published because you're a celebrity"?*

A:    I haven't yet, because it just came out. But I wouldn't be surprised if I get that. But I couldn't complain, because the fact that I am a familiar name is part of why it was so damn easy to get published. I'm in a position to reap the benefits of that familiarity and not take the sort of grousing that might go with it from other people.

Q:    *To change the subject, what do you, as a Minnesotan, think of Jesse "The Body" Ventura?*
A:    I wish I knew. I haven't lived in Minnesota for a long time. I watched a lot of professional wrestling when I was a kid there, but he was after my time. I was back with Verne Gagne and the Crusher and the Bruiser.

Q:    *I've noticed in* Barton Fink *you have John Goodman showing John Turturro how to do American collegiate wrestling. Then later in the film you contrast that with the fake professional-wrestling movie* Barton Fink *is trying to write.*
A:    Yeah, we did wrestling in high school, actually. Now this is exciting, this is really good: I read this book, *City of Nets*. It was a book about Hollywood in the 1940s. I read this story in passing that Faulkner was assigned to write a wrestling picture, and I thought, "What the fuck is a wrestling picture?" I mean, we all know what boxing movies are, but have I ever seen a wrestling movie? That was part of what got us going on the whole *Barton Fink* thing. But if you're interested in wrestling, I wrote another movie with a friend of mine, J. Todd Anderson, who went on and directed it, called *The Naked Man*. It's about pro wrestling. It's going to come out sometime late this year, early next year. So you'll have to watch for it.

Q:    *So, following in Faulkner's footsteps, you wrote a wrestling picture?*
A:    Yeah. [Laughs.]

Q:    *Are there professional wrestlers in it?*
A:    Michael Rappaport plays the main guy—he's the main wrestler. There are some professional wrestlers in small parts, but like I said, I'm not very conversant with the prowrestling scene now, so I don't remember their names.

Q:    *You have an interesting way of portraying violence in your stories and movies. In* Blood Simple *you have the guy's hand impaled with a knife, and in* Fargo, *of course, the wood chipper scene. Do you intentionally try to turn your audience's stomach?*

A:    That's a good question. No, it's not like you're trying to turn their stomach. Clearly at the end of *Fargo* there is something right about coming around behind the house and seeing Peter Stormare stuffing the rest of Steve Buscemi into a wood chipper. But why is that right? I don't know. It's good. I mean, it's right, right? Anything else wouldn't have been as good. It has to be that grotesque, but why? I couldn't really tell you. It's compelling, man. And there is something really appealing about presenting something that grotesque in a very deadpan, matter-of-fact fashion. That stuff works in movies and in stories.

Q:    *It's kind of neat to see stuff like that happen. I can't believe I just said that, but it's true.*

A:    Yeah, it's true. [Laughs.] We all take part in it.

Q:    *It's not just sadistic. I mean, when you see movies that are really dumb, it's just . . .*

A:    Then it's offensive. There's always something good, be it violence or whatever—there is something that makes it more intense. Being specific—you know, like a knife in a hand—is something more than "she hurt him, he got punched, he got stabbed," or whatever. An audience can feel it sympathetically.

Q:    *Did you ever torture little animals when you were a kid?*

A:    No, no, not at all. I don't equate it with—I don't think [violence] is a bad or reprehensible thing in a movie or a story, and I don't equate it with personal evil or reprehensible acts. I don't think one is in any way related to the other. But I do wonder why it works so well. It's a drama and you want the stakes to be high and palpable.

Q:    *How do you research this stuff? Do you try things out on your friends?*

A:    No, we don't. We don't do any research, in a word.

Q:     *The characters in your stories and in your movies speak in idiosyncratic ways. Why do you focus on diction and accents so much?*
A:     You mean, what's the deal, maaaaan? You know, it's how you establish a character. Part of what a character is is how he expresses himself. It's a different issue from something like *Miller's Crossing*, where everybody shares a vernacular, all the characters in the movie share a vernacular. In that respect, it's how you establish the world they're in, as opposed to just each specific character. I have the feeling that what I am saying is incredibly obvious and banal, but there it is. You think about dialogue in conjunction with the character who is speaking it. You've got a finer characterization through how they express themselves as opposed to the raw content of what they are saying. You want to establish a character by showing him or hearing him instead of saying he is X, Y, Z.

Q:     *Do you research different accents?*
A:     No. I go with what I hear. None of this stuff is really very arcane. It's just what I've been exposed to in life and movies, books, whatever.

Q:     *You seem to play with ethnicity and prejudice a lot in your stories and films. Why do you do that?*
A:     Well, nobody does in movies, but that's because movies are really expensive to do, so studios really feel—probably with some reason—that they have to pander to people's sensitivities. They feel they can't offend anybody with a $60 million investment in the movie. It just gets kind of dull in movies—nobody is specific ethnically because nobody wants to offend anybody. We've never felt constrained by it in the movies that we do because our movies are sort of a little off the beaten track anyway, and have been fairly inexpensive and don't have to be $100 million movies at the box office in order to make their money back. But in terms of the stories, I don't think it's that remarkable. I guess some people would be offended there, too, but people's sensitivities are really their problem. If you want to make a character specific, his ethnicity is part of who he is. If a character is specifically Jewish, say, I don't feel that I have to make him 100 percent attractive in order to appease people who would be satisfied by nothing less. And frankly, there are such people. You want to make characters who are real, have some validity, have some light, have

some spark, have some life to them. Part of how you do that—all of how you do that—is by making them specific, you know? You have to be specific about how they talk, which we've touched on, and how they behave, how they do everything. And their ethnicity is naturally going to be part of that. I mean, it seems natural and self-evident to me, although some people are, as you suggest, a little more nervous about it. It's a nervousness I just don't share.

Q:    *I thought that the ethnic conflict in* Miller's Crossing *was one of its most appealing aspects.*
A:    Yeah, and they call each other sheenies and guineas and whatever. In real life people are more relaxed about their ethnicity than they are for purposes of public debate or public presentation.

Q:    *Does your career as the Samuel Gelbfisz Professor of English as a Second Language at the University of Colorado at Boulder take up a lot of your time?*
A:    No, that's an emeritus position. I don't actually have to teach classes; I don't even have to show up.

Q:    *Was English your second language?*
A:    No, but I speak it as if it was. Oops, as if it were. It's a subjunctive.

Q:    *Have you thought of or are you working on a novel?*
A:    No! I must say . . . No. No. Here's one big reason: the stories are something I do in my spare time as we are working on other things that are really my career—that is, movies. So a sustained, long, concentrated period of time that I would imagine one would have to devote to a novel is something I don't think I am going to have in the foreseeable future, even if I were interested. Which I'm not, particularly.

Q:    *Do you think you'll keep working on stories?*
A:    Yeah. I actually have started one. I feel that I have another story for the weights-and-measures guy [the protagonist of *Gates of Eden*]. He goes to Amsterdam and goes to a hash bar and visits a prostitute and various horrible things happen to him. So that's in the works.

Q:    *Have you ever been to Amsterdam?*
A:    Yeah, a long time ago. I liked it. I didn't get to spend much time there.

Q:    *Your characters have interesting experiences with drugs and alcohol. Would you say that drugs and alcohol have had any influence on your work?*
A:    Drugs and alcohol? Yeah . . . not really. I have firsthand experience with drugs and alcohol, but I'm not really dissolute. I mean, actually, far from it. It's almost the reverse. But it's interesting. The whole hash thing, it's going to be good.

Q:    *How's that?*
A:    It's just in the context of the story I'm working on now. You know, pot is a good thing, isn't it? Although, like I say, I'm hardly a drug-culture writer. I've never read any Irvine Welsh, but having seen the movie *Trainspotting*, I'm sure I'm no Irvine Welsh.

Q:    *One last question. If I send you this profile after it's done, and you like it, is there any chance of getting a part in your next movie?*
A:    [Laughs.] To be honest, next to none.

# Double Vision

JONATHAN ROMNEY/2000

THE COEN BROTHERS may not have the strangest film in Cannes this year, but they can certainly boast the drollest promotional giveaway. It's a three-ounce tub of waxy, orange-colored, sweetly-scented stuff labeled "Dapper Dan Men's Pomade." It carries the portrait of a rakishly coiffed George Clooney, looking determined and modeling a convincing facsimile of Clark Gable's moustache.

As promo novelties go, it makes a change from T-shirts and tote bags, and it relates more precisely to the advertised film than is usually the case. In the Coens' new film, *O Brother, Where Art Thou?*, Clooney's character Ulysses Everett McGill, an escapee from a southern chain gang, wouldn't go anywhere without a dab of Dapper Dan to sweeten his locks. His flight across the deep south is, you can imagine, rather more facetious than in the '30s chain gang movies that the Coens take as their model.

Minnesota-born brothers Joel and Ethan are known for liking their bit of fun, and in their latest film, they haven't stinted themselves. *O Brother* is several films in one: a tale of three desperadoes on the lam in rural Mississippi; a blues and country musical; and, allegedly at least, a rewrite of Homer's *Odyssey*. Not that they've actually read the *Odyssey*, they admit. Fortunately, Ethan Coen says, one of the film's leads, Tim Blake Nelson, is a classicist. "I wonder if he read it in Greek? I know he read it." "Yeah," confirms Joel. "Did he?" Ethan insists. "I don't know if he read it in Greek," says Joel. "I know he read it."

From *The Guardian*, May 19, 2000. http://film.guardian.co.uk. Reprinted by permission of the author.

"Between the cast and us," says Ethan, "Tim Nelson is the only one who's actually read the *Odyssey*." There's little point, then, kicking yourself if you can't place all the allusions. The Sirens are easy enough, a trio of singing Amazons doing their laundry in the Mississippi. And the Cyclops is John Goodman in an eye patch.

Scylla and Charybdis I was less certain about. "Scylla and Charybdis? Where were they?" puzzles Ethan. The whirlpool at the end, surely? "Oh," the brothers chorus, "the whirlpool." Ethan grins pensively. "Oh, yeah, sure, Scylla and Charybdis." Joel says, "It's very, you know, selectively based on the *Odyssey*." Interviewers often lament that with the Coens, there's no point even asking: they don't give anything away.

They have this reputation as tight-lipped, enigmatic sorts who make enigmatic films. And yet the films pretty much speak for themselves; they are flawlessly accessible, even if you don't catch all the references to old movies and pulp paperbacks. The only thing that properly seems bizarre about the brothers' work is the breadth of their imagination: they specialize in pinpointing the kind of images and cultural references that are usually outside the remit of contemporary American cinema.

There's nothing that bizarre, if you think of it, about choosing to set a crime thriller in snowbound Minnesota, as the brothers did in *Fargo*, and having villains who relax by going to see Jose Feliciano in concert; it's just that it took the Coens to think of it. Every Coen film describes a world so thoroughly conceived that each one is its own fictional microclimate; in a sense the brothers don't really need to add much commentary. Hence, perhaps, the sense that when they give interviews, they are aware of the futility of the venture.

Here they are in Cannes again, sitting in the casino on top of the Carlton hotel, and although they have visited several times in the past (their *Barton Fink* won the Palme d'Or in 1991), they don't quite seem to belong. Older brother Joel looks as though he's done all the interviews he wants to in a lifetime, Ethan as though he's never done one in his life. Joel seems to have dressed for the part of the hot auteur in town and then let it all get messed up over a rough morning: shoulder-length hair more scrupulously crimped than previously, in a black jacket that could be either very cheap or very expensive; both the beard and the low mutter are reminiscent of Frank Zappa, and he keeps looking absently around the room as if he's wondering how long it is till lunch.

The friendlier Ethan, in a murky brown plaid shirt, with a scraggy beard and a face full of freckles, constantly grins broadly, occasionally giving a wheezy laugh, and seems to be relishing various private jokes as if they've only just crossed his mind. Despite the grandiose title, *O Brother, Where Art Thou?* is as down home and earthy a film as has come out of recent American cinema, although it lacks the lightness of touch of the Coens' best comedies.

It shares its title with the apocryphal movie planned by Joel McCrea's idealistic Hollywood director in Preston Sturges's 1941 comedy *Sullivan's Travels* (currently on re-release). Sullivan heads out across America to research his serious Steinbeckian hobo drama, only to conclude that it's a far nobler calling to make 'em laugh.

But the Coens' *O Brother* is not entirely the film that Sullivan would have made. "It pretends to be a big important movie," says Ethan, "but the grandiosity is obviously a joke. It is what it is, it's a comedy. There is a chain-gang interlude in *Sullivan's Travels*, but that's it." *O Brother* is another example of the Coens' partiality to period: *Miller's Crossing, Barton Fink,* and *The Hudsucker Proxy* all explored past decades, and even their last film, *The Big Lebowski,* had a certain distance, being set in the early '90s as opposed to 1998.

"We tend to do period stuff," says Ethan, "because it helps make it one step removed from boring everyday reality." Their latest film carries a considerable weight of historical authenticity, not least in the soundtrack of vintage southern music—gospel, Delta blues, and early country swing—assembled by singer-songwriter and one-time Dylan collaborator T-Bone Burnett.

One of the film's themes is the congruence of prewar American pop with history and politics, as the errant jailbird trio encounter various real-life characters, among them gangster George "Baby Face" Nelson and blues singer Tommy Johnson, who, like the better known Robert Johnson, was reputed to have sold his soul to the devil in exchange for blues prowess. Another real character is Texas governor Pappy O'Daniel, who would go electioneering accompanied by a "stump band," a music show to whip up popular support. "They'd draw the crowds," explains Joel. "People came to listen to the music and then they'd have to listen to the speech."

The film's southern history, musical and political, looks detailed enough to have been thoroughly researched, but the Coens insist it wasn't. "It's all stuff that to one extent or another we were aware of," Joel says. "It was all back there somewhere and filtered up into the script. We weren't going out and doing research and trying to apply it to a story, it's all much more haphazard. It wasn't like we were trying to create a realistic picture of the time and place so much as an imagined world where all those things intersect—real people and made-up people."

Both are keen that the film shouldn't be taken too seriously, even though for the first time (give or take the socialist convictions of their playwright Barton Fink, and the trendy crypto-fascists in *The Big Lebowski*) they seem to be focusing on political realities in *O Brother*. "The political undercurrent of the movie," says Joel, "functions primarily for dramatic purposes, because the politics are frankly pretty primitive. The bad guys are racial bigots and KKK Grand Dragons, and the good guys are the heroes of the movie. So it's all kind of a story thing."

Even so, the film pulls off something of a coup in managing to be more politically flippant than American comedies have managed since Mel Brooks's heyday. The scene where the heroes blithely wander into a torchlit KKK rally might, I suggest to the brothers, strike some viewers as being of questionable taste.

"Taste," says Joel, "has never been something we've worried about." "We're not big on taste," agrees Ethan, his grin broadening even further. "And actually, if you don't pander to undue sensitivities then it ends up usually not being much of a problem. In *The Big Lebowski*, we dumped the crippled guy out of the wheelchair, and no one seemed to mind that." "Everyone was saying, 'You're going to get a huge amount of mail from disabled people about this.' But it's all in the context of the story, and done by the John Goodman character who's clearly an idiot," says Joel, and Ethan cracks up in laughter.

They are among the most film-literate of mainstream U.S. directors—not indiscriminate movie-guzzlers of the Tarantino school, but scholars of a longer history whose films have referenced Warner Bros gangster pics, Busby Berkeley musicals, and even William Faulkner's fraught Hollywood tenure as a hired script hand.

But the only time they directly used other films as a starting point, the brothers say, was in their 1994 film (probably their least-liked, unjustly so) *The Hudsucker Proxy*. "We knew we were doing a sort of

Capra-esque thing," says Ethan, "but even that was not a specific one of his movies, just the whole sort of 'just his thing,' right?" They no longer consume films so tirelessly, they admit, largely the result of having children (Ethan has two; Joel has one, with his wife and occasional lead actress Frances McDormand). "We don't watch them together a lot," says Ethan, "and neither of us watches as many as we used to. It's actually gotten more and more hit-and-miss—movies that I planned to see and never end up seeing."

It is generally assumed that the Coens equally represent the presiding genius of their films, but while they share writing credits, Ethan is billed as producer and Joel as director. This means that in Cannes, each film is officially billed as "un film de Joel Coen," although their own production notes specify, "A Film by Joel Coen and Ethan Coen." Confusingly, only Joel's photo appears in the *O Brother* press kit.

Of the two, it's Ethan who has explored outside ventures. He recently wrote *The Naked Man*, a film by the duo's regular storyboard artist J Todd Anderson, about a character actor who moonlights as a pro wrestler. The film got a critical thumbs-down. "I thought it was very funny," Ethan says. "I enjoyed it, and not just in a pride of ownership, 'cause it's really J Todd's thing. It didn't get a theatrical release, for reasons I can understand. It's nobody's idea of a big audience mainstream movie."

More prominent was *Gates of Eden*, the short story collection that Ethan published in 1998. It is frustrating, in a way, because it suggests there's much more to his imagination and linguistic prowess than he is necessarily prepared to put into his movies. More striking than the dry squibs and Chandler parodies are the complex, concise character sketches, and the adolescent anecdotes which hint at the personally revealing movie the Coens have yet to make—although in all honesty, it's hard to imagine them coming up with a screen evocation of a synagogue-going Jewish upbringing in '60s Minnesota.

The next Coen brothers film starts shooting in six weeks. Known as The Barbershop Project, it stars Frances McDormand and Billy Bob Thornton. "It's set in a barbershop and is concerned with the minutiae of the barbering trade in the late '40s." Is that why their distributor has been handing out Dapper Dan's pomade—as a teaser? "It's just a coincidence," says Joel. "There're a lot of hair products in this next film." "Actually," says Ethan, "we use pomade in *Raising Arizona* as well, as a means of tracking the characters. It's a tired old gag." I scan Joel's faintly slicked locks for traces of his own hair-care product. Would he personally recommend Dapper Dan? "I take no responsibility for that pomade," he says.

# Brothers in Arms

## JIM RIDLEY/2000

Last summer, filmmakers Joel and Ethan Coen (*Raising Arizona, Fargo*) were in Nashville to find musicians for their latest film, *O Brother, Where Art Thou?* An episodic yarn that borrows from Homer's *Odyssey*, it stars George Clooney, John Turturro, and Tim Blake Nelson as escaped convicts on a seriocomic journey through 1930s Mississippi, a flight that includes brushes with bluesmen, bigots, gangsters, crooked politicians, and seductive sirens. (The title comes from Preston Sturges's *Sullivan's Travels*. It's the name of the movie Sturges's comedy-director hero Sullivan intends as his "serious" picture about the struggles of the Depression.)

Before filming began, the Coens took the unusual step of recording the music first. For the movie's mix of blues, gospel, and bluegrass, the filmmakers and music producer T-Bone Burnett assembled a stellar lineup that includes Ralph Stanley, Norman Blake, Alison Krauss, Emmylou Harris, Gillian Welch, the Cox Family, and the Whites, and they recorded the music here last year. All those artists and more—plus the Coens themselves—will appear at a benefit show next Wednesday, 24 May 2000 at the Ryman Auditorium, which will be recorded by documentarian D.A. Pennebaker for a concert film.

Soon, the Coens may have even more reason to celebrate. *O Brother, Where Art Thou?* screened last weekend to strong notices at the Cannes Film Festival, some of which mentioned the movie as a contender for the top prize, the Palme d'Or. If the Coens win, it would be their

From *Nashville Scene*, May 22, 2000. Reprinted by permission of the author and the *Nashville Scene*.

second Golden Palm (after 1991's *Barton Fink*). The movie itself will be released this fall. The *Scene* spoke to Joel and Ethan Coen last week from their home base of New York, where they're practicing their sibling harmonies for the Ryman stage.

Q:    *How did you choose the music for the movie?*

JOEL:    Well, actually, in the movie we used a sort of mixture of period recordings and rerecorded music. But the stuff that was redone and produced by T-Bone is all featured essentially live—it's music you see performed in the movie itself.

ETHAN:    It's not background, it's not working as underscoring, it's actually happening on camera.

JOEL:    In other words, it's in the context of the story. At one point, George Clooney sings and records a record that becomes a big hit, a song called "I Am a Man of Constant Sorrow." That's all part of the story, so it had to be a combination of prerecorded background instrumentals that the actors or musicians would sing live to on set, or prerecorded with the vocals and then lipsynched.

Q:    *Which musicians actually appear in the movie?*

JOEL:    The Cox Family, the Whites, Chris Thomas King . . . [John] Hartford was gonna be in it, but he was ill at the time we wanted to shoot his scene. The Fairfield Four are in the movie; they play gravediggers. They do a great version of "You've Got to Walk that Lonesome Valley." Most of Alison's band is in the movie.

Q:    *Were there any artists you wanted specifically?*

JOEL:    A lot of them were people that we knew and like and are fans of, like Alison and Emmylou and Gillian, and obviously we knew Ralph Stanley and John Hartford and all these guys. But they were actually brought in by T-Bone. At an early stage we sort of decided what music we wanted. Then T-Bone brought in a lot of different musicians and sort of collectively decided who was going to do what.

Q:    *What was the selection process like?*

JOEL:    Well, that was great, actually. At one point T-Bone basically had two days where he brought in lots of different people who all sort of played and sang together. And we got kind of a feeling for who was right. But it was a great experience, meeting all these people and hearing 'em play. It was unbelievable.

ETHAN:    Ralph [Stanley] coming in was kind of funny. You know, everyone's sort of hanging out and playing, picking, whatever, and then Ralph walked in. It was like they'd wheeled in one of the heads from Mount Rushmore. The whole room just kind of fell silent for a moment.

Q:    *What are some of the most memorable songs in the finished film?*
ETHAN:    There are a number of set-piece songs that are almost . . . not production numbers, because it isn't literally a musical, but have that kind of feel to them. One of the most notable ones is the Ralph Stanley thing, "O Death." Chris Thomas King [who plays a blues musician modelled on Robert Johnson] did a Skip James song, "Hard Time Killing Floor Blues." And there's the Jimmie Rodgers song . . .
JOEL:    . . . that Tim Nelson sings. It's really interesting, because he sings that live himself. He's not a trained singer, he's not a recording artist, he's an actor. But he's got this great country-western voice. He's going to sing in the concert, actually.
ETHAN:    It's this weird fantasy come true for Tim—he gets to stand on the stage of the Ryman and perform.

Q:    *We heard something about a sirens' song. . . .*
JOEL:    Oh, that's interesting! [The convicts] come upon these three women washing clothes in the river. That's Gillian, Alison, and Emmylou as the three voices. And they're singing this song which is from this old kind of black, bluesy lullaby from the period. Gillian wrote like four or five other verses for it.

Q:    *She's actually in the movie, right?*
JOEL:    Yeah, she is. She's trying to buy the hit record that Clooney has recorded, without any success.

Q:    *If you have sirens involved, the* Odyssey *parallels must hold pretty close.*
JOEL AND ETHAN:    [chortling] Yeah, well . . .
ETHAN:    We avail ourselves of it very selectively. There's the sirens; and the Cyclops, John Goodman, a one-eyed Bible salesman. . . .

JOEL:     Whenever it's convenient we trot out *the Odyssey*.

ETHAN:     But I don't want any of those *Odyssey* fans to go to the movie expecting, y'know . . .

JOEL:     "Where's Laertes?" [laughter]

ETHAN:     "Where's his dog?" [more laughter]

Q:     *How seriously do you intend the reference to* Sullivan's Travels? *Your movie sounds more like Sturges than the symbolic movie-within-a-movie that gives* O Brother *its title.*

JOEL:     In a way, that's true. There are things in it that are very reminiscent of *Sullivan's Travels*, but in a sense I would say "reminiscent of" instead of rip-off. [laughs] In our minds, it was presumably the movie he would've made if he'd had the chance. The important movie. The one that takes on the big, important themes.

ETHAN:     And if he'd been steeped in Homeric literature and early country music. [laughter]

Q:     *Aren't they the same thing?*

JOEL:     Yeah, that's what T-Bone likes to say. They're both verbal traditions. Oral traditions.

ETHAN:     That's about as far as it goes, though.

Q:     *What are you working on next?*

JOEL:     We're doing a movie about a barber in northern California in the early 1940s. [Pause, then accusingly:] I think I heard a little snicker there. I was in Texas a while ago, and I told that to Ann Richards, the former governor. She looked at me for about twenty seconds and said, "I'm trying real hard to get excited about this."

ETHAN:     There's more to it than Joel lets on. He actually is a barber, but he's interested in getting into dry cleaning.

Q:     *While you're on stage at the Ryman, are you going to favor us with a tune? "The Coen Brothers" does sound like an old-time hillbilly act.*

JOEL:     Oh, yeah.

ETHAN:     Yeah, I'm bringing my washboard, and Joel's bringing his spoons. [Issues a laugh like a car alarm going off.] Wait for us, we're coming on last!

# Joel and Ethan Coen

## NATHAN RABIN/2000

THE ONION:    Blood Simple *is very much a film noir. What attracted you to the genre?*
ETHAN COEN:    Well, we never really thought of it as film noir, although it is. It's plain, mean, ordinary people doing bad things to each other in the dark, so I guess that qualifies it as film noir. But we were really thinking, in a conscious way, about more of a . . . We both like James M. Cain stories, which sort of confuses the issue because a lot of his stories were subsequently made into film noir. To tell you the truth, we were thinking about what kind of thing we could do on a low budget. We knew we were going to be raising the money ourselves and that there wouldn't be much money. The sort of claustrophobic, heavily plotted murder melodrama seemed tailor-made for something you might be able to do successfully on a small budget, in real practical terms.

O:    Fargo *and* The Big Lebowski *both have elements of film noir in them, as well.* Fargo, *in particular, deals with nasty people doing nasty things.*
EC:    With *The Big Lebowski*, we were really consciously thinking about doing a Raymond Chandler story, as much as it's about L.A. And, again, Chandler's stories became film noir fodder, but it was more thinking about that, specifically, than about the subsequent films that were made from the stories that got us going. With *Fargo*, we weren't thinking generically in any terms at all, except if you want to think about the true-crime story, which is kind of a genre.

---

From *The Onion* 36, no. 24, (July 19, 2000). http://www.theavclub.com. Reprinted by permission.

O:    *How did winning the Oscar for* Fargo *affect your career?*
JOEL COEN:    Not much, really.

O:    *You don't think it enabled you to get certain projects made?*
EC:    Let me see. We made *The Big Lebowski* after *Fargo* . . .
JC:    We travel in limos now, go to fancy Hollywood parties.
EC:    Other than that . . .

O:    *The film you made before that was* The Hudsucker Proxy, *which was a very big film [produced by] Joel Silver.*
JC:    Oh, we had a great time with Joel. We'd work with him again.
EC:    Yeah, he's a lot of fun. He's the last movie mogul, in the old sense. The old sort of cigar-chomping . . .
JC:    He doesn't literally chomp cigars.
EC:    I mean in a Harry Cohn, Louis B. Mayer kind of sense.

O:    *Do you feel like you're at a point in your career now where you can basically make whatever kind of movie you want to make?*
JC:    No. It all has to do with the budget. We can make whatever we want to make as long as it's cheap, because our movies only make. . . . They kind of reliably make so much money, so if the budget is so big and no bigger, we can do what we want.
EC:    There are so many different factors involved in whether or not you can get something going—how much competition there is in the business at one particular time, how well your last movie did—but mostly it all comes down to the price, how much you want to spend.

O:    *You both grew up in Minnesota. Were you at all self-conscious about filming* Blood Simple *in Texas?*
EC:    Oh, no. I'd lived in Texas for a little while. We actually went down there because we were familiar with it, having spent time down there and knowing people there. That was part of the reason for going. I went to UT for a semester and lived down there for about a year, so I knew people who I knew would work on the movie. I knew what the production climate was like down there. I think maybe part of the attraction of going was the fact that it was sort of. . . . It's a very different place and somewhat exotic, having grown up in Minnesota. Beyond that, no. We were perfectly comfortable in terms of the production.

O:    *Being from Minnesota, but having obviously lived in different places for a long time, do you still feel like Midwesterners?*

EC:    Umm . . . We both lived in New York—well, Joel longer than me—for about twenty years.

JC:    Yeah, I've been in New York about twenty-five years.

EC:    So not so much.

JC:    After twenty-five years in New York, you're kind of . . .

O:    *It all sort of fades.*

JC:    It does a little bit. I've certainly . . . It doesn't fade entirely. It becomes more connected with your identity somehow.

O:    *Would you say you were more in touch with your Midwestern roots while you were filming* Fargo *in Minnesota?*

EC:    It was familiar, although it was also weird. We'd been back occasionally, and our parents still lived there, so it's not like we hadn't been back in the interim, but it still changed quite a bit from when we were kids. It was the same, but different.

O:    *I've read that Barry Sonnenfeld began his career directing porn films. Is that something you knew about when you hired him? [Sonnenfeld, director of such films as* Men in Black, Get Shorty, *and* The Addams Family, *served as cinematographer on the Coens'* Blood Simple, Raising Arizona, *and* Miller's Crossing.]

EC:    Oh, yeah.

JC:    That's not true. He didn't direct them; he shot them.

O:    *So somebody else was off screen screaming directions, and he was just the cinematographer?*

EC:    Yeah, he was the cinematographer.

O:    *Was that a factor at all in your hiring him?*

EC:    Oh, yeah. We were big admirers of his. [Laughs.]

O:    *Any particular film that stood out?*

JC:    I have to say, I don't think we saw any of those, but we certainly knew all about them. We'd heard the stories. We'd seen stuff that Barry had shot, but not the porn films.

O:    *The interesting thing about DVDs and restorations is that you can go back and change, however minutely, films that you've done. Are there any . . .*
EC:   Yeah, it feels like cheating, doesn't it?

O:    *It's like with George Lucas and the* Star Wars *movies: After a certain point, you should just be done with them.*
EC:   You've got to stand by it.

O:    *Do you feel like there's anything you'd want to redo about any of your other films?*
JC:   Yes, but it's cheating. We decided only to cheat on this first one.

O:    *As beginners, you could do that, right?*
JC:   Yeah, exactly.
EC:   There were also practical reasons. We had to go back anyway, because it's our only movie that wasn't released by a studio, so physically, the elements for it weren't archived anywhere. They weren't housed anywhere, so we had to go back and find the print and sound elements. It was impossible to find a good print of the movie, a print that wasn't dirty and fading and worn out, and we were afraid that if any more time passed, we wouldn't be able to find the original elements to make new prints. That was part of the impetus of the whole thing.
JC:   We were organizing all this material again anyway and fixing up the sound for the DVD, so we figured we might as well cheat a little bit and fix up the picture, as well.
EC:   It's not an issue with our other movies.

O:    *One of the interesting things about your films is that nearly every one is in a different genre. Are there any genres you'd like to work in that you haven't done yet?*
EC:   A farm comedy.
JC:   Or a dog movie. We haven't done that. Like *Old Yeller.*
EC:   We keep arguing. Joel wants to do a dog movie and I want to do a farm comedy like *Ma and Pa Kettle.*

O:    *Do you think there'd be an audience for a* Ma and Pa Kettle *update?*
EC:   Yeah, you know, we'd cast David Straithairn and Kathy Bates.

O:    *I could see that.*

EC:    Either that, or we've both talked about doing a remake of *Guess Who's Coming to Dinner?*

O:    *It'd be a little on the less timely side, I would imagine.*

EC:    Well, it'd be an interesting exercise in postmodern aesthetics.

# Filmmaker Ethan Coen

TERRY GROSS/2000

THE FILMMAKING TEAM OF JOEL AND ETHAN COEN have a new movie comedy called *O Brother, Where Art Thou?* Most of the Coen brothers' movies reflect their quirky sense of humor and love of film noir. We're going to do a mini-retrospective of their films with Ethan Coen. First, let's hear a scene from the new movie. *O Brother, Where Art Thou?* is set during the Depression. It tells the story of three petty criminals who escape from a chain gang in search of buried treasure. George Clooney plays Ulysses Everett McGill, the leader of the group. In this scene, Clooney's character meets Big Dan Teague, a one-eyed Bible salesman played by John Goodman:

BIG DAN: I don't believe I've seen you boys around here before. Allow me to introduce myself: name of Daniel Teague, known in these precincts as Big Dan Teague, or to those who are pressed for time, Big Dan, *tout court.*
MCGILL: How ya doing, Big Dan. My name's Ulysses Everett McGill, and this is my associate, Delmar O'Donnell. I detect, like me, you're endowed with the gift of gab.
BIG DAN: I flatter myself that such is the case. In my line of work it's plum necessary. The one thing you don't want . . . is air in the conversation.
MCGILL: Once again we find ourselves in agreement. What kind a work you do, Big Dan?
BIG DAN: Sales, Mr. McGill, sales. And what do I sell? The truth, every blessed word of it, from Genessie on down to Revelations. That's right, the

---

From National Public Radio, *Fresh Air,* December 22, 2000. Copyright © 2000 by Ethan Coen. Reprinted by permission of Ethan Coen.

Word of God—which let me tell you, there is damn good money in during these times of woe and want. People are looking for answers, and Big Dan sells the only book that's got 'em. And what do you do—you and your . . . tongue-tied friend.

DELMAR:   We . . . ah . . .

MCGILL:   We . . . we're adventurers, sir, currently pursuing a certain opportunity—but we're open to others as well.


The Coen brothers co-write their films. Joel is listed as director, and my guest Ethan as producer. But they say that in reality, they share all the work. Their crime comedy *Fargo* won an Academy Award for best screenplay. Their other movies include *Raising Arizona, Barton Fink, Miller's Crossing*, and *The Big Lebowski*. Their first film, *Blood Simple*, was re-released earlier this year. That one's about a betrayed husband who hires a shady character to kill his wife and her boyfriend. That shady character, played by M. Emmet Walsh, delivers the opening monologue:

VISSER (PLAYED BY M. EMMET WALSH): The world is full of complainers. The fact is, nothing comes with a guarantee. Now I don't care if you're the Pope of Rome, President of the United States, or Man of the Year, something can all go wrong. And go ahead, you know, complain, tell your problems to your neighbor, ask for help—and watch him fly. Now in Russia they got it mapped out, so that everyone pulls for everyone else: that's the theory, anyway. But what I know about is Texas. And, down here, you're on your own.

TERRY GROSS:   *How do you go about plotting movies like* Blood Simple *when, you know, there's the set up, and things get complicated. . . .*

ETHAN COEN:   Yeah, we're actually incredibly irresponsible about it. We just start writing at the beginning, without an idea, without any idea really, about how it's going to go. We don't, for instance, outline the script before we start writing it, we just sort of start in with the first scene and see where that leads—which is actually, oddly enough, maybe the reason things get sort of complicated. You end up painting yourself into corners, if you don't know where you're going, and you perform weird contortions to get yourself out, which land you in odd places that, well, you certainly, and then hopefully the audience, never expected to find you in.

TERRY GROSS:   *Your brother, I think, had been working on editing cheap horror films before you made* Blood Simple *together. Are there any particular shots or scenes or stylistic touches that relate to those horror films?*

ETHAN COEN:   The best of the bunch was a movie by Sam Raimi called *The Evil Dead*, which had a couple of camera things that we just more or less sort of stole from Sam. One of them was just a really crude, homemade method for moving the camera quickly without a camera dolly. But actually, Sam's movie generally being the best of the ones Joel worked on, it was something we learned a lot from.

TERRY GROSS:   *Is the shot that you're talking about that you borrowed from Sam Raimi that kind of really jumpy, fast . . . it looks like it would be a steady-cam shot, except it's really jumpy, and it's a really fast kind of . . . I don't know what to call it. It's not a zoom exactly. . . .*

ETHAN COEN:   No, it is just a fast track. You're right. Sam called it a shaky-cam. It's a sort of homemade steady cam. And what it is, it's just a camera mounted in the middle of a two-by-four, which one person grabs at either end and runs like hell with. [laughter] So it has, you can sort of jump over, clear obstacles, skim over or under whatever, and it's sort of much more fluid than a lock-down track would look, that sort of standard dolly move would look, and more energetic, largely because the lens is so wide. You have to use a really wide lens or it would become just unbearably bumpy.

TERRY GROSS:   *Now I think you used that shot when Frances McDormand is getting strangled in the movie.*

ETHAN COEN:   Yeah, we did indeed.

TERRY GROSS:   *Now one of your movies,* Barton Fink, *is about a very pretentious playwright, played by John Turturro, who wants to write for a "new living theater of and about the common man." And his successful plays lead a studio head to bring him out to Hollywood. I want to play the scene where the studio head, played by Michael Lerner, welcomes Barton Fink to Los Angeles:*

LIPNICK (PLAYED BY MICHAEL LERNER):   My name's Jack Lipnick. I run this dump. You know that, you read the papers. Lou treatin' you all right? You got everything you need? What the hell's the matter with your face? [to Lou] What the hell's the matter with his face, Lou?

BARTON:   It's not as bad as it looks . . . it's just a mosquito. . . . in my room.

LIPNICK:   Place OK? [to Lou] Where'd you put 'em?

BARTON:   I'm at the Earle.

LIPNICK:   Never heard of it. [to Lou] Let's move him to the Grand or the Wiltshire. Hell, he can stay at my place.

BARTON:   Thanks . . . but I wanted a place that was a little less. . . .

LIPNICK:   Less Hollywood—sure, say it. It's not a dirty word. Stay wherever the hell you want. The writer is *king* here at Capitol Pictures. You don't believe me, take a look at your paycheck at the end of every week. *That's* what we think of the writer. [to Lou] So, what kind of pictures does he like?

LOU:   Mr. Fink hasn't given a preference, Mr. Lipnick.

LIPNICK:   So how about it, Bart?

BARTON:   Well, ah . . . to be honest I, I don't go to the pictures much, Mr. Lipnick.

LIPNICK:   That's OK. That's OK! That's OK, that's just fine. You probably walked in here thinking that was going to be a handicap, thinking that we wanted people who knew something about the medium, maybe even thinking there was all kinds of technical mumbo jumbo to learn. You were dead wrong. We're only interested in one thing: can you tell a story, Bart? Can you make us laugh, can you make us cry, can you make us want to *break out* in joyous song? Is that more than one thing? OK, the point is, I run this dump and I don't know the technical mumbo jumbo. Why do I run it? Because I got horse sense, damn it—*showmanship*! And also, and I hope Lou told you this, I am bigger and meaner and louder than any other kike in this town. Did you tell him that, Lou? Coffee?

TERRY GROSS:   *Ethan Coen, did you ever get a disingenuous introduction like this from a Hollywood studio head?*

ETHAN COEN:   Ah, no—that's certainly not based on life. I don't know that that kind of character exists anymore. Hollywood is a little more bland and corporate than that now. It's funny. I hadn't actually seen the movie since we finished it. Hearing it was . . . Michael Lerner's quite funny.

TERRY GROSS:   Michael Learner's great, yeah. Did anyone every try to convince you that the writer is king? [laughter]

ETHAN COEN:   Ah . . . no. In a word, no. [laughter] Nobody's that bald, at any rate.

TERRY GROSS:   *After your first crime film,* Blood Simple, *the crime films became a lot funnier, and I guess the most successful of your crime films is* Fargo, *in which Frances McDormand, your sister-in-law, plays Marge Gunderson, the chief of police in Brainerd, Minnesota. And she's investigating a couple of murders, and she's also very pregnant. So I want to play a scene in which she's investigating with another cop, and she's finding bodies at the crime scene:*

MARGE GUNDERSON:   Here's the second one. It's in the head and . . . the hand, there. I guess that's a defensive wound.

COP:   Oh ya?

MARGE:   Where's the State Trooper?

COP:   Back there, a good piece, in the ditch, next to his prowler.

MARGE:   OK. So we got our Trooper pulls someone over. We got a shooting. These folks drive by, there's a high-speed pursuit, it ends here, and then this execution-type deal.

COP:   Yep.

MARGE:   I'd be very surprised if our suspect was from Brainerd.

COP:   Ya.

MARGE:   And I'll tell ya what—from his footprint he looks like a big fella. [she bends over]

COP:   Ya see something down their, Chief?

MARGE:   No . . . I just think I'm gonna barf.

COP:   Jeeze. . . . you OK Margie?

MARGE:   Yeah, I'm fine. It's just morning sickness. Well . . . that passed.

COP:   Yeah?

MARGE:   Yeah, now I'm hungry again.

TERRY GROSS:   *That's a scene from your award-winning film* Fargo. *One of the things I really like about this film is that although the criminals are all actually pretty dumb, Marge, the police chief, who looks like she might be mocked in the movie, is actually a very good cop with a very big heart, and*

*very likeable. I just really loved the way you handled this character in the*
*movie. So, tell me about creating Marge.*
ETHAN COEN:    Well, it's funny you say that. A lot of people liked her,
and I'm sure that's why the movie did well. I always thought she was
the bad guy. [laughter]

TERRY GROSS:    *Did you, really? Why did you think she was the bad guy?*
ETHAN COEN:    I don't know—I just related to Steve Buscemi's character
more. [laughter] He seemed like the classic sane person in an insane land.
Marge, Fran's character definitely is sort of embodying the insane land. I
kind of found her a little bit alarming, as did Fran. We were all a little surprised that people liked her quite as much as they did. But, you know. . . .

TERRY GROSS:    *Tell me something you found alarming about her.*
ETHAN COEN:    Well, she's . . . well, there are admirable things about
her, but she's also definitely, ah . . . sure of herself to an alarming
degree, certainly not given to introspection.

TERRY GROSS:    *You really thought the Steve Buscemi character is the most*
*sane. It's Steve Buscemi who's actually hired to kidnap the wife so that people*
*can collect the ransom money, and everything gets out of control. What did*
*you write into the Steve Buscemi character that made him so likable to you,*
*and so seemingly sane to you?*
ETHAN COEN:    Well, I'll tell you, in one respect he's sort of an audience
surrogate. He's the one character who's not local. Even Peter Stormare,
his sidekick, is not of the region, but he's Swedish, so in that sense he's
connected to the region. So as a sort of alien in the landscape—he even
dresses inappropriately for the climate—he's again an outsider, an audience surrogate in that respect. And, you know, there's just something
sort of refreshingly chatty and direct about Steve, his character.

TERRY GROSS:    *And you've worked with him in several films.*
ETHAN COEN:    Yeah, and we always end up killing his character for
some reason.

TERRY GROSS:    *And does he resent that? [laughter]*
ETHAN COEN:    He hasn't complained yet. Maybe that's why we continue to do it.

TERRY GROSS:    *What's your approach to casting? Do you do the casting yourselves? You've worked with some terrific actors in your movies—Nicolas Cage, W. H. Macy, Frances McDormand, M. Emmet Walsh, Dan Hedaya (one of his early roles was in* Blood Simple), *John Turturro, John Goodman. . . .*

ETHAN COEN:    Yeah, we've been lucky. We've worked with great actors. But it's really a buyer's market for that. There're a lot more good actors out there than there are good parts, so if you write something that's interesting to an actor, you'll have good actors to choose from. In terms of the casting, it's always been a mix with us of writing parts for specific people that we know—or sometimes that we don't know but whose work we know, as was the case with Emmet Walsh in our first movie— and writing parts for whomever, somebody that we don't have any specific actor in mind for as we're writing which we then subsequently go out and cast.

TERRY GROSS:    *Well, Ethan Coen, thanks so much for talking with us.*
ETHAN COEN:    Thanks.

# Pictures That Do the Talking

## ANDREW PULVER/2001

THERE'S A PRESENCE IN THE ROOM; a ghostly, disembodied presence. Joel Coen, sitting unconcerned in an armchair, doesn't appear to feel it. Maybe it's just me, but aren't there normally two of them? "I don't spend much time with Ethan outside of work," says Joel, in a barely audible drawl. Where is Ethan? Joel mumbles something indistinct, but it doesn't seem right to press the question. Maybe they've had a row; maybe Ethan's mangled corpse is trussed up and stuffed in the ornate wooden chest under the window ledge. More urgently, will Joel be able to manage to complete a sentence on his own? Past evidence suggests it might be tricky.

If this isn't unsettling enough, there's more big news. Joel Coen has got rid of the ponytail. Throughout the Coen brothers' dazzling film-making career, Joel's haircut was something everyone just pretended they didn't see. No one talked about it. Now it's gone, no one will ever mention it again. Not that *los hermanos* Coen haven't made secret capital out of their appearance: a duo of skinny, unshaven four-eyes, looking like a couple of systems analysts who have got lost in the early 1970s on the way to the Jefferson Airplane freakout. Ethan has tended to sport a harmless frizzy mess, giving him a faintly rabbinical air. Joel's appalling ponytail was the best way to tell them apart. Well, I can report that he's cut it off. At forty-seven, Joel Coen has graduated to a wavy, shoulder-length mop.

From *The Guardian*, October 13, 2001. Copyright Guardian Newspapers Limited 2001. Reprinted by permission.

It turns out that brother Joel has been on a family holiday in Scotland with his wife—*Fargo* and *Blood Simple* star Frances McDormand—and adopted son Pedro, and Joel has headed to London for a back-slapping session with producers Working Title, and a private screening of the new Coen film *The Man Who Wasn't There*. He's also—with customary Coen reluctance—forcing himself to shill for his movie.

In fact, nobody could be less enthusiastic to talk about a Coen brothers movie than the Coens. Maybe it's all to the good that there's only one of them here. In tandem, the Coens are a tricky proposition. Most directors at least make the pretense that they like to chat about their work: they slog for endless months through the production, explaining their wants to all and sundry; jabbering to the media, you soon gather, is merely a continuation of the filmmaking process. Film directors tend also to be a little—to put it mildly—on the egocentric side. The Coens, in stark contrast, just don't seem to be interested. Arguably the most unconventional of mainstream American directors, they don't offer snarling hostility or even sullen wariness, just a helpless, unspoken consternation that they should have to talk about themselves and what they do.

But on his own, a single Coen brother does turn out to be a different animal. Without the other one with whom to trade in-jokes or exchange wondering glances, Coen solo is almost chatty, and prepared to acknowledge the nature of their relationship. How do they stand spending so much time with each other? "Well, we work together, but it's limited to that. We spend the working day together, so at the end of that you never feel the need to say, 'let's go out to dinner,' you know what I mean? It's all kind of limited to work."

Are your films simply the sum of two sibling personalities that are peculiarly perfectly meshed? "No . . . it's difficult to explain. The work that we do together reflects the point at which our interests intersect. It's been eighteen years we've been working together, and it's a reflection of the point at which we're interested in the same things . . . That is to say, we're interested individually in different things, but that's not what gets worked at." So you don't necessarily always run on the same track? "It's always reflected in the work—in that it's a dialogue, it's an egging-on process, in that one person will suggest something and the other will respond to it or amplify it."

So who actually does what? Do the credits, Joel as director, Ethan as producer, mean anything? "No. We're both on the set; the movies are codirected in every sense of the word. Actors often get paranoid before they start working with us—they're apprehensive that things'll be confusing. You know, that I'll say, 'Slower,' and he'll say, 'Faster' . . ."

When did you realize you had a special affinity as a filmmaking team? "It was really the point when we started writing together, when I was working as an assistant editor. We started writing scripts for other people, for people who were coming in to work on projects I was working on. It was that point we realized: this works out pretty well."

Here Joel is referring to his own apprenticeship in the film industry: his first recorded job was, in 1980, to assistant-edit the debut of another tyro director, Sam Raimi. Raimi had the resource to raise money from family connections to finance his film—which became the savage comedy-horror classic *The Evil Dead*. Joel, a few years after studying film at New York University, was married at the time (this was well before he met McDormand, but the woman concerned wishes to retain her privacy). Meanwhile, Ethan, three years younger, had graduated from the philosophy department at Princeton (and written a paper on Wittgenstein), and joined his big brother in New York. It was there, as the '80s dawned, that the writing began, often in collaboration with Raimi, who has coscripting credits on *Crimewave* (which became his second movie in 1985) and *The Hudsucker Proxy* (which became the Coens' fifth, in 1994).

Inspired by Raimi's method of fundraising, the Coens took a third script, *Blood Simple*, back to Minneapolis to try and persuade friends and family to pony up. Another key member of the team, Barry Sonnenfeld, became their director of photography, and filmed a three-minute trailer for them in 1982. (Sonnenfeld has gone on to outdo all his former *compadres* as a big-budget director, squiring *The Addams Family*, *Get Shorty*, and *Men in Black* to massive success.) According to legend the Coens turned to the local branch of Hadassah, the American women's Zionist charity, who gave them a list of a hundred wealthy Jewish philanthropists. Thus it was the brothers scraped together the $1.3 million needed to get *Blood Simple* off the ground.

By later standards of low-budget, deferred-payment filmmaking, this sounds like a lot, but in the early 1980s the independent film movement was in its infancy. This was well before template-setting shoestring productions such as *Stranger Than Paradise* or *She's Gotta Have It*—let alone bargain-basement stuff like *El Mariachi* or *Clerks*—had made their appearance. In their adolescence, Ethan and Joel had messed around with Super 8 (titles are said to include "Ed . . . A Dog" and "The Banana Film"), but *Blood Simple* was the real deal. Looking back at the film now, all the Coen trademarks are there: an agglomeration of literary and cinematic references (with a heavy tilt to the hard-boiled school); idiosyncratic photography—including the now-immortal skip over a sleeping drunk as the camera tracks along a bar top—itself indebted to *The Evil Dead's* cartoonish style; and studied acting performances that layer unfussy naturalism alongside high-key grotesque.

Their follow-up, *Raising Arizona*, set out along a different road entirely—so much so that it fell squarely into the wave of late '80s baby comedies along with *Three Men and a Baby* (released the same year, 1987, as *Arizona*), and *She's Having a Baby* (1988). But the same stylistic tics that marked out *Blood Simple* are there, and the Coens' method was set. A chiseled script, actors that were required to fill out the dialogue but not improvise from it, and a new set of cultural baggage reformed and retooled in the service of storytelling.

It's a method that has served them beautifully right through their career. The Coens are shortly to release their ninth movie, *The Man Who Wasn't There*. Rumor-mill aficionados may know of it as The Barber Project, the work-in-progress title that reflects the business occupation of its lead character, Ed Crane (played by Billy Bob Thornton).

The title was changed shortly before its premiere at the Cannes Film Festival last May—to reflect, as the Coens said, Crane's emotional vacuum as well as a key element of its thriller plot. It's set in 1940s California (the same town in fact, Santa Rosa, as Hitchcock's 1943 noir *Shadow of a Doubt*), shot in a luminous black-and-white by the Coens' longtime cinematographer Roger Deakins, and, like *Blood Simple*, is infected with the spirit of pulp novelist James M. Cain, a key Coen touchstone. Thornton, stone-faced and laconic, is quite exceptional in his role as a barber who suspects his wife is cheating on him—so much so that, though it's a radically different performance from his trademark demon-haunted twitchiness, the Crane part fits him like a glove. It's a

now established feature of the Coen modus operandi that they often
tool their extraordinary characters with specific actors in mind, so was
Thornton always the model?

It seems not. "With this one," says Joel, "we wrote the part for Fran
[McDormand, who plays Crane's wife Doris], and we wrote the part that
Michael Badalucco plays [Ed's barber-shop partner Frank], but that was
about it. We didn't know who was going to play the lead character. In
that respect it was like *Fargo*: we wrote a part for Fran, we wrote a part
for Steve Buscemi, but we didn't know who was going to play the part
Bill Macy ended up with.

"But Billy Bob is someone we've known for a while, we haven't
worked with before but we knew him, and . . . I don't know why he
occurred to us, because he's not our image of the character. He's a
southern guy from Arkansas, and Ed is not supposed to be that. But on
the other hand, Billy Bob's such a transformative actor—both physically and in every other way—that we started to think that this would
be rather interesting. And he certainly has the confidence to do this
kind of character. Which, as an actor, you need to do it. Because Ed says
very little, he's very still, and that would just drive most actors crazy.
They'd be very insecure about it, thinking they weren't doing enough;
we had a feeling that Billy Bob would understand."

Was Cain—the literary progenitor of classic American noir, in the
shape of *Double Indemnity*, *The Postman Always Rings Twice* and *Mildred
Pierce*—as much of an influence on the film as it appears? "Yes, definitely. Cain was very much in our minds, because he was interested in
crime stories that involved people in their everyday lives at work, and
not about underworld figures. People who work in banks, or the insurance business, or restaurants . . . or the opera business, which was
another obsession of his. In that respect, like the domestic melodrama
that turns into a crime story, it owes a lot to Cain.

"But there are ways in which it's not film noir: for one thing, the
main character couldn't be further from your conventional film noir
hero, in terms of his obsessions and personality . . . but, it's got all that
modern dread, that feeling of disassociation and paranoia about what's
happening in the world about you. Also foreground in our thinking
were science fiction films from the '50s, all the postwar paranoia things.
You get the pulpier, cheesier elements of American postwar culture, as

reflected in men's magazines, and health movies you'd see in school, and science fiction movies you'd see about aliens, and civil defense movies, that kind of thing. . . ."

By now, certain things are apparent. First, *The Man Who Wasn't There*, like every Coen film before it, readily lends itself to explication in terms of film and literary reference: a narrative line borrowed from here, a character from there, a camera move from somewhere else. Second, Joel can't stop saying "we" or "our"; even with his brother thousands of miles away, the sibling connection is a hard habit to break. Here's Joel talking about how *The Man Who Wasn't There* began to take shape: "It's like a lot of the stuff we do: it starts in some form or other quite a while ago, but we very frequently will work on something for a while, we write a little bit of it, and then we come back to it much later. We probably first started thinking about it four or five years ago at least. It was pretty much finished by the time we started *O Brother*. But then George [Clooney] was available so we went ahead with that. Frequently, the order in which you do movies is dictated by when certain actors you want to work with are available to do them, and so the whole thing comes together."

It's a tantalizing thought, the Coens and their scripts. You can't get rid of the feeling that in some bulging bottom drawer lies a stack of unseen treasures waiting for their chance to get in front of the camera. It's happened before; *The Hudsucker Proxy* lay unused for a decade, written in the early 1980s with Raimi before *Blood Simple* had even begun filming. While *Blood Simple* was waiting for release, the three of them knocked off *Crimewave*, which became Raimi's second film a year later. A few years ago Ethan wrote a script about a wrestler-superhero called *The Naked Man*. (That became a feature film directed by their storyboard artist J Todd Anderson.) They have completed an adaptation of *Cuba Libre*, an Elmore Leonard novel about a bank-robbing cowboy set in the 1890s. They did a draft (presumably rewritten again by someone else) for a still-to-be-shot film called *Intolerable Cruelty* that's been hanging around Hollywood for years. They've talked cryptically about something they've written "for Ed Harris."

As film history records, the Coens had to wait until special-effects technology had advanced to realize *Hudsucker*'s expensive fantasy sequences—and to command the budget to cover them. (This, at

$25 million, wasn't achieved until the mid-1990s, with the help of the unlikeliest of partners, action-movie superproducer Joel *Die Hard* Silver.) And despite all they've achieved, the brothers have just run slap-bang into the same barrier; their next project, an adaptation of James Dickey's *To the White Sea*, starring Brad Pitt and with a budget of $60 million, has lost its backing from Twentieth Century Fox. The story of a U.S. airman attempting to make his way home after crash-landing in Japan during the Second World War, it ran into problems after Fox apparently baulked at the Coens' decision to film on location in Hokkaido.

What would be the Coens' biggest film to date is by no means dead yet, but reinforces Joel's wariness about getting involved with the big boys. "You know, the ease with which we finance projects is completely dependent on what the budget of the movie is, and who's in it, I guess, more than who we are or what we've done. For a certain price it's easy for us to get things financed because now we're established . . . you know, let us play in our corner of the sandbox so long as no one gets threatened or hurt. It's hard for someone to lose money so long as the movies are done very cheaply. But when the movie gets up above a certain amount of money it gets more difficult, more dependent on other factors. *To the White Sea* is quite a bit more expensive and very difficult subject matter."

The turning-point, from a financial point of view, was undoubtedly the success of *Fargo*; up until then, they had thoroughly boxed themselves in to a high-prestige-but-low-money ghetto, imprisoned by the increasingly modest box-office figures of *Miller's Crossing, Barton Fink*, and *Hudsucker*, none of which took more than $10 million in their home country. And this despite the solid backing they obtained from British outfit Working Title, who came on board the Coen operation to help fund *Hudsucker*, and have stuck with them ever since.

Despite the Cannes Palme d'Or they won for *Barton Fink* in 1991, the particularly depressing results for *Hudsucker* (released in 1994, cost $25 million, took $2.8 million, in the U.S.) meant that, like it or not, they had to think small. Against all expectations, *Fargo*—set in and around their home town of Minneapolis—at less than a third of the budget, took in ten times their previous film, won two Oscars, and suddenly elevated the Coens to the front rank of American independent filmmakers. Hence the flurry of activity since; you sense the brothers are making up for lost time, as well as striking while the iron is hot, and the light is green. Hence also the Coens' regular attendance at Cannes; European admiration has kept them afloat financially as well as critically, and they're grateful for it.

Since Fargo, the Coens have given the world *The Big Lebowski*, *O Brother, Where Art Thou?*, and now *The Man Who Wasn't There*, each with their own pool of background reading, film technique, and one-liners. They are, the French would agree, the consummate auteurs, their freaky-deaky brotherliness only serving to accentuate the idiosyncrasy of their films. But, strange to say, it's hard to believe the Coens have really developed as filmmakers—other than in expanding the reading list. Where, you might ask, is the heart? You might ask, but you won't get an answer.

If the Coens are consistent about anything, it's the almost total self-effacement, authorially speaking, as regards their highly wrought films. Each seems independent of the others and of the people that made them. Joel is defensive on the point. "I just see it as moving from story to story. There's no development, except that you try to do something a little different each time, different at least from what you did just previous to it so you keep the exercise interesting to yourself."

If the Coens stand for anything, perhaps, it's a persistent desire to stand up for classical filmmaking. "We still cut on film and not on computer. It's to do with idiosyncratic things about what kind of screen I want to look at all day. I like handling the film, too; how I learned how to edit was on flatbed editing machines and Moviolas, all the dinosaurs of the trade." Since the industry has pretty much converted wholesale to computer editing, Joel is letting old habits die hard. That's also what makes the Coens' editing pseudonym—Roderick Jaynes, a mythical crusty old buffer from the British film old school, who was actually nominated for an Oscar for Fargo—a joke of such powerful longevity.

It's a principle that also extends into the shoot: no mucky DV cameras for them. "The actual craft of movie making is part of what we're interested in," he says. "I'm not that interested in digital filmmaking because there's something . . ." Here he pauses to think. "The technology's evolving and some day all movies will be made like that, but right now I don't find the results it yields are at the same level as shooting on film." *The Man Who Wasn't There*, he says, was shot on color stock, then printed on high-contrast black and white title stock. "That's basically because no one in the last forty years has developed new black and white film, so you can't find high-speed, fine-grade black and white stock. No one shoots it any more." In contrast to their seemingly Ludd-ite attitude to cinema technology, the Coens have quietly absorbed a lot of fancy computer-generated effects into their movies (principally *Hudsucker*), and even pioneered a particular software application by color timing *O Brother* on computer to give the movie its washed-out sepia-photograph look. "You just take what you need," says Joel, tittering.

However much of an inscrutable face the Coens like to present to the world, their long-term success has seen the spawning of a quiet but per-sistent spin-off industry. Books have come along—most notably *The Making of* The Big Lebowski by William Preston Robertson—which have built a picture of their detail-obsessed working methods. They can be glimpsed in the background of *Down from the Mountain*, a Pennebaker and Hegedus documentary about the "old time mountain style" bluegrass performers featured on the soundtrack of *O Brother, Where Art Thou?* (It will be released in U.K. cinemas in the same week as *The Man Who Wasn't There*.) Most significant of all, maybe, brother Ethan committed a collection of short stories to print last year, comple-menting the occasional articles that the Coens have issued to various magazines and published screenplays over the years.

It's through these writings that the avid fan can glean the kind of details that turn the Coens into human beings. In Robertson's book, for instance, the Coens' creative process is gone through in great detail; it also reveals that this most lolloping of Coen films is by far their most personal, in the sense that the two lead characters are based directly on acquaintances of theirs. A real life stoner, Jeff Dowd—a.k.a The Pope of Dope—metamorphosed into Jeff Lebowski; another bunch of friends (including he-man director and gun nut John Milius) contributed key aspects of John Goodman's Walter Sobchak.

All this is well documented; what's less often noted is the way the Coens' heavily orthodox Jewish upbringing has found its way into the character. Sobchak is forever quoting Zionist founding father Theodore Herzl—"if you will it, Dude, it is no dream"—or shoehorning in references to his supposed Jewish background ("I told that kraut a fucking thousand times I don't roll on shabbas.") Turn if you will to Ethan's short story "I Killed Phil Shapiro" in the *Gates Of Eden* collection: there you will find, with the pungency of true authenticity, an account of a trip to a summer camp in Wisconsin—Camp Herzl. "The camp director, Rabbi Sam," writes Ethan, "was a dark slender man with a yarmulke and hairy legs and a tall gnarled intensity. He spoke a few words of welcome in which figured the phrase 'If You Will It, It Is No Dream.'" It all clicks into focus, like those corny binocular shots in 1970s thrillers. Joel, as ever, is having none of it. "Yeah, people sometimes want to feel like the stories have a direct relationship to your own life, or people that you know, or some continuing story which is a continuing reflection of your concern. Some filmmakers work that way, very effectively. It's just not at all the way we approach the—whatever you want to call it—storytelling, or whatever it is. The stories are constructed out of what is interesting to us at the time, and different elements that we're interested in from things that we've read or seen or experienced and, ah . . . yeah. . . ." He trails off.

But this stuff must come from somewhere? Reluctantly, Joel gives in. "Yeah, we grew up in the Minneapolis suburbs, with a fairly religious upbringing. A lot of the Jewish references in *The Big Lebowski* come from things we heard over and over again in synagogues." You don't strike me as religious now. "No." He giggles. "It was just a big part of who we were growing up. We went to Hebrew school from second grade, five days a week after school. For a while there they were really drilling it into us. My mother comes from a pretty orthodox family, so it came from her mostly; my father not so much, though he was a fairly willing accomplice."

Joel, however, grows fidgety fast under this line of questioning. He's even less interested in talking about anything to do with McDormand ("Fran's been there from the very beginning, from the first day of the first movie.") So it's a bit of a shock that he suddenly becomes animated on the subject of his social life—after I ask him if he's ever had anything to do with Woody Allen, a filmmaker of whom the Coens are a kind of bizarre inversion. "I've never met him, but I saw him once in an elevator. He was slouched in a corner with a hat pulled over his face so no one would recognize him. It's funny, as a film director, you don't meet other directors at all often. In New York you can live your life in the film business and, if you choose, have nothing to do with other people involved in the same business. That's one of the nice things about New York—it's not a company town like L.A. It's actors who meet lots of film directors, because they go from movie to movie. So most of the directors I know are people I've met through Fran. I'm very good friends with John Boorman, for example, because of Fran doing a movie, *Beyond Rangoon*, with him. That's the way it works."

After that small insight into the auteur filmmakers' dinner-party circuit, Joel shuts up. He can go now, and he does.

# Joel and Ethan Coen

## GERALD PEARY/2001

MANY OF MY FELLOW JOURNALISTS, in meeting up with the Coen brothers, Joel and Ethan, come away disappointed, or even disillusioned. Considering their smart, subversive, playful films like their *Raising Arizona, Fargo*, or *The Big Lebowski*, we anticipate two happily verbal guys bubbling with fascinating things to say about their movies. But their *O Brother, Where Art Thou*? press conference at Cannes in 2000 was a typical Coens' showing: the duo smug and diffident, strangely disconnected from the Q&A. Their short-cut, frustratingly evasive answers made them appear tired of discussing their movie—although it was the world premiere!

In an interview for *Moving Pictures* magazine, the reporter, Damon Wise, challenged the Coens' stand-offish attitude. The Coens were unrepentant:

ETHAN:  "You make the movie and journalists have to write about something . . . There it is. I don't know."
JOEL:  "What I think you are referring to is to the fact that we often resist the efforts of . . . people who are interviewing us to enlist us in that process ourselves. And we resist it not because we object to it but simply because it isn't something that particularily interests us."

So I was braced—braced to get nothing!—at Cannes 2001, when a gathering of American journalists interviewed the leads and, again, the Coen brothers about *The Man Who Wasn't There*, their Billy Bob

From *Boston Phoenix*, November 2001. Reprinted by permission of the author.

Thornton–starring homage to the hardboiled "noir" view of novelist James M. Cain.

First we got Thornton, an off-the-screen little guy in a Metallica t-shirt and anxious to talk . . . about how he adores his wife, Angelina Jolie. He leaned over the table to show the gathered fourth estate the vial of spouse-blood which hangs about his neck. "For our anniversary, she gave me her will," he said, proudly. "She got us both burial spots in Arkansas next to my brother, who died in 1988."

What about Thornton's character in this movie, small-town barber, Ed Crane? "It's this guy and the guy in *A Simple Plan* who are closest to myself. I feel like 'the man who wasn't there.' I got my wife, my kids, my mom. I'm not interested in things outside the basement and the back yard. I always identify with John Lennon, who loved to stay home.

"I really don't care about commerciality. God knows if anyone will see this film. But I love these guys, the Coens, and their sense of humor. I agreed to do the film when Joel told me, 'It's about a barber who wants to be a dry cleaner.'

"I love all the Bogart movies, and Fred MacMurray in *Double Indemnity*. I think MacMurray is a great actor. For this movie, I didn't try to look like Bogart. I was thinking more about Frank Sinatra. When you get into that mood, you look like those guys. In real life, we're not in black-and-white, but somehow that feels more real in this movie, more monochromatic. You can feel people sweating in black-and-white."

Next up was Frances McDormand, wife of director Joel Coen, Oscar winner as the cornflakes Minnesota cop, Marge, in *Fargo*, and acclaimed as the protective mom in *Almost Famous*. "Marge was the embodiment of all things an actress is supposed to be," McDormand said, nostalgic for that once-in-a-lifetime part, "and in *Almost Famous*, I felt voluptuous and free, very alive and jiggly and complex." In marked contrast, she said of her femme fatale, Doris, in *The Man Who Wasn't There*, that "the role was more technical than usual, me caring that my lipstick was right, the hair was perfect. The challenge was mostly the black-and-white. The movie is about Ed Crane, not Doris."

What about the Coen Brothers' communicativeness? McDormand, who is straight and open, shook her head, bemused. She knows, because the vacuum that journalists feel is also present on the set. Even for McDormand, being directed by her husband, Joel. "Sometimes it's easier getting direction from Ethan," she confided. "He's more direct. Since *Blood Simple*, it's a huge improvement how they have dialogue with actors. Their not communicating was to the peril of certain performances."

Are they really opening up? McDormand told us that *The Man Who Wasn't There* is a more personal project than earlier Coen brothers films.

Finally, the Coens: Joel, the taller one with the longer hair, director and co-writer; Ethan, producer and co-writer.

A journalist nudged them. "Frances says this film is more personal. How is it personal?"

ETHAN:    "I don't think it's more personal or less personal. There's nothing autobiographical."

JOEL:    "It's set in the 1940s, and that's not personal. These are stories which take us away from first-hand experience."

The Coens at Cannes spill all! You've read it here first.

# Joel and Ethan Coen

KRISTINE McKENNA/2001

A BARBER POLE TWIRLS outside the window and three bar-
ber chairs are in a row, facing a wall of mirrors. On a shelf is a collection
of razors, clippers, scissors, and aftershave lotion. When a man lazily
sits in one of the chairs, the barber, who is dressed in white, asks,
"What'll it be?" The guy answers, "Just a trim."

It's a scene replayed throughout America every day, but this isn't a
real barbershop. This barber isn't really a barber, either. It's Billy Bob
Thornton, the actor and director renowned for the 1996 movie *Sling
Blade,* whose lack of training as a barber doesn't stop him from cutting
hair. There's a line of people—mostly extras who are here with the hope
of a quick scene in the movie—waiting for haircuts. "The sad thing is
that Billy Bob thinks he's good," says the movie's co-writer Ethan Coen.
"He's like one of those guys who trains to be a boxer for a boxing
movie, then thinks he can beat people up." Ethan and his brother, Joel
Coen, cackle about Thornton's "victims." "We've seen some pretty
gruesome haircuts."

Bad haircuts are only one of the offbeat things moviegoers are likely
to find in a Coen brothers movie. Joel and Ethan, who jointly write,
direct, edit, and produce their movies, have been called the Merry
Pranksters of filmmaking. Working mostly outside of the traditional
studio system, the Coens produce movies that are black, hilarious,
and violent, with thin or confused plots and twisted, grotesque,

From the Playboy Interview: Joel and Ethan Coen, *Playboy* magazine (November 2001).
Copyright © 2001 by Playboy. Reprinted with permission. All rights reserved.

if unforgettable, characters. The movie business is known for adhering to formula and its aversion to risk, but many of the Coens' movies seem not only noncommercial but anticommercial. Woody Allen may be the only other director who is consistently able to make whatever movies he wants without regard for box-office potential (which isn't to say that some Coen brothers movies haven't done well at the box office). And while Woody Allen's movies are sweet and somewhat predictable, the Coens' are neither.

Who else would have brutally and messily exploded a cow in *O Brother, Where Art Thou?*, or hand-grenaded a rabbit in *Raising Arizona*? But their most violent moments have been saved for humans, leaving such indelible images as John Goodman charging through an inferno while blasting a shotgun in *Barton Fink*. Or Steve Buscemi being stuffed into a wood chipper (blood spraying everywhere) in *Fargo*. Or Dan Hedaya being buried alive in their first movie, *Blood Simple*. (When he tries to rise up, he's furiously beaten back down with a shovel.) In their latest movie, *The Man Who Wasn't There*, the Coens knock off Tony Soprano. The character in the film played by Sopranos star James Gandolfini dies slowly, thick blood gurgling from a tiny hole in his jugular vein.

Shot in black and white and set in the California town of Santa Rosa in 1949, the movie is inspired by Alfred Hitchcock and James M. Cain. Thornton, as barber Ed Crane, starts out as one of the bleakest characters in movie history. His wife, played by Frances McDormand (Joel's wife, who won an Academy Award for her performance in *Fargo*), has an affair with Gandolfini, who winds up on the wrong end of a cigar cutter. The movie does the film noir genre proud not only with a generous amount of infidelity, greed, and bad luck but with a sleazy tooth-pick-chewing detective, an oily defense lawyer, and a sexy but sad shaving scene (in which Thornton shaves McDormand's legs). Ethan says the movie is about "ordinary middle-American people who get into a situation that spirals out of control."

There is nothing ordinary about the characters in any Coen brothers film, beginning with 1984's *Blood Simple*, another film noir about infidelity and greed. "It is the most inventive and original thriller in many a moon," wrote David Ansen in *Newsweek*, "a maliciously entertaining murder story."

Next came *Raising Arizona*, a surreal comedy with Holly Hunter and Nicolas Cage that moved at the pace of a Roadrunner cartoon, then *Miller's Crossing*, a meditation on loyalty and betrayal set in America's organized crime community of the thirties.

In 1991 the Coens released *Barton Fink*, a scathing look at the Hollywood film industry of the early forties that quickly became a classic and won the Palme d'Or at the Cannes Film Festival. Throughout their ascent, the Coens worked with a regular crew of unusual actors, including McDormand, Goodman, John Turturro, Hunter, and Buscemi, whose careers were propelled by their performances in Coen brothers films. The Coens' successes gave them access to bigger stars, including Tim Robbins and Paul Newman, who appeared in *The Hudsucker Proxy*, a lyrical fable in the tradition of Frank Capra and Preston Sturges. It was McDormand, however, who helped catapult their biggest hit, *Fargo*, to six Independent Spirit Awards and seven Oscar nominations. It won two—McDormand for Best Actress and Joel and Ethan for Best Screenplay.

*The Big Lebowski* (1998) cast Jeff Bridges as a Venice Beach stoner and John Goodman as a slightly unhinged Vietnam vet pitted against avant-garde artists, pornographers, and German nihilists. Last year's *O Brother, Where Art Thou?*, a Depression-era tale of a mismatched trio who escape a chain gang and then have a series of adventures rambling around the Old South, features a hilarious performance by George Clooney.

After *The Man Who Wasn't There* opens, the Coens head for Japan to shoot an adaptation of James Dickey's third and final novel, *To the White Sea*. Published in 1993, it's a stark story that chronicles the adventures of a World War II tailgunner shot down on a mission over Tokyo. The movie, starring Brad Pitt, has a budget of $45 million, which makes it their most expensive film to date. A big chunk of the budget will be spent re-creating the 1945 firebombing of Tokyo. The film is almost dialogue-free, a modernday silent film.

The Coens were born in a suburb of Minneapolis called St. Louis Park—Joel in 1954, Ethan in 1957. Their father was an economics professor at the University of Minnesota and their mother an art history professor at St. Cloud State. Smart, sophisticated kids but unexceptional students, they mostly skied and watched movies. They saw Truffaut's

*400 Blows* in a high school cinema club but claim to have been more inspired by Dean Jones and Doris Day comedies, cheap horror flicks, and Tarzan movies.

In their early teens the Coens mowed lawns and saved money to buy a Vivitar camera. With it, they began shooting Super 8 movies, including such early efforts as a remake of *Naked Prey* called "Zeimers in Zambia," a remake of *Lassie Come Home* called "Ed, a Dog" that featured Ethan as the female lead (costumed in his older sister's tutu) and "The Banana Film," the story of a man with an uncanny ability to smell bananas.

As teenagers, both Coens attended Simon's Rock College of Bard, a college for high school age students in Great Barrington, Massachusetts. Joel spent a lot of his free time in Manhattan and in the mid-seventies he enrolled in the film studies program at New York University. Of his years at NYU, Joel says, "I was a cipher there. I sat at the back of the room with an insane grin on my face." After college, he spent the early eighties working as an assistant in various capacities on a series of low-budget films. As related in Ronald Bergan's book on the brothers, filmmaker Barry Sonnenfeld hired Joel to be a production assistant on an industrial film. "Without a doubt the worst PA I ever worked with," Sonnenfeld recalls. "He got three parking tickets, came late, and set fire to the smoke machine."

Ethan, meanwhile, headed to Princeton, where he studied philosophy and wrote a senior thesis titled "Two Views of Wittgenstein's Later Philosophy." During that time, he temporarily left school and then applied for readmission. When he was late getting the forms in, he wrote that he'd had his arm blown off in a hunting accident. He was readmitted only after a meeting with the college psychiatrist. In 1979, he moved to Manhattan and had a series of temporary jobs. The brothers soon began writing scripts together in their spare time. By 1981, they had written *Blood Simple*. They shot a three-minute trailer for their non-existent movie and used it to secure funding for the film. In September 1982, the Coens went to Austin, Texas, and shot *Blood Simple* in eight weeks. They divided up the credits on the movie the way they've subsequently appeared on all their films: written by Joel and Ethan Coen, produced by Ethan Coen, directed by Joel Coen. In fact, it's an arbitrary listing, because both of them share all the duties on all of their films. They even jointly edit their movies under the pseudonym Roderick Jaynes.

Joel's first marriage fell by the wayside. When Frances McDormand was cast as the female lead in *Blood Simple*, he fell in love with her. They married in 1984 and now live on Manhattan's Upper West Side with their seven-year-old son. Ethan met his wife, editor Tricia Cooke, on the set of *Miller's Crossing*. They live in lower Manhattan and have a five-year-old son and an infant daughter.

The Coen brothers work nonstop and are notoriously reluctant interview subjects, but *Playboy* managed to sit them down while they were completing *The Man Who Wasn't There*. Kristine McKenna, who recently spoke with Tim Burton for the magazine, was tapped for the assignment. Here's her report:

"Besides their strange sensibility and moviemaking talent, the most remarkable thing about the Coen brothers is their relationship. They spend an extraordinary amount of time together, yet they don't interrupt each other, they laugh at each other's jokes, listen to each other's ideas with interest, and seem to genuinely like each other. They talk like they make their films—one of them mentions a fragment of an idea, the other takes it further and they bounce it back and forth until it metamorphoses into something interesting, provocative, silly, or—often—weird."

PLAYBOY:    *How important is commercial success to you?*
JOEL:    We want the movies to be seen. At the same time, we're resigned to the fact that we're not making commercial movies and the appeal will be limited.
ETHAN:    On the other hand, if a movie does better than you thought it would, it's gratifying. Conversely, it's disappointing if it doesn't perform up to your expectations.

PLAYBOY:    *What hasn't?*
ETHAN:    *The Hudsucker Proxy* was the worst commercially. *Miller's Crossing* didn't do any business, either. From a financial point of view, they were disasters.

PLAYBOY:    *Do you know why they failed?*
JOEL:    That's the same as trying to find out why one worked. After the fact, it's bogus. Who knows?

PLAYBOY:    *Is there no relationship between commercial success and good movies? Can you see reasons why* Fargo *was a hit and* The Hudsucker Proxy *wasn't?*
ETHAN:    No.
JOEL:    No.
ETHAN:    Within certain broad parameters you know a movie might appeal to a wider audience than another one, but we're not kidding ourselves.
JOEL:    We thought *O Brother, Where Art Thou?* could appeal to a wider audience, and we knew *Barton Fink* never would.
ETHAN:    But we had no idea *Fargo* was going to do any business at all.
JOEL:    That's true. We thought it was like *Barton Fink*. We thought, We're going to make it really cheaply and nobody will get hurt. We used to try to figure this stuff out. We thought it was important to know why some movies were successful and some weren't if we wanted to survive in the business. We gave up. After the fact, it's easy to come up with reasons. Fran's performance had a lot to do with *Fargo*. People loved it. However, while we were shooting the film we had no idea the public was going to love that character. On the other hand, I thought Jennifer Jason Leigh was really funny in *The Hudsucker Proxy*, but the performance seemed to rub people the wrong way. Why? Who knows?

PLAYBOY:    *Do the awards feel random, too?*
JOEL:    You have a better sense of the awards. We knew *The Big Lebowski* wasn't an awards kind of movie.

PLAYBOY:    *Why not?*
JOEL:    It's a silly comedy. *Raising Arizona* was another silly comedy.
ETHAN:    Comedy in general doesn't get invited on that circuit.
JOEL:    On the other hand, we knew that *The Man Who Wasn't There* would be invited to Cannes, where it won a big prize.
ETHAN:    It's in black and white.

JOEL:    Black and white invites prizes.

ETHAN:    Especially from the French.

PLAYBOY:    *Where does quality come in?*

ETHAN:    Awards are not about quality.

JOEL:    We go to competitions because the movies get more attention. That's the main reason. The press attention is important with our movies. We don't have the advertising budget that, say, *Pearl Harbor* does.

ETHAN:    The awards put a movie on people's radar. Festivals are good, even though the idea of putting movies in competitions—this one is the best this, that one is the best that—is ridiculous.

PLAYBOY:    *Are you able to make virtually any movie you want without interference from movie studios?*

JOEL:    We're mercifully free of the Hollywood committee development process and the process of making the movie. They understand that if they are going to do a movie with us, they'll let us do it our way.

ETHAN:    We've never been messed with.

JOEL:    For a couple reasons.

ETHAN:    For one, we write the script. We tell the story the way we want and no one tells us what we should be doing. Also, our movies are cheap. It's nothing for them. Most of the movies they're making give them bigger headaches.

JOEL:    No one will get fired over one of our movies.

ETHAN:    Nobody even had much to say about *O Brother*, which cost more than the others, because the financial health of the movie studio didn't depend on such a small movie.

PLAYBOY.    *Joel once said, "Ethan has a nightmare of one day finding me on the set of something like* The Incredible Hulk, *wearing a gold chain and saying 'I've got to eat, don't I?'" Could you ever sell out?*

JOEL:    The whole selling-out thing really isn't an issue because neither of us finds money that interesting.

ETHAN:    The movie people let us play in the corner of the sandbox and leave us alone. We're happy here.

PLAYBOY:    *Do you agree that it's a small and uncrowded corner? Who else besides you and perhaps Woody Allen can make whatever movies they want?*

JOEL:    Maybe Woody Allen and us. Yeah.

ETHAN:    There are some big directors who've made huge hits who can do what they want.

JOEL:    But they aren't as marginal as we are. There aren't many who have marginally commercial movies and have our freedom. We're lucky. We know it. It's back to the fact that we work cheap.

ETHAN:    That's really the long and the short of it.

JOEL:    Our movies are inexpensive because we storyboard our films in the same highly detailed way Hitchcock did. As a result, there's little improvisation. Preproduction is cheap compared with trying to figure things out on a set with an entire crew standing around.

ETHAN:    So we're left alone, which is indeed sort of miraculous.

PLAYBOY:    *Do the distributors have a say at all?*

ETHAN:    No. They say things, but we don't necessarily listen. They were nervous about the new movie.

JOEL:    Principally because it was in black and white.

ETHAN:    People were terrified of that. Black and white stigmatizes a movie in the eyes of the exhibitors. It means it's an art film. They are leery of it. They may have good reasons, I don't know. However, it was important to us to make it black and white, though it was harder to get the financing.

PLAYBOY:    *Did you consider switching to color?*

ETHAN:    No. We just wouldn't have made it, at least not now. We would have put it in a drawer.

JOEL:    We got away with it because, once again, the movie was cheap. It was under $20 million. That said, we know we're lucky. We're in an enviable position. We've made enough of these things—it's not as if we're just starting out. We're a known quantity. When we first started, we were lucky because there was a lot less activity in the independent film world. There weren't seven hundred movies submitted a year to the Sundance Film Festival. It was easier to get some attention. There was less noise.

PLAYBOY:    *Would it be tougher to release* Blood Simple *now?*

JOEL:    I imagine it would be. We're lucky because now people know who we are. We have a track record in the market, for what it's worth.

ETHAN:    Our record goes both ways, though.

JOEL:    Yes, they know they can lose a little money on us, too [*laughs*].

PLAYBOY:    *You have been called the "grandfathers of the independent film-maker movement." Are you proud of your progeny?*

ETHAN:    God! You're not going to make us responsible for that, are you?

PLAYBOY:    *Is that a bad thing?*

ETHAN:    The thing is, people have always been making films outside of the studios.

JOEL:    For decades there was marginal, nonnarrative stuff. The current variety of independent films started in the sixties with people like Roger Corman, Russ Meyer, and, later, John Sayles.

ETHAN:    We aren't the grandfathers of any movement. In the eighties, the so-called indie film movement was a media creation. What I found irritating is that "independent" became an encomium. If it was independent, it was supposed to be good, and studio films were bad. Obviously, there are bad independent films and good studio films.

PLAYBOY:    The Hudsucker Proxy *was the first time you worked with a big-name Hollywood producer, Joel Silver. Were you apprehensive about working with him?*

JOEL:    We were a little, because of his reputation. However, Joel is a smart guy and he knew what we were looking for when we got into business with him. We weren't looking for a partner in terms of the nitty-gritty of the production. We were looking for someone to help us with the studio and help us finance the movie. He offered his services on that basis. When he says he'll do something, he does it.

PLAYBOY:    *Another thing that has come with your success are big-name actors. Is it different working with people such as George Clooney, Brad Pitt, or Paul Newman?*

JOEL:    The bigger stars we've worked with have been without the movie-star vanities or meshugaas that you read about and dread.

Clooney, for example, was the opposite. He has no entourage. He's a big movie star, but he's a nice guy.

ETHAN:    Paul Newman, too. It's in part self-selecting. We pay so little. The people who want to have their movie-star things indulged wouldn't work with us.

JOEL:    We couldn't give them the stuff they're used to.

ETHAN:    Someone who wanted a big salary and a lot of attention would tell us to get lost. If they work with us, they are doing it for other reasons. They wouldn't be doing it if they were coming with some movie-star agenda.

JOEL:    Definitely not for the money.

ETHAN:    Or more fame. Our movies don't make them recognized on the street, necessarily.

PLAYBOY:    *Are you recognized on the street?*

JOEL:    If people recognize me, it's because they're looking at my credit card. Frankly, nobody gives a shit. I get a little more of it when I'm with Fran, because people recognize her. Her fame can occasionally be intrusive, but she's not in the category of people who can't go out.

PLAYBOY:    *Do you ever take advantage of her celebrity?*

JOEL:    Sometimes Fran will be in a crowded New York restaurant and the manager will give her a card with a number she can call so she can get a reservation even if there aren't any available. Has she ever used that? Yeah, probably.

PLAYBOY:    *Do you write movies with actors—Fran or anyone else—in mind?*

ETHAN:    Half-and-half. We often think about people we know and have worked with before. With Fran, with John Turturro. With some of the other people.

PLAYBOY:    *Did you discover Turturro?*

JOEL:    We knew him before we did *Miller's Crossing*. He went to school with Fran. You get to know one actor and you're on a slippery slope.

PLAYBOY:    *Is it gratifying to set people like him off on successful careers?*
JOEL:    It's a mutual thing.

PLAYBOY:    *How about Steve Buscemi?*
JOEL:    We met him in an audition. When there's a great collaboration like the one with him, you want to work together again.

PLAYBOY:    *When you first cast John Goodman, he was about to begin work on* Roseanne.
ETHAN:    The TV show hadn't begun and he wasn't well known. He just came in on an audition.
JOEL:    We work with someone and—I don't know. It works or not. There's sympathy to a working style and getting along well. There's also the actor's ability, of course. Something just happens.
ETHAN:    They understand the material in a full way. In addition, they surprise you by what they bring to the roles.

PLAYBOY:    *How have you cast people like Billy Bob Thornton, Jeff Bridges, or Paul Newman?*
JOEL:    We write these things and we need actors. Other than the parts for the people we always work with, we don't really have an idea who will play the parts. Sometimes we think about the role and about actors we know from their work.

PLAYBOY:    *Did you ask Paul Newman?*
ETHAN:    Yes. We asked and he said yes. We couldn't believe it.

PLAYBOY:    *Did you feel intimidated working with him?*
JOEL:    Not at all. Paul is a regular guy in the very best way. He is completely unaffected. The only actor I imagine might make us nervous is Brando. You'd never know whether he was going to show up and want to play the part as a bagel or something. I think he's gone off the deep end.

PLAYBOY:    *How did you cast* Fargo?
JOEL:    We wrote Fran's part for Fran and Steve Buscemi's part for Steve. But Bill Macy came in during a casting session.

PLAYBOY:    Fargo *was loosely based on a 1987 kidnapping that took place in Minnesota. Are you often inspired by real events?*
JOEL:    We found the story compelling, but we weren't interested in rendering the details as they were. We're not big on research and we just don't care at a certain point.

PLAYBOY:    *Did a real person inspire the Dude, Jeff Bridges's character in* The Big Lebowski?
ETHAN:    Yes.
JOEL:    Definitely [*they laugh*].
ETHAN:    A couple people in L.A. did, especially one guy. We spent time in L.A. and met a few people who were quintessentially L.A. people. One guy in particular—a producer—was like the guy in the movie.

PLAYBOY:    *Did you do a lot of research about the drug culture, or do you know about it from personal experience?*
ETHAN:    It's just this guy. The guy is a pothead and stuck in the sixties. A former SDS guy. There are a lot of those people out there like him.

PLAYBOY:    *Do you often base your characters on real people?*
JOEL:    Often the characters are composites. Normally.
ETHAN:    And sometimes they're not.

PLAYBOY:    *Are there actors you've written parts for who have repeatedly turned you down?*
JOEL:    It took us a long time to get Jeff Bridges to take the part in *The Big Lebowski*. He danced around it for a while. I've heard that he does that on every movie. He's slow to take a part and has a lot of insecurity about it before he commits to it. But once he does, the insecurity evaporates. That was another fun working experience.

PLAYBOY:    *Which star from the past do you most regret having missed the opportunity to work with?*
ETHAN:    Richard Burton would have been good.
JOEL:    I'd like to have worked with Fred MacMurray.

PLAYBOY:    *Do you think you're better filmmakers when you're working with actors you like?*

ETHAN:    We only work with actors we like.

PLAYBOY:    *After* Miller's Crossing, *Gabriel Byrne said, "It was not a fun set." Why not?*

JOEL:    Gabriel can be moody, but we had a good time with him. Tex Cobb, who played the biker in *Raising Arizona*, is the only person we've worked with who posed problems. He's not an actor, and he was going through some shit at the time. He was a bit of a pain in the ass.

PLAYBOY:    *How about Nicolas Cage in that movie?*

ETHAN:    He was great. We're hoping to do something else with him. We've written a Cold War comedy called *62 Skidoo* that we want him to do. It deals with amnesia, mistaken identity, and that very sixties question, "Who am I?" It's vaguely in the tradition of *Seconds* and *The Manchurian Candidate*, which are incredibly groovy movies that were very much of their time.

PLAYBOY:    *Did you write* Raising Arizona *with Cage in mind?*

JOEL:    We actually wrote it for Holly Hunter—with her in mind.

PLAYBOY:    *Was it challenging to direct all the babies you had in that movie?*

JOEL:    It was bizarre. Whenever you have an infant, you have to triple or quadruple them. When we had five kids in the movie, we had to have fifteen babies on the set.

ETHAN:    The picture babies and the stand by babies. Cacophonous, nightmarish.

JOEL:    We had the baby pit—a big padded pit that they were tossed into when we weren't using them. The mothers all sat around the perimeter knitting.

ETHAN:    Whenever we needed a baby, we reached into the pit and grabbed one. It was kind of like a barbecue pit.

JOEL:    You can't really direct a baby, which is the problem. You take one out of the pit, put it in front of the camera and see if it behaves.

If not, you toss it back into the pit and get another one. It's a lot like working with animals, actually.

ETHAN:    Yeah. If an animal doesn't do what you want it to do, you just grab another one. But the rules for working with animals are a lot more stringent than those for working with babies.

JOEL:    There is definitely no comparison.

PLAYBOY:    *What can you do with a baby that you can't do with an animal?*

ETHAN:    A million things.

JOEL:    The pit. We could never do that with animals.

ETHAN:    Believe me. It's a remarkable thing to see how animals are monitored. You cannot kill a mosquito on-screen.

JOEL:    When you do a Screen Actors Guild movie that uses animals in any way you have to get the American Humane Society to sign off on it. We blew up a cow in *O Brother*, which meant we had to send the Humane Society work tapes while the film was being shot. When they saw the cow scene they didn't believe it was computer generated, but I assure you it was.

ETHAN:    There is a rule that you can't get a cow anywhere near a moving car.

JOEL:    It might cause the cow stress.

ETHAN:    You can't upset the animals.

JOEL:    We had to have a lizard crash pad for *Raising Arizona*.

PLAYBOY:    *What's a lizard crash pad?*

ETHAN:    A lizard shoots off a rock in the movie, and we had to have a preapproved soft place for it to land.

PLAYBOY:    *Is there a reason you tend to put animals in peril?*

JOEL:    No. For fun.

ETHAN:    We don't put them in any more peril than we put people.

PLAYBOY:    *That's true. With the exception of* The Hudsucker Proxy, *all of your films have included a fair amount of violence and killing.*

ETHAN:    It's called drama.

PLAYBOY:     *Do some of your movies' dark scenes—burying someone alive in* Blood Simple, *for example—come from your nightmares?*
JOEL:     Not really. They are the general phobias people experience, I suppose, but it's not personal to us.
ETHAN:     It's just stuff that creeps people out. We like that.
JOEL:     The reason we killed the cow in *O Brother, Where Art Thou?* is that we think it's funny.


PLAYBOY:     *How would you respond to someone who is offended?*
JOEL:     I recognize that some people might not think it's funny, but really [*laughing*], what's not to like? It's interesting to me that people are so upset about the cow scene. We blew up a rabbit in *Raising Arizona* and people were upset about that, too. In a focus group, people were really upset about the rabbit. Shooting people was fine, but they didn't like seeing a rabbit get hurt. Eating cows is fine, but hitting a cow with a car is not.
ETHAN:     It's easy to offend people. People get uncomfortable, for instance, when the main character in a movie is not sympathetic in a Hollywood formula way. Our movies are loaded with things that aren't to everyone's taste. On the other hand, there's a scene in *O Brother* where a frog gets squished that everyone seems to like. It's all right to do frog squishing.
JOEL:     In our next movie, Brad Pitt plays a character who identifies intensely with animals, yet he kills many animals over the course of the story. Those killings are potentially more alienating to an audience than the scenes in which he kills people.
ETHAN:     I don't know exactly why.


PLAYBOY:     *You murder James Gandolfini in your new movie. Are you fans of* The Sopranos?
JOEL:     Not really.
ETHAN:     We don't watch TV. I don't have HBO. We knew him from character parts he had played in other movies.
JOEL:     Before *The Sopranos* he played small parts, and we always really liked him. I hear he's great in *The Sopranos*, though.

PLAYBOY:    *Is it a moral or practical decision not to watch TV?*
JOEL:    I don't know what it is.
ETHAN:    I'm just not interested.
JOEL:    I watch the news.
ETHAN:    I watch the news, too. But I couldn't tell you about any of the regular shows that are on now.

PLAYBOY:    *How about movies? Do you try to keep up with them?*
ETHAN:    I go when I get a chance. I see whatever is nearby and playing at the right time, which means I don't necessarily see the movies I'm particularly interested in seeing.
JOEL:    Our moviegoing habits have changed over the past five or six years, mostly because we have kids.
ETHAN:    We see a lot of kid movies.

PLAYBOY:    *Is that good or bad?*
ETHAN:    It's not good. With some exceptions. *Chicken Run* was good. It might be the last good movie I've seen.
JOEL:    I'm curious about *Shrek* because my kid saw it four times. The kids want to see every Disney movie that comes out. Some are hard to sit through.
ETHAN:    There were many years when we saw a lot of movies—the cold weather of the Midwest drives you inside to watch movies. Now we don't.
JOEL:    Recently I liked *Amores Perros*. I also liked *Sexy Beast*.

PLAYBOY:    *Do you generally prefer art and foreign movies?*
JOEL:    Yeah. If I have a chance, I try to see those kinds.

PLAYBOY:    *We've discussed violence in your movies, but how about sex? British film writer Ronald Bergan wrote, "The Coens avoid the obligatory sex scenes found in most adult films." Why?*
ETHAN:    What about the orgy scene in *The Big Lebowski*?
JOEL:    Yeah, and there's a sex scene in *Barton Fink*, too, although it does end up with the woman being decapitated.

PLAYBOY:    *What about—*

JOEL:    And the scene in *Barton Fink* where John Turturro and John Goodman wrestle? We consider that a sex scene. [*Ethan laughs heartily.*] I don't know. We're of the school of panning away to the waterfall or the steaming kettle or the flock of geese flying.

PLAYBOY:    *Is it that you dislike sex scenes?*

JOEL:    It's that there aren't many scenes of that sort that are done well. Pedro Almodóvar does them well, but he's the only one. It's not that I don't find that aspect of film interesting, but I'm not interested in doing it.

PLAYBOY:    The Man Who Wasn't There *has been described as a return to your beginnings. Is it?*

ETHAN:    I suppose so. It's definitely more hard-boiled than *O Brother* is.

JOEL:    The movie takes place in Santa Rosa in 1949, the same time and setting as Hitchcock's *Shadow of a Doubt*, which, along with *Psycho*, is probably my favorite Hitchcock film.

PLAYBOY:    O Brother, Where Art Thou? *is said to be loosely based on* The Wizard of Oz. *Is that true?*

JOEL:    That was definitely an inspiration and a big influence on the movie. In fact, one of my favorite shots in the film is strongly reminiscent of *The Wizard of Oz*. It's a shot of George Clooney, Tim Nelson, and John Turturro peering through some bushes while looking down on a Ku Klux Klan meeting.

PLAYBOY:    *The Klan members perform an elaborately choreographed dance. What inspired that bizarre scene?*

JOEL:    The dance combines aspects of the witch's castle scene in *The Wizard of Oz*, a number from a Busby Berkeley musical and some interesting old films we saw of the Klan. They marched in formation like that. It really was like a synthesis of Busby Berkeley and Nuremberg.

PLAYBOY:    Barton Fink *features a character named W. P. Mayhew who's played by John Mahoney and is loosely based on William Faulkner, who you've both expressed great admiration for. What's your favorite Faulkner book?*

JOEL:    Light in August, but don't ask me why. The other one I like a lot is *The Wild Palms.* We steal many names from Faulkner, but we haven't attempted to steal a whole book, yet [*laughing*]. O Brother, for instance, has a character named Vernon T. Waldrip, and we got that name from *The Wild Palms.*

PLAYBOY:    *At what point does an homage to a genre become a spoof of a genre?*

JOEL:    We've always tried to emulate the sources of genre movies rather than the movies themselves. For instance, *Blood Simple* grew out of the fact that we started reading James M. Cain's novels in 1979 and liked the hard-boiled style. We wanted to write a James M. Cain story and put it in a modern context. We've never considered our stuff either homage or spoof. Those are things other people call it, and it's always puzzled me that they do.

PLAYBOY:    The Man Who Wasn't There *was also based on Cain's work. What do you like about his stories?*

JOEL:    What intrigues us about Cain is that the heroes of his stories are nearly always schlubs—loser guys involved in dreary, banal existences. Cain was interested in people's workaday lives, and he wrote about guys who worked as insurance salesmen or in banks, and we took that as a cue. Even though there's a crime in this story, we were still interested in what this guy, who's a barber, does as a barber. We wanted to examine exactly what the day-to-day was like for a guy who gives haircut after haircut.

PLAYBOY:    *On the set, Billy Bob Thornton was giving real haircuts to extras and crew members. Did you get one?*

ETHAN:    Are you kidding?

JOEL:    No way. We had to hire someone to fix the haircuts he was giving people.

PLAYBOY:    *You've said that you're more attracted to film noir as a literary form than as a film genre. Are noir books better than the movies that are based on them?*

JOEL:    Most of the movies aren't as good as the books, although there are exceptions. John Huston's film noirs like *The Maltese Falcon* and *The Asphalt Jungle* are great, but many film noirs are crummy. Everyone loves *Out of the Past*, for instance, and Kirk Douglas is good in it, but it's a little overcooked.

PLAYBOY:    *Critics write about your films as if they are challenged to crack some sort of code in order to grasp your real intentions. Are they reading in too much?*

JOEL:    That's how they've been trained to watch movies. Several critics interpreted *Barton Fink* as a parable for the Holocaust. They said the same thing about *Miller's Crossing.* The critic J. Hoberman cooked up this elaborate theory about the scene where Bernie is taken into the woods to be killed. In *Barton Fink*, we may have encouraged it—like teasing the animals at the zoo. The movie is intentionally ambiguous in ways they may not be used to seeing.

PLAYBOY:    *Your critics seem to hold you to a higher standard. Do you think about them when you're making movies?*

ETHAN:    Never.

PLAYBOY:    *Are you consciously trying to do something different each time out?*

JOEL:    Not really. We were out filming this scene in *Fargo* where a car is approaching in the distance on an empty stretch of highway as Steve Buscemi is dragging a state trooper's body off the road. As we were shooting that scene, Ethan and I looked at each other and we both said, "It seems like we've been here before." There's an almost identical scene in *Blood Simple.* It's a complete accident.

ETHAN:    We don't generally worry about repeating ourselves. Being original and always doing the new thing is incredibly overrated.

PLAYBOY:    *All of your movies are set in the past. Are you less interested in the present or future?*

JOEL:    The past has a kind of exoticism. Setting a story in the past is a way of further fictionalizing it. It's not about reminiscence, because our movies are about a past that we have never experienced. It's more about imagination. Right before we made *Barton Fink*, for instance, we read a book called *City of Nets* by Otto Friedrich that was essentially a history of Los Angeles and Hollywood in the forties. It was an intensely evocative book and played a role in how we conceived the film.

ETHAN:    Books often play a role in our becoming interested in a period or a place. We considered trying to get the rights to *Mildred Pierce*, which wasn't much of a movie but was a great James M. Cain novel set in Glendale in the forties. The book *Mildred Pierce* is actually the saga of Glendale, but the movie didn't bother getting into any of that.

PLAYBOY:    *Several of your films incorporate elements of screwball comedies. What's your favorite of that genre?*

JOEL:    *The Miracle of Morgan's Creek*, although I'm not sure that it's technically a screwball comedy.

ETHAN:    As for contemporary attempts at screwball comedy, *I Wanna Hold Your Hand* was pretty funny, in a screwball kind of way. *Used Cars*, too.

PLAYBOY:    *Did you watch them when you were kids?*

ETHAN:    I like all of Preston Sturges's comedies.

PLAYBOY:    *What's your earliest memory?*

ETHAN:    I remember moving across the street. We moved from one house into the house across the street.

JOEL:    Our parents liked the neighborhood. I remember climbing on top of the stove and setting my pajamas on fire when I was three years old. [*Laughing*] I remember the expression on my parents' faces.

PLAYBOY:    *What was the first film that made an impression on you?*

JOEL:    I remember going to see *David Copperfield* when I was four and being completely freaked out by the scene where David's father beats the shit out of him. It upset me so much that I had to leave. Right after that I saw *All Hands on Deck*, which was much more my speed.

ETHAN:    I have a vivid memory of seeing a film called *Hatari*. There's an elephant stampede at the end of it.

JOEL:    From an early age we were into what we thought were adult movies—things like *Splendor in the Grass* and *A Summer Place*.

ETHAN:    They don't make that shit anymore. It's been usurped by significant, disease-of-the-week theme TV movies.

JOEL:    Yes, but when we were kids, films like *Tea and Sympathy* served the purpose. *Tea and Sympathy* was a lot better than a TV movie about somebody who gets spina bifida.

PLAYBOY:    *Were you movie fanatics in those years?*

ETHAN:    There are movie nuts who are filmmakers—Scorsese and Truffaut, for instance. Not us. We're not collectors of film and we're not as knowledgeable about movies as many of those guys. We're fond of stories; movies are a way of telling stories. We found out that we had some facility for writing them and we got an opportunity to actually make one. It's not as if we have some mystical attachment to film.

PLAYBOY:    *You've described your childhood as bland. Is that an accurate characterization?*

JOEL:    I've described it as bland to people who were digging for some explanation of why we do what we do. I remember the blandness fondly. At the same time, I was quite eager to leave when I was in my teens. As soon as I saw New York City, I wanted to be there.

PLAYBOY:    *How important was religion in your childhood?*

ETHAN:    Judaism was a central part of the house we grew up in. We had a religious upbringing. I went to Hebrew school every Saturday and had a bar mitzvah, but that just meant I got presents. I never took it seriously. Some part of it probably seeps in, but I think that's more of an ethnic than a religious thing.

JOEL:    Yes, I imagine some of it influenced my point of view to a degree. But neither Ethan nor I have maintained a great deal of interest in the traditions.

PLAYBOY:    *Will your sons be bar mitzvahed?*

JOEL:    My wife is the daughter of a Disciples of Christ minister, and her sister is a minister in that church. Our son [who's adopted] was born in

Paraguay to a Catholic family, so it's complicated. Fran's more into summer solstice. I guess you could say our son's being brought up as a pagan.

PLAYBOY:    *Do you believe in God?*
JOEL:    Not in the Jewish sense. I don't believe in the angry God, Yahweh.

PLAYBOY:    *What do you think happens after death?*
JOEL:    You rot and decompose.

PLAYBOY:    *Do you believe in the law of karma—that we reap what we sow? Or do some people get away with murder?*
JOEL:    Some people do get away with murder.

PLAYBOY:    *Do you believe in capital punishment?*
JOEL:    No.
ETHAN:    No.

PLAYBOY:    *How did having your children change you?*
JOEL:    I certainly see fewer movies.

PLAYBOY:    *Has it changed your filmmaking at all?*
JOEL:    Mmm. No.

PLAYBOY:    *Does filmmaking ever become tedious?*
JOEL:    Parts of the business are tedious. We had no idea how much promotion you have to do. It wasn't until we were assaulted with all that during the release of *Blood Simple* that it crossed my radar. We say no to a lot and we won't do television, but you have to do a certain amount.
ETHAN:    If they give you millions of dollars to make a movie, they expect you to promote it. You make these movies and a year later you have homework.
JOEL:    Watching dailies can be tedious, too. Frequently you'll shoot something over and over because you're looking for a small detail. It can be nothing more than an insert, but you'll have to sit through hours of dailies with a room full of people wondering why you shot an hour of a hand holding a coffee cup.

ETHAN:    There's another thing, too. You wait around a lot. Mostly you just sit around and bullshit during those long stretches of waiting.

JOEL:    It takes time to light the scene—whatever.

PLAYBOY:    *How do you spend the time?*

JOEL:    You can gain twenty pounds in six weeks, so I try to stay away from the craft services table. I used to drink a lot of coffee. Ethan still does, but my stomach can't take it. I drink a lot of tea.

PLAYBOY:    *Have you two ever had a ferocious disagreement?*

JOEL:    This seems to disappoint people, but no, we haven't.

ETHAN:    Occasionally we get a little testy with each other, but that's about the extent of it.

JOEL:    We wouldn't be doing this if we had ferocious disagreements. We share the same fundamental point of view toward the material. In fact, the credits on our movies don't reflect the extent of our collaboration. We take separate credits, but we actually do everything together.

PLAYBOY:    *Why do you edit under a pseudonym?*

ETHAN:    Because it would be bad taste to have our names on our movies that many times.

PLAYBOY:    *What's the process? Who sits behind the word processor? Who sits behind the camera?*

ETHAN:    We both sit behind the camera. We both watch the actors. I tend to be at the word processor more because I type faster.

JOEL:    On the set it's completely equal. We talk to the actors and cinematographer and designers. Whenever a decision has to be made, it's made by the one of us who is closer to the problem. The movies really are codirected.

ETHAN:    After they are shot, it's a mirror, in a way. When we're editing, Joel actually makes the physical cuts and splices.

JOEL:    Because I have had more practice on the machine from when I was an assistant editor. But we're editing the movies cut by cut together.

PLAYBOY:    *How about dreaming up your projects?*

JOEL:    We don't do high-concept movies. It's not that one of us will say, "*Das Boot* in a spaceship." We just talk about ideas.

ETHAN:    It's impossible to say after the fact whose idea it was. Ideas just get expanded and developed, and there's an informal discussion until we have the framework to start writing.

JOEL:    Sometimes we just start writing to see where it goes. It might start off with, literally, "John Goodman and John Turturro in a hotel room."

PLAYBOY:    *You have said that your next movie, a film adaptation of James Dickey's* To the White Sea, *is a silent movie. Why a silent movie?*

JOEL:    I wouldn't call it a silent movie, but after the first ten or fifteen minutes there isn't any dialogue. It's about an American airman who's shot down over Tokyo the night before the city is firebombed. He then walks from Honshu to Hokkaido. Because he's alone, there's no dialogue for 90 percent of the movie.

PLAYBOY:    *What made Brad Pitt right for the leading role?*

JOEL:    The lead character is a tailgunner in a B-29, and there's something all-American about Brad that's appropriate. Brad is actually far too old to play the part, so the fact that he has a boyish quality is good. Basically, he's supposed to be a kid who was drafted.

ETHAN:    He also kills a lot of people, so the actor can't be somebody you're going to detest. He's killing to survive, but the killings are fairly graphic.

PLAYBOY:    *More violence?*

JOEL:    The issue of violence in movies bores me. The discussion about it is endless. We get asked about it frequently. There's all this political stuff around it. It's a bore.

ETHAN:    I was just reading one of Philip Roth's novels, and there's a character in it who talks about trees. He says, "Who gives a shit about a tree," and I feel the same way. I find trees boring.

PLAYBOY:    *If not in your movies, do you ever have qualms about violence in other movies? Where do you draw the line on movie violence?*

JOEL:    I don't draw a line anywhere. I won't watch a film like *Faces of Death* or depictions of actual violence or newsreels of people killing themselves, because I don't want that stuff in my psyche. But generally

I find myself more repulsed by maudlin, overly sentimental films than by violent films.

PLAYBOY:    *When was the last time you cried in a movie?*
JOEL:    I hate when people cry in movies. It's particularly disconcerting when you're sitting at a really awful movie and you hear people all around you sobbing and blowing their noses.

PLAYBOY:    *Do you ever cry?*
JOEL:    I cried during *Dancer in the Dark* [*laughing*]. Actually, I barely sat through it. I hate to say this, but the best part of the movie was when Björk beat David Morse to death with a metal box.

PLAYBOY:    *Joel, you once said, "Ethan is unbelievably sentimental and sloppy and he's always trying to sneak that into our movies." Were you kidding?*
JOEL:    Actually, it's true.
ETHAN:    I admit it—there's that exploding cow, for instance.
JOEL:    He's trying to sneak a love interest into our new movie. It doesn't make any sense at all because it's not in the novel, but he wants Brad Pitt to meet a girl along the way.
ETHAN:    Yeah, I want him to run into a Japanese girl walking through the snow dressed in animal skins and a sable hat. Kind of a *Clan of the Cave Bear* thing. I also wanted to give the lead character a buddy, it being a war picture and all.
JOEL:    Then we could kill the buddy.
ETHAN:    And Brad Pitt would get to say, "They killed my buddy."
JOEL:    That's funny! We should do it. Then everyone can talk more about violence in the movie.

# Interview with Joel Coen

## SMRITI MUNDHRA/2001

I WISH THAT THERE WERE SOME SECRET to the way Joel and Ethan Coen make movies. I wish that there were some bizarre ritual or habit or some kind of classified information I could take credit for letting IGN *FilmForce* readers in on. Having worked on two of their films before turning to journalism for my livelihood, I've had the rare experience of seeing how the Brothers operate during the filmmaking process, which, considering the kind and quality of the films they produce, ought to yield at least one eyebrow-raising anecdote. But alas, the quirkiest thing about the Coen Brothers is that they are seemingly quirkless. From my vantage point over the two summers that brought us *O Brother, Where Art Thou*? and the upcoming noir drama *The Man Who Wasn't There*, Joel and Ethan Coen perfectly fit the profile of Normal Guys. Maybe too normal.

"Come on, you've seen the way we work," Joel Coen tells me during an interview in Los Angeles. "You know there's nothing mysterious about it." I ask him what he's trying to hide by continually refusing to provide audio commentary on the DVDs of his films. "I don't know," he replies vaguely, further propagating my hypothesis that Something Is Up. "Generally speaking, it's not something I listen to. Usually, I don't want to sit down and listen to the director gas on about his movie. I just can't actually imagine myself sitting down and having that much to say."

From *FilmForce*, November 2, 2001, http://filmforce.ign.com. Reprinted by permission of *FilmForce* and IGN.

Could it be that the creative team that has brought to us the bizarre worlds of *Blood Simple*, *Raising Arizona*, *Barton Fink*, and *Fargo* are really just regular Joes? Joel Coen would like to have us think so. "Maybe there should be less of a mystique around making movies," he asserts. "I just don't think that there's any real mystery there."

Fans of Joel and Ethan Coen are perpetually looking to figure out what makes the brothers so creative. There are Joel and Ethan Coen film societies and college classes devoted to the subject of decoding their films. "I think those things should be discouraged," says Joel. "I'm afraid one of the members of those clubs is going to be the person that assassinates Ethan in five years."

The latest addition in an incredibly prolific few years for Joel and Ethan Coen is *The Man Who Wasn't There*, which brings them back to the noir genre of their debut, *Blood Simple*, which put them on the map as filmmakers. For his favorite film noir, Joel cites *The Maltese Falcon*, "and I like the Billy Wilder movie *Double Indemnity*," he adds. "And then I like the sort of skanky film noirs, the real low budget Edgar G. Ulmer kind, you know, *Detour* kind of movies." In the vein of the classic noir films of half a century ago, *The Man Who Wasn't There* aims to recall not only the look, but also the feeling of its time. "With this one, we were thinking noir to a certain extent, but we were also thinking about science fiction movies from the early 1950s. You know, the flying saucers and the pod people." According to Joel, the purpose of adding science fiction elements to his noir film was to evoke the mindset of 1950s suburbia. "We were interested in the whole idea of post-war anxiety, you know, atom bombing anxiety and the existential dread you see in '50s movies, which curiously seems appropriate now."

Having noir elements isn't the only recurring theme from previous works in *The Man Who Wasn't There*; the film boasts another of the spectacular array of odd supporting characters that have become the toast—and, to some, the malfunction—of the Coen Brothers' films. Joel and Ethan are as often chastised as they are regaled for their interesting choice of characters. "I've never really understood that," says Joel, of the numerous letters he and Ethan receive protesting their supposed usage of unflattering stereotypes. "It's a funny thing; people sometimes accuse us of condescending to our characters somehow—that to me is kind of inexplicable." He admits, "I guess there's a certain amount of poking fun at certain characters, but that's because there is something amusing about them or about the way they behave, so I guess you can say that that's poking fun at the character. But the character is your own invention, so who cares?"

The boys have come under fire for misrepresenting everyone from Minnesotans to southerners to Vietnam veterans. "If you have a character that's specific ethnically, or regionally—let's say this character is from Minnesota, or this character is Jewish, or this character is a Unitarian from Omaha—that character is supposed to stand in and represent all Jews, or all Unitarians from Omaha, or all Minnesotans, and of course that's ridiculous," he explains. "You're doing it to make the character as specific as possible, so that it's a specific individual that you're talking about, not that whole class of people."

"We create monsters and then we can't control them," he says, laughing at the theory that he and his brother are like Dr. Frankenstein figures. "No, really, you love all your characters, even the ridiculous ones. You have to on some level; they're your weird creations in some kind of way. I don't even know how you approach the process of conceiving the characters if in a sense you hated them. It's just absurd."

A trend in Coen Brothers movies seems to be that these odd characters, often played by regulars in the Joel and Ethan's talent circle such as Steve Buscemi, John Turturro, Michael Badalucco, and John Goodman, support big-name stars that assume lead roles in their films. "That's true, and it's become more common in that last five to ten years," Joel reflects. "What's sort of deceptive is that the point at which we worked with some of these actors, they weren't really stars yet. Nicolas Cage was not a big star when we did *Raising Arizona*. A lot of these people were also virtually unknown, too, when we worked with them first—Fran [McDormand], Holly [Hunter], John Goodman."

"It's a funny thing, yeah. We do tend to work with bigger stars now." One of them being Joel's wife, Frances McDormand, who won an Academy Award for her work in *Fargo*. McDormand, who hadn't worked with her husband and brother-in-law since then, re-teams with the brothers again for *The Man Who Wasn't There*. "This movie is sort of an exception to that because Billy Bob [Thornton] and Fran are very well known actors, but aren't the kind of 'movie stars' in the sense that George Clooney and Brad Pitt are."

Speaking of Brad Pitt, what about the highly publicized collaboration between the actor and the brothers? "That one went down the old drainerino," he says of *To the White Sea*, a World War II drama that was scheduled to commence principle photography this winter. "It was really a budget thing at the end of the day," he adds. Namely, the film required more money than what the studio was willing to put forth. "It wasn't anybody's fault, it was just that a certain amount of money was available to make the movie, and a certain amount was necessary to actually make it properly, and it came to a point where we had to either radically reconceive how we were going to shoot the movie or move on to something else." That something else is a comedy called *Intolerable Cruelty*, which will reunite them with *O Brother* star George Clooney. As for *To the White Sea*, "I think it's dead."

Getting an elusive figure like Joel Coen to sit down for a lengthy interview is no easy task, and part of that can be attributed to the kinds of questions he is asked. Just to be on the safe side, I asked the director to give me a list of questions that he was sick of answering. "Well, I'd be perfectly happy never to have to answer anything again about how I work with Ethan," he says, almost instantaneously. I immediately cross three or four questions off of my list. "Or whether we have arguments, or . . . you know what I mean? I've been answering those questions for twenty years. I suppose it's interesting to people, but you would think that if they were that interested, they would go back and read any of the hundreds of interviews we've given over the past twenty years, and we'd never have to answer it again." So if you're looking for that kind of information, use your favorite search engine.

Part of the reason fans are so interested in the process behind constructing the library of stories that the Coen Brothers have assembled is because, as filmmakers, they are considered to be at the very top of the game. Joel insists that acquiring a station like that is a gradual process, and one that he hasn't totally reconciled himself with. "I think we learned a lot between our first and second films," he says, referring, of course, to *Blood Simple* and *Raising Arizona*, respectively. "There's a big jump in your confidence in terms of your craft after you've made your first feature—or at least it was for us. And then after that you continue to learn new things and become more confident, but it's a slower, more incremental process."

One fear for the director is complacency. "People do get lazy, and I'm sure that happens to us to a certain extent. But, you know, if the material is challenging, it forces you to challenge yourself when handling it."

Complacency is one thing, but does Joel Coen ever fear mediocrity? "Oh sure!" he answers readily. "Definitely, because you want to keep it fresh and you hopefully can keep doing new stuff that's going to continue to stimulate and keep people interested." Joel claims to feel the most responsibility towards "people that have been interested in our work for awhile, because those are the last people you want to disappoint."

Creative people are known for doing crazy things to keep the juices flowing, and to get themselves out of slumps. "A sort of creative Viagra as it were?" asks Joel, laughing heartily at his witticism. "No, we do it completely without chemicals."

Though they may be at or near the apex of their career right now, with story ideas and energy overflowing, Joel worries that that may not always be the case for him and his brother. "It's a funny thing because you look at the careers of other filmmakers, and you see them sort of slow down, and you realize, 'maybe this becomes harder to do as you get older.' That's sort of a cautionary thing. I hope it doesn't happen to me."

All things considered, where does Joel Coen see himself in twenty years? "Well that's a good question," he says, pondering over the answer for a while. "I have no idea. Part of me hopes I'm still making movies, and part of me hopes that I'm not!" He issues another hearty laugh of the kind he's famous for amongst his acquaintances. "I don't know. I mean, it would be nice to still be making movies in twenty or thirty years. It's kind of a funny business because it's a business of young people. I've got friends that are filmmakers older than I am by twenty years, and I see how, for absolutely no logical reason—because they are so much better than most filmmakers working now—have trouble getting projects off the ground, and it's because it's a very youth-oriented business."

He doesn't knock young Hollywood though, acknowledging that there are new filmmakers that he admires. "I like Spike Jonze, I really liked that *Being John Malkovich* movie, and I like Wes Anderson."

Of the old timers, Joel regards Stanley Kubrick as a master, not only for his storytelling prowess, but also for his knack for treading the fringes of the mainstream without actually being a part of it. "I always admired Stanley Kubrick for the fact that he managed to beat the system somehow," he says. Similar compliments have been issued to the Coen Brothers for their ability to retain creative control over their projects, despite the fact that they are almost always funded by major studios. "I think he kind of had it all figured out."

Dwelling on the state of filmmaking past, present, and future, though certainly interesting, still doesn't answer the core question that fans of Joel Coen's films are always asking—why is he creative? "I don't know that I am," he responds. "That's for other people to decide. I guess it beats throwing trash for a living."

# Stealing the Show: Tom Hanks and the Coen Brothers Gang Up to Remake *The Ladykillers*

DIXIE REID/2004

THE COEN BROTHERS, Ethan and Joel, paid homage to the 1955 British crime caper *The Ladykillers* in their first movie, 1984's *Blood Simple.*

They borrowed the line "Who looks stupid now?" which M. Emmet Walsh mutters as he shoots Dan Hedaya.

It would be twenty years before the brothers returned to *The Ladykillers*—this time rewriting William Rose's Oscar-nominated script and making it into a broad, modern-day comedy set in the Deep South.

The Coens are in San Francisco for the afternoon along with star Tom Hanks, who is in particularly high spirits. He walks into the room, tossing his sunglasses, reading glasses, cell phone, and PDA on the table. He takes new $20 bills from his checkbook and jokingly hands them out to the Coens.

"Thank you for the role. Thank you very much," he says, chuckling.

In keeping with the original, the Coens' version of *The Ladykillers* is a comic yarn about a slippery fellow, this time called Goldthwait Higginson Dorr III, Ph.D., who masterminds (sort of) a heist. He and his hapless band of thieves, masquerading as musicians, tunnel from an old lady's root cellar into the cash-filled vault of a Mississippi River casino.

From the *Sacramento Bee*, March 21, 2004. Copyright The Sacramento Bee 2005. Reprinted by permission of the *Sacramento Bee*.

When their widowed landlady, Mrs. Munson (Irma P. Hall), discovers the crime and threatens to turn them in, they must kill her. Trouble is, these bumbling criminals are more of a danger to themselves.

Hanks plays Dorr as a cross between an affected Rhett Butler and Snagglepuss—with a laugh that sounds like he's gargling a hairball.

"We came to call it the rat quiver laugh," says Ethan Coen.

"The first time I did it," Hanks says, "there was a joke at the end of one scene, and I think Professor Dorr surprised himself that he had actually stumbled on such a witticism. It was like, 'Oh, I'm actually making a joke here,' so it began there, and it was a question of, how deep is that well? How often can you go to it, to the rat quiver source? It kind of took over the entire body like a petit mal seizure."

Hanks, of course, replicates the rat quiver on request and has the brothers nearly falling over in laughter.

The Coens had wanted to make a movie with Hanks for some time, says Joel, who is three years older than Ethan.

"This was one of those situations where that desire to work with someone in particular and a part we had just written was dovetailed," Joel says. "Don't ask me why, but we thought this could be something really interesting for him and not anything we've seen him do before."

"It's a kind of outlandish part, a grand part," says Ethan. "It's a big part, in the sense of being almost theatrical, and we felt there was a danger if it were in the wrong hands."

"You've got to be able to be big, but be real," Joel adds.

"That's right," Hanks chimes in. "Go big or go home."

Together, the Coens wrote, directed, produced, and edited (under the pseudonym Roderick Jaynes) *The Ladykillers*. It's the twelfth script they've written together. Ethan is often credited as the producer and Joel as the director, but their roles often overlap.

The brothers are known for their dark humor and quirky plots in such films as 1996's *Fargo* (for which they shared Oscars for writing and editing, and Joel's wife, Frances McDormand, won for best actress.) Other movie credits include *Raising Arizona, Miller's Crossing, Barton Fink, The Big Lebowski*, and *O Brother, Where Art Thou?* (which earned them an Oscar nomination for screenwriting).

And even though as youngsters they saw the original *The Ladykillers,* with Alec Guinness starring as the professor, and borrowed the line for *Blood Simple,* the Coens hadn't considered a remake.

Their friend Barry Sonnenfeld, who directed *Get Shorty* and *Men in Black,* asked the Coens to rewrite *The Ladykillers* with the idea of directing it himself. Sonnenfeld served as cinematographer on three of the Coens' films.

"So it wasn't actually something that ever crossed our minds until he brought it to us," Joel says, "and then Ethan and I looked at the movie again, which we hadn't seen probably since we were kids. We thought this was something we could do something with and have fun with. Then Barry decided not to do it, and we decided we wanted to do it."

From the beginning, they wanted to set the movie in sleepy Pascagoula, Mississippi, home to the kindly Mrs. Munson, a devout and devoted member of a Southern Baptist congregation. Her propensity for churchgoing allowed the Coens to introduce the gospel music of such standard-bearers as the Soul Stirrers, Blind Willie Johnson, and Bill Landford and the Landfordaires.

And while the Coens started the story with Mrs. Munson, they moved quickly to the character of Professor Dorr.

"Because he also seemed to have a lot of possibilities drawing on the regional aspect," says Joel. "And that in turn led to the musical part of the movie that was interesting to us, the gospel music. With the rest, we felt kind of free to branch out, to Southeast Asia and wherever the rest of the gang was from."

The would-be thieves making up the professor's "gang" are the General (Tzi Ma), a stoic fellow adept at swallowing lighted cigarettes; Garth Pancake (J. K. Simmons), the barely capable munitions expert; Lump (Ryan Hurst), who does the heavy lifting; and Gawain (Marlon Wayans), the inside man working as a janitor at the casino.

Gawain is what Mrs. Munson calls "a hippety-hop," an urban fellow with a slew of tiny pigtails on his head and a foul mouth.

"He was the audience's point of view," says Wayans, who's eating a late lunch down the hall from Hanks and the Coens at the publicity stop. "He said what everybody else was thinking. He's a lot smarter in some ways than Hanks's character, who spits out all the big words. He's like, 'I don't know big words, but I know a thing or two. I know a shady man and that Pancake is shady.'

"No matter how wrong he is, Gawain don't know how to apologize, and it ain't his fault," Wayans continues. "I kinda based him on an old assistant of mine, who would do something wrong and look at me like I was wrong for asking him to do the job. God puts people in your life for a reason. They're there to be characters."

Like Wayans, Hanks gave his character considerable thought. He came up with the professor's mustache and Vandyke beard, which he saw in Civil War daguerreotypes. He worked with the costume designer on creating the professor's wardrobe, an Old South cape and formal suit, and invented Dorr's British-flavored Mississippi accent.

He also concocted a background for the character.

"He says he is from Mississippi, although where, who knows?" Hanks says. "He says he's on sabbatical from the institution where he teaches, the University of Southern Mississippi in Hattiesburg, which is true, but I think he's been on sabbatical for fourteen years. He was fired because of that hasty decision by the dean in order to avoid the sexual harassment suit. I do believe he studied at the Sorbonne, but I think he studied drinking. He was essentially accepted, read a couple of the Flaubert books, and then spent the rest of his time in bars."

"Hey," says Joel, "that's an idea for a sequel: 'The Professor, the Paris Years.'"

Hanks laughs and begins again. He's on a roll now.

"Yes, a movable feast. And I think that ever since then, he's been trying to get somebody else to pay for his bus station cafeteria dinner. And somewhere along the line, I think he was in jail at some time. He's been spending a lot of time in what are essentially $15-a-month boarding rooms in Memphis and Nashville and throughout that fertile Delta area that is Mississippi and Louisiana. Not so much one step ahead of the law as one step ahead of the people he owes money to, who are legion."

The three men are laughing loudly. Joel slaps the table.

Hanks continues: "Let me tell you about Professor Dorr. He doesn't believe in cheap shoes, nor multiple pairs. He has a single pair of wonderful handmade shoes, and he wears nothing other than those, because he's discovered they last nearly a lifetime. He never buys store-bought. He gets them from this guy up in Oxford, Mississippi, who still makes handmade shoes."

"Are you sure they aren't from the Salvation Army?" Ethan asks.

"Handmade," Hanks insists.

Audiences might surmise that a man on the run simply wears all of his clothes on his back in lieu of carrying a valise. And so while Mrs. Munson and her lady friends are decked out in their light summer florals, the professor seems to labor in the Mississippi humidity under many layers of fabric.

"You can wear twelve layers in Mississippi, provided you never walk faster than this," says Hanks, who makes his way to the beverage cart at a halting pace. "Then, it's actually quite possible, because it's cotton, a natural fiber. And, remember, he is a slow-moving man who spends much of his time in a root cellar."

The Coens wrote considerably more dialogue for the professor than their other characters. Hanks' Dorr pontificates endlessly at times.

"Not that that was any reason to take the movie. Line count, please!" Hanks says. "The good news is that it's not unlike doing Shaw or Shakespeare in that the ideas are so easily connected that, once you do the mechanics of memorizing, it just flows out of you.

"He is never at a loss for words, but the downside is that I knew I'd be talking and talking and talking," Hanks says, "and at the end of the day, they'd cut to Marlon going like this." He shrugs one shoulder. "Or I'd be be knocking myself out, and Tzi Ma just had to swallow a cigarette."

Hanks spreads his arms dramatically. "And that, ladies and gentlemen, is how comedy beats are made."

# My Father Lived in Croydon

## PETER BRADSHAW/2004

THE COEN BROTHERS' VERSION of the classic Ealing comedy *The Ladykillers* transplants it from '50s London to the present-day Deep South. But director Joel Coen tells Peter Bradshaw he feels perfectly at home with this very English comedy because he is British himself. Sort of.

It is hard to imagine a director less interested in the process of publicizing a new movie than Joel Coen, who, as one half of the legendary Coen brothers, is now presenting the remake of the 1955 Ealing black comedy classic *The Ladykillers*, which opens here this month.

It is not that he is difficult or tetchy. Quite the contrary. As he conducts our interview in a five-star hotel room, he is very charming, with tousled hair, chunky glasses and a sleepy smile: so laid-back as to be almost horizontal, answering each question with the distracted but amiably bleary air of someone awakened from a pleasant reverie to which he is confident about returning soon.

The Coens' *Ladykillers* transplants the action from postwar King's Cross in London to the present-day Deep South of the U.S., and Tom Hanks takes the Alec Guinness role of the mad, snaggled-toothed professor who assembles a motley crew of criminals. In this new version, they rent a room from the formidable old lady Mrs. Munson and pretend to rehearse a Renaissance music ensemble in her basement, while secretly tunneling into the count room of a nearby casino.

---

From *The Guardian*, June 15, 2004. Copyright Guardian Newspapers Limited 2004. Reprinted by permission.

It's very different from the original. Marlon Wayans is the equivalent of Peter Sellers' ruthless spiv. Unlike Wayans, Sellers never used the MF-word. If he had, the Ealing studios would probably have spontaneously combusted. The result is a strange merging, or maybe rather juxtaposition, of two pungently individual styles: Ealing's and the Coens'. How on earth did Joel and Ethan Coen, the people who gave us *The Big Lebowski, Fargo, Barton Fink*, and *The Man Who Wasn't There*, arrive at *The Ladykillers?*

"Well . . ." drawls Joel, smiling indulgently, as if the question was interesting but eccentric, and had never occurred to him, "the director Barry Sonnenfeld, who's an old friend of ours, had a deal at Disney to remake the movie. He asked us to do the script: it was essentially a writing assignment. But for various reasons he had to pull out and asked us if we wanted to do it. The funny thing about writing a movie-screenplay is that it's not like television commercials, where you can really stand back and not have any investment in it at all. So having written the script we thought: sure! Let's make it!"

So what did he think of his source material? Joel laughs: "OK, it's an Ealing comedy so there's something very British and very genteel about it, which isn't particularly our thing. The more genteel aspects of the movie kind of got trashed! Ha! Ha! But other things stayed."

Did he feel alienated from its Britishness, I wondered? Coen shakes his head, leans forward and reveals that he is British. Or at least the Coen family is. "Our father Edward Coen is an American citizen by virtue of having been born in the United States," he says. "He joined the U.S. army in the Second World War and went to college in America and became a professor of economics. But my grandfather, Victor Coen, was a barrister in the Inns of Court in London. I remember when he retired, my grandparents went to live in Hove and we used to visit them there."

Hove. You don't get more English than that. As he dredges up these exotic antecedents from his mind, Coen smiles to himself, having apparently not thought about these things for decades.

"My father actually grew up in London. Lemme see—this is a long time ago. He's still alive, by the way, in his late eighties. I think he lived in, oh yeah, Purley and Croydon." Coen mouths these names wonderingly, as if they are moons of Jupiter. "Yeah! That was it. You know what? He told me once about going to Croydon airfield to see Charles Lindbergh landing! He had very British tastes in movies, and it must've been because of him that we watched all those Ealing movies on TV."

So there you go. If things had been different, Joel and Ethan Coen might have been brought up in homely Hove or Croydon or Purley, and not Minnesota.

So does he think that British audiences might react against this appropriation of one of their great films? At this stage, Coen comes the nearest he is going to get to a sharp reply: "Well, the original movie was written by an American and directed by an American. The British feel very proprietary about it!" It is broadly true. Director Alexander Mackendrick was born in Boston, Massachusetts, to Scottish parents, and grew up in Scotland; he worked in Ealing and Hollywood and lived the final thirty-odd years of his life in California. Screenwriter William Rose was born in Missouri, but left for Canada before the Second World War and joined the army before coming to England.

For many, this will be more evidence that the Coens are preparing to jettison the distinctive auteurist modus operandi that has made them beloved in Europe and at the Cannes Film Festival, but which has always prevented them winning big box-office success. "We'll gladly enter the mainstream any time the mainstream will have us!" Coen disarmingly replies: He gives a great honking laugh. "I don't know if we're capable of entering the mainstream, but it's not for want of trying!"

As it happens, the Coens' *Ladykillers* seems to have been hatched and dispatched pretty efficiently. The script took them just two months, on a tight deadline, where other projects have evolved over years. "When we say we're writing something," chuckles Coen, "we mean we're just sitting around a room talking and mostly napping. For years my friends accused me of going to the office essentially to nap and I denied it, and then I just admitted it was true."

So it may be that in this middle period of his career, Joel Coen is a much more dynamic and conventionally focused Hollywood professional. But as I leave, he runs a hand distractedly through that mop of hair and does seem to be glancing rather longingly at that five-star hotel bed.

# INDEX

CONVERSATIONS WITH FILMMAKERS SERIES
PETER BRUNETTE, GENERAL EDITOR

*The collected interviews with notable modern directors, including*

Robert Aldrich • Woody Allen • Pedro Almodóvar • Robert Altman • Theo Angelopolous • Bernardo Bertolucci • Tim Burton • Jane Campion • Frank Capra • Charlie Chaplin • Francis Ford Coppola • George Cukor • Brian De Palma • Clint Eastwood • Federico Fellini • John Ford • Terry Gilliam • Jean-Luc Godard • Peter Greenaway • Howard Hawks • Alfred Hitchcock • John Huston • Jim Jarmusch • Elia Kazan • Stanley Kubrick • Fritz Lang • Spike Lee • Mike Leigh • George Lucas • Sidney Lumet • Roman Polanski • Michael Powell • Jean Renoir • Martin Ritt • Carlos Saura • John Sayles • Martin Scorsese • Ridley Scott • Steven Soderbergh • Steven Spielberg • George Stevens • Oliver Stone • Quentin Tarantino • Andrei Tarkovsky • Lars von Trier • Liv Ullmann • Orson Welles • Billy Wilder • John Woo • Zhang Yimou • Fred Zinnemann